MIKHAIL BAKHTIN

Mikhail Bakhtin is one of the most influential theorists of philosophy as well as literary studies. His work on dialogue and discourse has changed the way in which we read texts – both literary and cultural – and his practice of philosophy in literary refraction and philological exploration has made him a pioneering figure in the twentieth-century convergence of the two disciplines.

In this book Graham Pechey offers a commentary on Bakhtin's texts in all their complex and allusive 'textuality', keeping a sense throughout of the historical setting in which they were written and of his own interpretation of and response to them. Examining Bakhtin's relationship to Russian Formalism and Soviet Marxism, Pechey focuses on two major interests: the influence of Eastern Orthodox Christianity upon his thinking; and Bakhtin's use of literary criticism and hermeneutics as ways of 'doing philosophy by other means'.

Graham Pechey was born in South Africa and educated at the Universities of Natal and Cambridge. He has published numerous articles on Mikhail Bakhtin, Romantic writing, literary and cultural theory, and South African literature. Having retired in 2000 from lecturing in English at the University of Hertfordshire, he now teaches English part-time at the University of Cambridge and is an Associate at the University's Centre of African Studies.

CRITICS OF THE TWENTIETH CENTURY
General Editor: Christopher Norris,
University of Wales, Cardiff

A.J. GREIMAS AND THE NATURE OF MEANING
Ronald Schleifer

CHRISTOPHER CAUDWELL
Robert Sullivan

FIGURING LACAN
CRITICISM AND THE CULTURAL UNCONSCIOUS
Juliet Flower MacCannell

HAROLD BLOOM
TOWARDS HISTORICAL RHETORICS
Peter de Bolla

F.R. LEAVIS
Michael Bell

POSTMODERN BRECHT
A RE-PRESENTATION
Elizabeth Wright

DELEUZE AND GUATTARI
Ronald Bogue

ECSTASIES OF ROLAND BARTHES
Mary Wiseman

JULIA KRISTEVA
John Lechte

GEOFFREY HARTMAN
CRITICISM AS ANSWERABLE STYLE
G. Douglas Atkins

EZRA POUND AS LITERARY CRITIC
K. K. Ruthven

PAUL RICOEUR
S. H. Clark

JÜRGEN HABERMAS
CRITIC IN THE PUBLIC SPHERE
Robert C. Holub

INTRODUCING LYOTARD
ART AND POLITICS
Bill Readings

WILLIAM EMPSON
PROPHET AGAINST SACRIFICE
Paul H. Fry

ANTONIO GRAMSCI
BEYOND MARXISM AND POSTMODERNISM
Renate Holub

KENNETH BURKE
RHETORIC AND IDEOLOGY
Stephen Bygrave

NORTHROP FRYE
THE THEORETICAL IMAGINATION
Jonathan Hart

ROMAN JAKOBSON
LIFE, LANGUAGE AND ART
Richard Bradford

JACQUES DERRIDA
OPENING LINES
Marian Hobson

RAYMOND WILLIAMS
LITERATURE, MARXISM AND CULTURAL MATERIALISM
John Higgins

MIKHAIL BAKHTIN
THE WORD IN THE WORLD
Graham Pechey

MIKHAIL BAKHTIN

The Word in the World

Graham Pechey

Routledge
Taylor & Francis Group

LONDON AND NEW YORK

First published 2007 by Routledge
2 Park Square, Milton Park, Abingdon, Oxon OX14 4RN

Simultaneously published in the USA and Canada
by Routledge
270 Madison Ave, New York, NY 10016

Routledge is an imprint of the Taylor & Francis Group, an informa business

© 2007 Graham Pechey

Typeset in Palatino by Taylor & Francis Books
Printed and bound in Great Britain by
Antony Rowe Ltd, Chippenham, Wiltshire

British Library Cataloguing in Publication Data
A catalogue record for this book is available from the British
Library

Library of Congress Cataloging in Publication Data
A catalog record for this book has been requested

ISBN: 978-0-415-42420-2 (hbk)
ISBN: 978-0-415-42419-6 (pbk)
ISBN: 978-0-203-96280-0 (ebk)

THIS BOOK IS DEDICATED TO THE MEMORY
OF MY LATE WIFE, THE ARTIST NOLA
CLENDINNING (1943–93)

CONTENTS

EDITOR'S FOREWORD

The twentieth century produced a remarkable number of gifted and innovative literary critics. Indeed it could be argued that some of the finest literary minds of the age turned to criticism as the medium best adapted to their complex and speculative range of interests. This has sometimes given rise to regret among those who insist on a clear demarcation between 'creative' (primary) writing on the one hand and 'critical' (secondary) texts on the other. Yet this distinction is far from self-evident. It is coming under strain at the moment as novelists and poets grow increasingly aware of the conventions that govern their writing and the challenge of consciously exploiting and subverting those conventions. And the critics for their part – some of them at least – are beginning to question their traditional role as humble servants of the literary text with no further claim upon the reader's interest or attention. Quite simply, there are texts of literary criticism and theory that, for various reasons – stylistic complexity, historical influence, range of intellectual command – cannot be counted a mere appendage to those other 'primary' texts.

Of course, there is a logical puzzle here, since (it will be argued) 'literary criticism' would never have come into being, and could hardly exist as such, were it not for the body of creative writing that provides its *raison d'être*. But this is not quite the kind of knockdown argument that it might appear at first glance. For one thing, it conflates some very different orders of priority, assuming that literature always comes first (in the sense that Greek tragedy had to exist before Aristotle could formulate its rules), so that literary texts are for that very reason possessed of superior value. And this argument would seem to find commonsense support in the difficulty of thinking what 'literary criticism' could *be* if it seriously renounced all sense of the distinction between literary and critical texts. Would it not then find itself in the unfortunate position of a discipline that had willed its own demise by declaring its subject non-existent?

But these objections would only hit their mark if there were indeed a special kind of writing called 'literature' whose difference from other kinds of writing was enough to put criticism firmly in its place. Otherwise there is nothing in the least self-defeating or paradoxical about a discourse, nominally that of literary criticism, that accrues such interest on its own account as to force some fairly drastic rethinking of its proper powers and limits. The act of crossing over from commentary to literature – or of simply denying the difference between them – becomes quite explicit in the writing of a critic like Geoffrey Hartman. But the signs are already there in such classics as William Empson's *Seven Types Ambiguity* (1928), a text whose transformative influence on our habits of reading must surely be ranked with the great creative moments of literary modernism. Only on the most dogmatic view of the difference between 'literature' and 'criticism' could a work like *Seven Types* be counted generically an inferior, sub-literary species of production. And the same can be said for many of the critics whose writings and influence this series sets out to explore.

Some, like Empson, are conspicuous individuals who belong to no particular school or larger movement. Others, like the Russian Formalists, were part of a communal enterprise and are therefore best understood as representative figures in a complex and evolving dialogue. Then again there are cases of collective identity (like the so-called 'Yale deconstructors') where a mythical group image is invented for largely polemical purposes. (The volumes in this series on Hartman and Bloom should help to dispel the idea that 'Yale deconstruction' is anything more than a handy device for collapsing differences and avoiding serious debate.) So there is no question of a series format or house style that would seek to reduce these differences to a blandly homogeneous treatment. One consequence of recent critical theory is the realization that literary texts have no self-sufficient or autonomous meaning, no existence apart from their afterlife of changing interpretations and values. And the same applies to those critical texts whose meaning and significance are subject to constant shifts and realignments of interest. This is not to say that trends in criticism are just a matter of intellectual fashion or the merry-go-round of rising and falling reputations. But it is important to grasp how complex are the forces – the conjunctions of historical and cultural motive – that affect the first reception and the subsequent fortunes of a critical text. This point has been raised into a systematic programme by critics like Hans-Robert Jauss, practitioners of so-called 'reception theory' as a form of historical hermeneutics. The volumes in this series will therefore be concerned not only to expound what is of lasting significance but also to set these critics in the context of present-day argument and debate. In some cases (as with Walter Benjamin) this debate takes the form of a struggle for interpretative power among disciplines with sharply opposed ideological viewpoints. Such controversies cannot simply be ignored in the interests of achieving a clear and balanced account. They point to unresolved tensions and problems which are there in the critic's work as well as in the rival appropriative readings. In the end there is no way of drawing a neat methodological line between 'intrinsic' questions (what the critic really thought) and those other, supposedly 'extrinsic', concerns that have to do with influence and reception history.

The volumes will vary accordingly in their focus and range of coverage. They will also reflect the ways in which a speculative approach to questions of literary theory has proved to have striking consequences for the human sciences at large. This breaking down of disciplinary bounds is among the most significant developments in recent critical thinking. As philosophers and historians, among others, come to recognize the rhetorical complexity of the texts they deal with, so literary theory takes on a new dimension of interest and relevance. It is scarcely appropriate to think of a writer like Derrida as practising 'literary criticism' in any conventional sense of the term. For one thing, he is as much concerned with 'philosophical' as with 'literary' texts, and has indeed actively sought to subvert (or deconstruct) such tidy distinctions. A principal object in planning this series was to take full stock of these shifts in the wider intellectual terrain (including the frequent boundary disputes) brought about by critical theory. And, of course, such changes are by no means confined to literary studies, philosophy and the so-called 'sciences of man'. It is equally the case in (say) nuclear physics and molecular biology that advances in the one field have decisive implications for the other, so that specialized research often tends (paradoxically) to break down existing divisions of intellectual labour. Such work is typically many years ahead of the academic disciplines and teaching institutions that have obvious reasons of their own for adopting a business-as-usual attitude. One important aspect of modern critical theory is the challenge it presents to these traditional ideas. And lest it be thought that this is merely a one-sided takeover bid by literary critics, the series will include a number of volumes by authors in those other disciplines, including, for instance, a study of Roland Barthes by an American analytical philosopher.

We shall not, however, cleave to theory as a matter of polemical or principled stance. The series will extend to figures like F.R. Leavis, whose widespread influence went along with an express aversion to literary theory; scholars like Erich Auerbach in the mainstream European tradition; and others who resist assimilation to any clear-cut line of descent. There will also be authoritative volumes on critics such as Northrop Frye and Lionel Trilling, figures who, for various reasons, occupy an ambivalent or essentially contested place in modern critical tradition. Above all the series will strive to resist that current polarization of attitudes that sees no common ground on interest between 'literary criticism' and 'critical theory'.

CHRISTOPHER NORRIS

ACKNOWLEDGEMENTS

Versions of the chapters of this book have appeared – in some cases more than once – in various journals and collective volumes between 1990 and 2003. Formal permissions have been granted by the following copyright holders: *Radical Philosophy* for Chapter 1, which appeared in that journal as 'Boundaries versus Binaries: Bakhtin in/against the History of Ideas', 54, 1990; Routledge for Chapter 4, which appeared in greatly abridged form as 'Modernity and Chronotopicity in Bakhtin' in David Shepherd (ed.), *The Contexts of Bakhtin: Philosophy, Authorship, Aesthetics* (Amsterdam: Harwood Academic Publishers, 1998); Taylor and Francis (Journals) (http://www.tandf.co.uk/journals), publisher of *Pretexts: Literary and Cultural Studies*, for Chapter 5, which appeared there as 'Not the Novel: Bakhtin, Poetry, Truth, God', 4:2, 1993; Raphael de Kadt, editor of *Theoria: A Journal of Social and Political Theory*, for Chapter 6, which appeared there as 'Eternity and Modernity: Bakhtin and the Epistemological Sublime', 81/82, 1994; and David Shepherd, editor of *Dialogism: An International Journal of Bakhtin Studies*, for Chapter 7, which appeared there in greatly abridged form as 'Philosophy and Theology in "Aesthetic Activity"', 1, 1998. I take this opportunity of formally thanking all of the above; and of thanking also those others – Paul Contino, Caryl Emerson, Susan Felch, Michael Gardiner and Ken Hirschkop – who encouraged me to believe that the project of this book was worthwhile by later reprinting four of these essays in volumes edited or co-edited by themselves.

All of the individuals cited above have had a larger role in the development of my understanding of Bakhtin than is circumscribed by the function of editor in relation to particular pieces of my work, and they are joined in this by so many others that it would be an insult to the inadvertently excluded to start naming too many names. Moreover, I have chosen to confine my specific acknowledgements to those friends who have discussed Bakhtin with me substantially; others, who share my other interests (in South African literature, and more generally in linguistic, literary-critical, literary-historical and theological matters) and who might feel rebuffed by their absence from these paragraphs, will find themselves duly acknowledged in two further volumes on those topics which I hope to bring out in the not too distant future.

The first of my less formal acknowledgements begins with a reflection of Bakhtin's on kinsfolk. We must not, he writes, say of our relatives, 'They are mine', but, rather, 'I am theirs'. It is from them – and of course in the first instance from one's parents – that one acquires the gift of an earthly name, for (as he writes elsewhere) I cannot name myself; only the other can name me. My own first others, who knew nothing of Bakhtin, and who had no literary pretensions, none the less by their radically different verbal habits drew the young Graham Pechey's attention to words – his mother by a strict literalism of their definition, his father by a relentless punning play on them – that he cannot do otherwise than remember Dorothy and Noel Pechey now with love and thankfulness. The last paragraph of Chapter 6 was written in Pietermaritzburg, South Africa, on the eve of my mother's funeral in 1992, and it takes some of its tone from my mood at that time.

Bakhtin loomed large in discussions with some of my former colleagues at the University of Hertfordshire (UH) between 1973 and 2000: these were the glory days of 'theory'; Bakhtin was understood to be a 'theorist', however limiting and inimical to his own self-image that description might have been; and 'theory' was part of the innovative diet we served up to our students. I am indebted to Gill Davies, Alan Hooper, Jean Radford, George Wotton and the late Dennis Brown both for such discussions and for their touching faith in the reality of this book, which was so long in its gestation. With the shift to university status, with the consequent pressure to build up a 'research culture' – above all with the peculiar self-consciousness of our status bred by the regular quadrennial 'Research Assessment Exercise' – 'Pechey's book on Bakhtin' seemed ever to be receding into the distance, impossible of completion. Now that it has at last appeared, I am long retired from UH, and it redounds of course to no institution's greater glory. Whilst the satisfaction is wholly my own, some at least of the credit for this book must go to those who taught and talked with me through all those years in harness together.

Outside that institutional context, but no less important for all that as significant interlocutors, are Paul Connerton, friend of forty years' standing, distinguished writer on social memory and co-conspirator with my daughter in the plot to get this book out; Charles Lock, critic and philologist *extraordinaire*, whom I met through the Bakhtin connection but who, in the uncanny conjunction of our diverse scholarly interests, has also helped me to see that there is life after Bakhtin; Anton Simons, writer of an excellent book on Bakhtin in Dutch; and Donald Wesling, from whose important interventions in the field of 'Bakhtin and poetry' I have drawn strength in making my own. My thanks also go to Christopher Norris, general editor of the 'Critics of the Twentieth Century' series, for so carefully reading and annotating the manuscript, and to Polly Dodson, my editor at Routledge, for her unstinting help with the practicalities of producing this book.

Finally, I remember in this place my late wife Nola Clendinning, miniaturist and painter of icons, whose knowledge of Orthodox Christianity altered my reading of Bakhtin, and who is both the posthumous inspiration of Chapter 7 and the hidden antecedent of its feminine third-person pronouns; my daughter Laura, who at eight drew a carnivalesque cover for this book (sadly now lost) and who then at twenty-five shamed me by her doctoral industry into finishing it at last; and my wife Rosie Sykes, craftswoman, literary scholar and wildlife enthusiast, from whom I have learned to balance my tendency too precipitately to look past the visible with an attentive gaze upon this world's particulars. To all of these, my love and thanks for bringing me to where I am today.

G.K.P.
Cambridge,
8 September 2006

ABBREVIATIONS

Full bibliographical details of volumes cited will be found in the bibliography at the end of this book.

AA	'Art and Answerability', in *Art and Answerability*
AH	'Author and Hero in Aesthetic Activity', in *Art and Answerability*
BSHR	'The *Bildungsroman* and its Significance in the History of Realism (Toward a Historical Typology of the Novel)', in *Speech Genres and Other Late Essays*
DN	'Discourse in the Novel', in *The Dialogic Imagination*
EN	'Epic and Novel: Toward a Methodology for the Study of the Novel', in *The Dialogic Imagination*
FMLS	P.N. Medvedev, *The Formal Method in Literary Scholarship*
FTC	'Forms of Time and of the Chronotope in the Novel', in *The Dialogic Imagination*
IENM	'Interview with the Editor of *Novy Mir*', in *Speech Genres and Other Late Essays*
MHS	'Toward a Methodology for the Human Sciences', in *Speech Genres and Other Late Essays*
MPL	V.N. Voloshinov, *Marxism and the Philosophy of Language*
NM70–71	'From Notes Made in 1970–71', in *Speech Genres and Other Late Essays*
PCMF	'The Problem of Content, Material, and Form in Verbal Art', in *Art and Answerability*
PDP	*Problems of Dostoevsky's Poetics*
PT	'The Problem of the Text in Linguistics, Philology, and the Human Sciences: An Experiment in Philosophical Analysis', in *Speech Genres and Other Late Essays*
RW	*Rabelais and His World*
TPA	*Toward a Philosophy of the Act*

INTRODUCTION

Not the last word

This book of essays records a twelve-year exchange in a much longer conversation with Mikhail Mikhailovich Bakhtin (1895–1975) – a conversation which began, indeed, when he was still alive, and which has now lasted half of *my* life. Given his own overriding contention that dialogue is a much broader phenomenon than the face-to-face, turn-taking interlocution which conventionally goes by that name, it scarcely matters that Bakhtin and I trod the same earth for thirty-five years without ever meeting; or that if, by some extraordinary quirk of fate, we had met, the Babelic confusion of tongues which put Russian in his mouth and English in mine would have forestalled understanding. If a certain deference to my more sceptical readers makes me reluctant to speak of a plane beyond the punctualities of time and space which will find both of us together again – and of the luminous transparency of understanding which, one trusts, that meeting will yield – then I have to say that those among such readers who have never (if only momentarily) suspended their disbelief in the afterlife will not have reaped the considerable philosophical rewards of placing oneself uncompromisingly on the other side of the known, and will have missed something quite crucial in their reading of Bakhtin. For the philosopher himself, such spiritual acrobatics yield the deepest understanding, and he expects of us a skill like his own in their execution.

Modern literature begins in the *Divine Comedy* with just such an intricately imagined excursion: Dante Alighieri's innovative use of the dialogue of the dead – by no means new in itself – places the solid, shadow-casting body of a living, ongoing consciousness among the variously judged shades of the next world; the upshot is a defamiliarization on both sides. In Bakhtin's terminology, a 'spirit' finds himself among dead 'souls', the otherworldly products of

1

finished worldly lives – directly fashioned works, as we might call them, of the 'aesthetic activity' of the Almighty. The author outside the work imagines himself as its hero, and his sphere of action is God's workshop of souls, where the great cosmic labour goes on. Dante's audacious fiction aimed at jolting a whole social order chaotically out of joint into seeing itself for what it is might have failed as a spur to praxis in the historical world of his time and ever after; as an adventure of knowledge, though, it is not only as new and effectual as ever, but also the paradigm for all modern acts of literature. Its essential gesture is repeated as much in *The Canterbury Tales* and the work of William Blake as it is in the last poem written by Geoffrey Hill. And it is at the root, too, of the European novel: Bakhtin's own most favoured heir to Dante's omni-temporal imagination is his fellow Russian Fyodor Mikhailovich Dostoevsky, and Dostoevsky had before him, of course, the example of Nikolai Gogol's *Dead Souls*, intended (in Bakhtin's view, misguidedly) (*EN*, 28) as the first part of a Russian *Divine Comedy* in prose.

In his earliest work, Bakhtin twice offers us an analysis of a short poem by Alexander Pushkin which has the lyric hero undergoing a twofold parting from his lover – she returns home to Italy, only then to die – and ending by holding her to her promise of a kiss in what will now be not the earthly future but the hereafter. The Dantean connotations scarcely need elaborating. Unsurprisingly, in the second of his two analyses, Dante's name crops up several times, along with the observation that the 'emotional-volitional reaction' of the author finds expression not just in that aestheticization of natural intonations which he calls 'rhythm' – Bakhtin extends the sense of this word as he was later equally to elasticize that of 'dialogue' – but in the very 'choice of a hero' for the work (*AH*, 225). If we read this *in tandem* with a point made in the same context about how in 'aesthetic seeing' there is always a 'potential hero' (*AH*, 229), even if that hero is not thematically manifested or is removed from the centre of attention – even, indeed, in a still life, or a piece of purely instrumental and non-programmatic music – we are moved to reflect in a Bakhtinian manner on Bakhtin's own choice of heroes in *his* work. For Bakhtin certainly chooses heroes: the litany of them is well known; Katerina Clark and Michael Holquist identify them with those of any educated Russian of his generation.[1] Bakhtin is an author whose heroes are authors; and Dante, I would argue, is the principal 'heroic' potentiality in all of his writing. Fitfully present in a citational sense, the subject only of occasional comments in the great monographs, Dante could be said to haunt them none the less as the human axiological centre around which they revolve and by which they are rhythmically energized. Bakhtin, I contend, learns more from Dante than from anyone else. Dante's relative absence and Dostoevsky's strong presence in the work of Bakhtin that has come down to us – these are absolutely Dantean situations: after all, according to Bakhtin himself Dante's earthly world is a world without centres (*AH*, 208); and, besides, what could be more in the spirit of Dante than the choice of a *vernacular* hero in Dostoevsky?

Bakhtin's later emphasis upon the novel should not encourage us in the view that he did not like poetry. Of his four major heroes, two are principally poets, two write prose; laid out chronologically, they form a revealing pattern, at once chiastic and alternating. Thus, first we have a late-mediaeval Italian poet; then an early-modern French prose writer; then a high-modern German poet; finally a Russian writer of prose. Or: framed by two writers to whom a synchronic, omni-temporal imagination is ascribed are two others who variously represent the linear track of history. Or, again: from a 'formally polyphonic' (*PDP*, 31) poetry of the 'vertical' of eternity (Dante) we pass on to the prose (Rabelais) and the poetry (Goethe) of the 'horizontal' of history, finally coming to rest in the novelist of cosmic synchrony in whom the polyphony of fully weighted voices has broken out of mere juxtaposition into interaction. The correlation of Dante and Dostoevsky is made quite explicit in *Problems of Dostoevsky's Poetics*. This temporal ordering of Bakhtin's pantheon dramatizes for us the fact that the modern literary hero closest to him in time and culture is in some sense a throwback to modern literature's first great figure: that the two figures most widely sundered in time link up over the heads of intervening figures who between them mark the stages of a growing self-consciousness of history in the West. The unmerged though still only externally juxtaposed voices of Dante's poem give way to the dynamically interlocutory voices of Dostoevsky's prose. That late-mediaeval polyphony has been freed from its stasis is for Bakhtin the signal cultural achievement of a modernity which has otherwise proved itself only too tragically productive of social and spiritual pathologies. As I hint in Chapter 7 of this book, Dostoevsky seems to signify for him the intersection and reconciliation of modern (sociopolitical) freedom and its premodern (theological) counterpart. Elevating the novel over other forms must then be seen as a strategic move designed to draw attention to the power of modern literary discourse to absorb social languages and dialogize them, in a challenge to all earthly centres – all absolute points of reference in *this* world. To challenge the latter is to reinforce the legitimate claim of the only such centre: that which is not of this world, and which believers call God. As a social phenomenon, 'poetry' in Bakhtin's sense is a code for the abuse of literary discourse in the celebration of worldly centres of power. If his early descriptions of aesthetic activity seem to imply poetry as a model, that is because Bakhtin is not invoking there the sociopolitical effects of literature in oppressive contexts but speaking, rather, of the general 'architectonics' of 'verbal art'. Singing, celebrating, 'rhythmicizing' real-life intonations: whilst perversions of these aesthetic acts are possible, such perversions are plainly not the concern of the early work. In any case, the *Divine Comedy* is so capacious a work that it might be said to anticipate all literature, including modern prose fiction; *Purgatory* is in some ways a proto-novel in verse. *Hell* shows us a place where the abusers receive their justified lot: namely, abuse of what remains of their whole personalities. *Paradise* shows us a place of unalloyed praise. Purgatory is the otherworldly place most like our earthly world, inasmuch as it is a hybrid state of ambivalent praise–abuse; reading *Purgatory*, we understand better the transcendental meaning Bakhtin attaches to the novel genre. What we find in purgatory is nothing less than the illuminating estrangement of this earthly condition in which we enjoy the God-given freedom to repent and to amend our lives. Those in hell have lost that freedom; those in paradise no longer need it.

It cannot escape an attentive reader that many of the perennial Bakhtinian motifs have their germ in Dante. Before all else, there is the idea of knowledge as experiential, incarnational, chronotopic – of truth as a matter of pilgrimage and of personal encounter with a great diversity of thoroughly, indeed intensely, individualized *persons*. Virgil's role in the poem puts before us very vividly the early-Bakhtinian notion of rationality as a moment of 'answerability': Dante's 'master' does not in any simple allegorical sense stand for (pagan) Reason; in his readiness to lend both physical and intellectual help to the poet-hero through Hell and Purgatory – that is, to put the matter more concretely, in his energetic *answering* with body and soul – he is important above all for what he *does*. Virgil is, in short, a paradigm for (indeed a paragon of) answerable action. Dante himself, as often as not, answers with his body to what he witnesses, particularly on those occasions when feeling overwhelms him in contemplation of the consequences of God's judgement in the other world. The poet and the Italian language stand in a relation of homology: just as the humble Tuscan vernacular is exalted as the vehicle of the highest, cosmic themes, so the poet inserts the somatic into the semantics of salvation. Reading Dante's transfiguration of the body of the mother tongue, we understand how literature is positioned at the moment of its (modern) inception. Writing the *Divine Comedy* is, after all, an enormous gamble: inventing a topography of the afterlife; populating it; raising the love of a woman into a figure of the love of God which is not the disposable bodiliness of allegory but the ontological equivalent of what it signifies: all of that amounts, in fourteenth-century Europe, to a calculated spiritual-political risk. Literature, we may say, is an act of controlled hubris, a laboratory for well-meaning experiments in overreaching, heresy endlessly courted without positive proof of commission. To the inquisitorially minded reader, what Dante writes would seem a sort of spiritual correlative of treason, and therefore grounds for his excommunication or worse – at the very least, of the prohibition of his work (the poem's actual historical fate). The writer, however, writes in the belief and trust that there is an ideal reader – Bakhtin's 'superaddressee' – for whom the hubris will show its other side, its truth, as humility. For Dante, poetry's beneficent heresy is the homoeopathic dose which will cure the illness of traditional faith, secure for it a future beyond the most corrupt of papacies and open a new Augustan era of universal peace.

This digression on the theme of 'Bakhtin and Dante' will perhaps seem less digressive by the end of this introduction. In the meantime, though, I must return from the fourteenth century to the late twentieth and to my own relationship with Bakhtin. The first of these essays was written in 1988; six further essays followed in the next seven years; and the last was finished in 2000. The order of their composition was partly contingent upon the order of appearance in English translation of the works on which each of them is principally focused; thus if the last chapter deals somewhat perversely with Bakhtin's earliest work, that is because *Toward a Philosophy of the Act* only became available to anglophone readers without competence in Russian in 1994. In their order as chapters there is only one departure from the chronology of composition: Chapter 2 was written early in 1994. Those who wish, then, to read this book as the story of one reader's developing encounter with Bakhtin may choose to read Chapter 2 after Chapter 6. Chapters 1, 5 and 6 have already appeared in print at least twice; they reappear here at the same length and largely unchanged, apart from a certain expansion and updating of their notes. Whilst Chapters 4 and 7 have also appeared elsewhere, they are presented here in versions that are so much fuller than those already published as to constitute altogether new reading experiences for those who in the past might have read the latter. Chapters 2, 3 and 8 will be new to all readers, being published here for the first time. With two exceptions – Chapters 1 and 5 – all the essays in this book are close readings of particular works (or parts of works) by Bakhtin and his 'circle'. I have striven in these chapters less to expound his 'ideas' for newcomers to them than to offer a commentary on Bakhtin's 'texts' in all their complex and allusive 'textuality' for the benefit of those who are already familiar with them. Bakhtin's voice sounds alongside the voices of other writers and thinkers of the twentieth century whose projects seemed to me in some way cognate with his. Among these are not only figures with whom he is manifestly in dialogue but also those (even if possibly unknown to him) with whose work his own work may be said to resonate. I have done this in the belief that Bakhtin is – and are not we all? – neither absolutely *sui generis*, nor reducible to the sum of his multifarious 'sources', nor (again) merely coincident with the words he managed to set down before he died: Bakhtin expands in our reading of him beyond the thinker he once was in life. I should say also that this dialogue I have set up inclines more to the pole of 'internal' dialogue or dialogism than to the externalities of a quotation-matching exercise; instead of voices with clear boundaries, alternately taking and yielding the floor, the reader will find a finely co-implicated weft of terms and tones. It is mainly because of this refusal on my part of the positively attributable position that the chapters are so lightly referenced, at least by comparison with most other academic monographs. Or, rather: the truly important references are not those in small print at the end but those in parentheses in the text which encourage the reader to go back to Bakhtin and enter into an intense and intricate conversation of the kind that this book itself attempts.

Bakhtin's *name* first came into my field of vision in 1971, when I was reading an essay by Lucien Goldmann in which he cites the work of his pupil Julia Kristeva; I first read his *work* about a year later.[2] I began by thinking – and I was by no means alone in this delusion – that he was some sort of 'Marxist' critic of Russian Formalism, a 'post-formalist' who was sometimes, confusingly, also numbered along with the Formalists themselves. None of the essays in this volume is written on this now-discredited premiss. The first to be written, 'Boundaries versus Binaries', marks the start of my trek away from Bakhtin's putative 'Marxism' inasmuch as it proposes a Bakhtin who has taken another route out of Hegel than that taken by Karl Marx; who is certainly not any kind of Soviet or 'Second-International' (Engelsian-scientistic) Marxist; and whose quasi-'Western Marxism' brings him into the orbit of those 'post-colonial' thinkers whose meditations upon the anti-colonial – so far from propelling the modern project forward with the nineteenth-century steam power of the master-category of 'class' – lead them ineluctably into critiques of cultural modernity at large. If the 'revo-lutionary' pathos that is part of this essay's specific tonality is not a tone I would adopt today, both the integrity of the case as a whole and the value of its incidental insights into the bearings of Bakhtin's thought demand that it be left unmodified; and so it has been. Being rude about 'philosophy' is another of this essay's habits of speech that I now regret, perilously elevating (as it does) 'method' over 'truth'. By the time I finished writing 'First philosophy' (Chapter 8) in 2000 I no longer considered the epithet *philosopher* 'lethal': Bakhtin himself, we were to learn, wore that badge with pride. 'Philosophy' connotes the seriousness and the scope of Bakhtin's project, even if it is (as I put it in that chapter) 'philosophy by other means'. These means are of course literary; for I believe we should hold his early philosophical intent firmly together with his later choice only of writers and their works as the vessels of his thinking; that, in other words, we should not see these acts of refraction through literature as a rejection of philosophy. Bakhtin is plainly an early representative of that later convergence in twen-tieth-century thought whereby – complementarily – literature is understood to be a form of knowledge and philosophy a form of writing. And one has to say 'literature' here and not 'art': that Romantic category threatens to subsume 'aesthetic *activity*' under a higher or 'theoreticist' generalization remote from ongoing life; acts of writing, on the other hand, constitute a vital transmission line running to and from the fundamental human and ethical given of the singular, non-iterable *deed*. With the reading of *Toward a Philosophy of the Act* that is undertaken in this chapter, I realized that Bakhtin's principal lessons are drawn from that which we now call 'literature' but which was once merely a generically distinctive sector of an undivided field of writing, and that it is not so much an 'alternative route out of Hegel' that defines him as something more epochal and encompassing: an alternative route *into* modernity.

This, then, is the path taken from the earliest- to the last-written chapters of this book – the development in my understanding of who Bakhtin was and what he was about. It now seemed to me that, in common with a generation of *pre*-revolutionary *post*-Marxists, he sees Russia's hegemonic (atheistic) intellectuals as false prophets fixing on and fetishizing the worst aspects of the West's modernizing trajectory. Reading that achieved modernity forward as a series of absolute breaks with the spiritual culture of the past was to be supplanted by a reading back along the same track with an eye to its continuities: Bakhtin's philosophy-in-deep-philological-dilution is a version of that second reading. The strongly incarnational emphasis of Russian Orthodox theology was clearly a help both to Bakhtin and those dissidents *avant la lettre*; at the same time, it was not a ready-made solution to the problems of a modernizing polity and civil society in the early twentieth century. Bakhtin's greatest insight was to see that it was the literature of modern Europe that was the true record of modernity and a sure antidote to the super-rationalization of the enlightenment. Now if this only became properly thinkable for me with the publication in English of Bakhtin's earliest works, it was something that I had already partly anticipated in the essay now published as Chapter 5. 'Not the Novel' – to give it its original short title – is an attempt, on the basis of what I then knew of Bakhtin's work, to come to an understanding of how his example might be followed in the reading of genres other than his favoured genre, and also of how 'God' survives in the light of a poetic that so resolutely privileges the overturning of all hierarchies.

Casting about for a way of concluding an argument largely dominated by the figure of William Blake – and also of giving that argument as strong a 'worldly' resonance as I could – I found myself beginning to 'think with' the whole process of transformation then proceeding in my own homeland, South Africa. That process in its last stages had thrown up a certain intellectual resistance within the resistance, a contestation of the culture of the slogan and of a literature of 'protest' characterized by stereotypical 'oppressor' figures and a language of revolutionary hyperbole. In short, the peril loomed of the rise to power of an orthodoxy of subversion as terroristic as the state it opposed. It was against this background that the dialogue of the dead I had initiated between Bakhtin and Blake seemed to promise an ethical space in which *eiron* and *numen*, parody and panegyric, could not only co-exist but also actively strengthen each other. The parallel with Russia's pre-revolutionary culture of dissent only struck me later; one quite uncanny coincidence is the particular objection raised by internal dissidents in both situations to the chillingly centralist description of writers and artists as 'cultural workers'.

Bakhtin's friend Valentin Voloshinov's *Marxism and the Philosophy of Language* bears a title that once drew a grimace from Bakhtin himself in later life; it might also seem an unlikely candidate for inclusion under the rubric of covert dissidence I have just been describing; this was, after all, 1929, and the work in question was in the public domain. 'Syntax and its subversion' (Chapter 3) suggests otherwise. Whatever the writer's intentions, the rhetorically chore-ographed ballet of abstracted ideas that makes up the main argument of that book is notably undone by the seemingly merely illustrative last section on reported speech, where (I argue) close encounter with literary quotation and a homing in upon the most hybrid of the routines of speech representation in fiction – so-called 'free indirect discourse' – dissolves all expository rhetoric in a genuine and open dialogism. It is also an occasion for the invoca-tion of exactly that body of Western European writing that we have seen was so weighty and ethically exemplary a record of modernity for Bakhtin. This great collective act of anamnesis is mediated, moreover, by those expert interpreters of its minutest particulars, those pioneers of the intercultural gaze: the German philologists – for it is they who clearly win the argument – whose field was litera-ture in the Romance languages. When we consider that the ultimate inspiration of these Vosslerite linguists was (as Erich Auerbach has shown) the lineage that runs from Herder back to Vico, and that the rationalistic Saussurean opposition to them is explicitly labelled 'Cartesian', it is clear that we have in this philological offshoot of the counter-enlightenment yet another occasion for the Bakhtinian reproach to the recklessly modernizing intelligentsia.

The only other essay to have been written in ignorance of Bakhtin's early work is the one here called 'Chronotopicity and conceptuality' (Chapter 4). The novelty in this case is not the dialogue that it stages between Bakhtin and Georg Lukács (others had done it before, and I myself had brought these two giants of novel theory together in an essay of 1987[3]); neither was the admis-sion of Gorky to that conversation anything at all new. We might instead isolate as that essay's genuine novelty my observation that the epic has no place in Bakhtin's account of the rich prehistory of the novelistic space–time complex, along with that observation's corollary: namely, that the childhood of the proto-genre of continuous self-reinvention that was at length to crystallize out as 'the novel' was nothing if not 'polymorphously perverse'. When Bakhtin conducts his covert case against Stalinist aesthetics through the loop of a no less hidden polemic with Hegel's conception (brought up to date by Lukács) of the novel as the 'bourgeois epic' – and it is a case that is developed further in *Rabelais and His World* – he is surely warning against the precipitate return of modern ideologies to premodern heroizing modes. Monochronic forms such as myth and epic belong legitimately, and function beneficially, in premodern societies; it is only when modern cultures 'try to reinvent myth' that they 'produce the monster of a monopolistic narrative with global pretensions'.

Bakhtin's notion of 'great time' – that omni-temporal dimension in which the remotest of contexts interact – is first dealt with in the chapter ('Eternity and modernity'; Chapter 6) from which that last quotation comes, and in which I look at Bakhtin's last writings in the light of my first reading of his earliest work. 'Great time' is the perspective in which liberating alternatives to infelicitous marriages of the archaic and the modern may be imagined; for it is plain that both archaizing and modernizing represent by themselves, or at least in the wrong correlation, a species of 'captivity' for Bakhtin (*IENM*, 5–6). The hermeneutic tradition into which Bakhtin recruits himself near the end of his life has just this methodological virtue of an endlessly reversible and bilateral movement of going out to a culturally or temporally 'other' work and then returning – Leo Spitzer's famous 'circle' – rather than unilaterally appropriating 'the past' for short-term ends. That hermeneutics and philology are intersecting disciplines, and that their best practitioners are acutely aware of the ethical force of their arguments in situations of international crisis, is nowhere made plainer than in the work of Auerbach and Bakhtin. As the reader will discover, the kinship between these two thinkers constitutes a recurring theme of this book.

I can now see with hindsight that all of these motifs are implicit in the work of the mid-1920s, which I discuss in two chapters from 1994: 'Aesthetics and the *avant-garde*' (Chapter 2) and 'Philosophy and theology' (Chapter 7). These motifs are only differently inflected, turning new faces to the reader. Bakhtin's polemic of 1924 against Russian Formalism is read in the first of these chapters as the site of a confluence of historical and biographical ironies affecting intellectual practice in the new Soviet state. An *avant-garde* poetics is criticized for its instrumentalizing tendency (a purposive rationality paradoxically consecrated to purposelessness), which identifies it with a vanguardist politics; its 'productionist' anti-aesthetic could not protect it from the repression of a political system notorious for its fetishizing of production in the economy. Against this, Bakhtin poses a notion of art as 'kind' and 'merciful', a practice of universal and unconditional understanding and remembering in which 'form' lovingly 'consummates' 'content' from outside. As the title of the other chapter – 'Philosophy and theology' – implies, the ethics of love upon which this alternative (Bakhtin would say truly 'aesthetic') aesthetic is founded is itself no less inclusive and anamnestic in its constitution, finding expression as it does in terms which freely cross present with past idioms, the Christological with the neo-Kantian. Far from being a shortcoming of our human condition to be made good by the abstract ideas and bloodless epistemology of modernity, our bodily 'outsideness' one to another is exactly the foundation on which we should build the whole house of value. That in Bakhtin's detailed phenomenology of other–self or 'author–hero' relations both in writing and in life we should find so understated a critique of the modern privileging of the narrowly knowing and disembodied ego is only partly to be explained by caution on his part: more positively, it enacts in its very style the devoted attentiveness, the intercreatural *care*, that is its overt and overriding theme.

Philologist, philosopher: 'lover of the word'? Or 'lover of wisdom'? Bakhtin is both together, and neither on its own. A passage from 'Discourse in the Novel' will not so much resolve this paradox as allow it to resonate creatively:

> Rabelais taunts the deceptive human word by a parodic destruction of syntactic structures, thereby reducing to absurdity some of the logical and expressively accented aspects of words . . . . Turning away from language (by means of language, of course), discrediting any direct or unmediated intentionality and expressive excess . . . that might inhere in ideological discourse, presuming that all language is conventional and false, maliciously inadequate to reality – all this achieves in Rabelais almost the maximum purity possible in prose. But the truth that might oppose such falsity receives almost no direct and intentional verbal expression in Rabelais, it does not receive its *own* word – it reverberates only in the parodic and unmasking accents in which the lie is present. Truth is

restored by reducing the lie to an absurdity, but truth itself does not seek words; she is afraid to entangle herself in the word, to soil herself in verbal pathos.

(*DN*, 309)

The deep scepticism about language as the home of the lie that Bakhtin obliquely ventilates here through the figure of François Rabelais has as its obverse a no less profound concern for what a Frenchman of much later times calls the *other of language*: the 'truth' which the word asymptotically approaches but with which it never quite overlaps.[4] In that little allegorical vignette at the end of the passage a personified Truth is imagined as a queenly figure enthroned apart, rapt in a sort of ultimate reserve. The explicitly heroic historical personage of Rabelais is joined by another 'potential hero', who here emerges from the *chiaroscuro* of intellectual discourse in all the light and *claritas* of a bas-relief, an unexpected grace adorning the formal construction of Bakhtin's argument.

Bakhtin was no doubt thinking of the confessional dialogue of the author with St Augustine in Petrarch's *Secretum*, over which the female figure of Truth presides, though without saying a word. Petrarch himself would certainly have been thinking of Dante; and indeed we do seem here momentarily to find ourselves before one of the blessed in the *Paradiso*. Conjured up for us once again is that familiar Bakhtinian symbiosis of irony and the numinous, a pairing which makes no sense to a vulgar enlightenment sensibility, but which encodes for the one who so variously rehearses it the greatest of truths about both Christianity and literature. The Rabelais celebrated here is so far from contradicting the spirit of Dante that we might actually think of the great French parodist as proleptically removing the philosophical dross which high modernity was later to strew in the path of the inventor of modern European writing, thereby clearing the space for the Italian poet's deeds of extraordinary spiritual daring to have their effect. It is for admitting us to such extraordinary perspectives as this that we, in our turn, celebrate the lithe acrobat of ideas who is the subject of this book.

1

BOUNDARIES VERSUS BINARIES

Dialogue and dialectics. Take a dialogue and remove the voices (the partitioning of voices), remove the intonations (emotional and individualizing ones), carve out abstract concepts and judgements from living words and responses, cram everything into one abstract consciousness – and that's how you get dialectics.

(*NM70–71*, 147)

Who or what is Mikhail Bakhtin? Two of the monographs we have on him agree on an identity: Bakhtin is a *philosopher*. The compliment, however well meant, is lethal, and this chapter (if it does nothing else) will contest not only that identity but also any other that might be offered. For Todorov, Bakhtin belongs to the 'intellectual family' of existentialism.[1] Tucked away as it is in a footnote, this affirmation might escape our notice if it were not implicitly announced in the bold script of a subtitle borrowed from Martin Buber: *The Dialogical Principle*. Bakhtin in Todorov's rendering becomes a proto-existentialist distinguished from all others by his elaboration of a theory of discourse, or what Bakhtin himself calls a 'translinguistics'. Even this is doubtful when we think of Maurice Merleau-Ponty's grounding of language in intersubjectivity and his contestation of dominant linguistic theories very much on their own terrain. Bakhtin is neither a phenomenologist with a flair for semiotics nor (like Emile Benveniste) a linguist who leavens and widens his technical interests with a little phenomenology. Rather than affirming an identity we should turn our attention to his *specificity* as a thinker, and we can do this by saying that language for him takes place not in the neutral space of 'communication' but in a charged and irreducibly sociopolitical space of its own endless making and remaking. It will not do to deny the existentialist and the semiotician in Bakhtin, but merely to add to each other these two moments of his thinking, without that third dimension modifying both, is to throw away the subversive potential of these Western responses to the twentieth-century crises of (respectively) the subject and of representation. Bakhtin then enters the history of ideas as a character with an honoured minor role in the Western narrative of human freedom.

Against this precipitate appropriation of Bakhtin by the liberal academy it is no use appropriating him as precipitately for 'Marxism'. What can safely be said is that his thinking is very closely akin to the independent tradition of Western Marxism and at odds with the Soviet Marxism dominant in his time. This uncritical internalization of late-modern scientism, incipient in Friedrich Engels, congealed in the period of the Second International into a dogmatic historical optimism and an economic determinism – in short, a metaphysics of the economic 'base'. Western Marxism, by contrast, is characterized by a preoccupation with the 'superstructure' and a deep dialogical engagement with those novel Western discourses which were beginning to call themselves the human sciences. A reductive account might suggest that this current of thought had simply internalized the opposing pole of the antinomy identified by Marx himself in the *Grundrisse*, that it was little more than a late-modern variant of that Romantic anti-capitalism which posed against the dystopia of a society commodified from top to bottom the utopian possibilities of 'art'.[2] This may be true of Georg Lukács, whose cultural conservatism helps to found such alliance as existed between Soviet and Western Marxism. It is in Walter Benjamin that we find a means of moving beyond Marx's paralysing antinomy. Benjamin's welcome to aesthetic modernism is a recognition that the text of dissident and experimental late-modern writing must be engaged in its textuality rather than dismissed in its ideality: the way out of the *Entfremdung* of reification is not through the category of the totality but through *Verfremdung*, an alienation-effect which makes art directly political.

Now Bakhtin also represents this insight, with the difference that *his* engagement with modernism is rather with its theoretical and philosophical than with its literary discourses. He constructs in this engagement an anti-Hegelianism which is compatible with, though by no means the same as, Marx's, and which is characterized by what we might call a return to a *pre*-Hegelian moment in the

German philosophical tradition. He makes this move in the context of a polity and an economy that thought of themselves as constituting the world's first exception to 'bourgeois' hegemony, and if in one respect he is the beneficiary of this placing – forever sharpening, as it must have done, his sense that the theoretical is inescapably the political – he is also in the short term its victim: in the atmosphere of suspicious defensiveness that reigned in the Soviet state under siege, his tactical heterodoxy might look like treason. In the subtext of the polemics of the 1920s – and then more overtly in the Dostoevsky book, where the signature of Dostoevsky as it were protected him – we can sense a critique that aligns itself with Lukács' in *History and Class Consciousness* (1923) while at the same time distancing itself from the Hegelianism of that text. The moment on which Bakhtin fixes is that of Kant and Goethe: he finds in the discourses of this moment a means of resisting Hegel's total absorption of the world in the absolute self-knowledge of Spirit, his abolition of a multiform objectivity in a uniform subjectivity.

Ernst Bloch's use of Goethe against Hegel and Ernst Cassirer's similar use of Kant provide close parallels for Bakhtin's project in this (early) period.[3] Cassirer's *The Philosophy of Symbolic Forms* (1923–29) is a text acknowledged by Bakhtin and Voloshinov as a Western ally of their own project,[4] and its publication in the year of Lukács's heterodox offering dramatizes its importance in that project's formation. In Bakhtin the word and the body live on their boundaries, just as the sensible and the intelligible do in Cassirer, and the present and future in Bloch. Bakhtin takes his cue from a stage of Western thought in which (as in Schiller, for example) the aesthetic had yet to lose its worldly moorings and be launched to lose itself in the sea of Spirit, as a mere cancelled phase of which philosophy is the subl(im)ation. He interrupts the passage of this stage into that hypostasis of cognitive consciousness which is idealism at its limit, 'philosophical monologism' at the height of its ambition. It is not for nothing that Bakhtin cites Kant at the beginning of his essay on the chronotope and insists in the *Bildungsroman* fragment on the chronotopic character of Goethe's thinking (*FTC*, 85; *BSHR*, 25–50).

Where does this leave Bakhtin? In my view he ends up somewhere between Western Marxism and post-structuralism, more politicized than the latter and with a more sophisticated theory of discourse than the former ever produced. Encoded in the polemic with Sigmund Freud and Ferdinand de Saussure and Russian Formalism – not as its truth, but simply as one of its bearings – is a complex dialogue and critical consensus with the neo-Kantianism of Cassirer, the heterodox Marxism of Lukács and (to bring another name into the equation) the existential theology of Buber, whose *I and Thou* was also coincidentally published in 1923. *Marxism and the Philosophy of Language* makes a tactical alliance with some of the motifs of classical Marxism in its Soviet variant in order to ventilate the claims of an alternative, at once anti-scientist *and* anti-Hegelian, to the dominant Marxist tradition. In the New Economic Policy (NEP) phase of early Soviet history the die had not decisively been cast, and a reinvention of Marxism fructified by a dialogue with Western discourses that offered an alternative route out of Hegel was still a possibility.

What we choose to call these discourses matters little: the important point is that they provide a ground for dissent from the official triumphalism of the (then) communist movement and for a rejection at once of the classical (Hegelian) speculative dialectic and of Engels's 'dialectics of nature'. In its polemic against the available versions of a proto-structuralism, Bakhtinism precociously invents a post-structuralism which also revives aspects of Marx's project that had been lost in the philosophizing of his heirs. One of these is the ambivalence of Marx's dialectic of history, its suspension between a 'tragic' and a 'progressivist' perspective. This comes through in the books on Dostoevsky and Rabelais and in the profound meditation upon the relationship of the serious and the comic that is contained in them. Bakhtin castigates utopian socialism as idealist, but it is equally clear that the alternative of supposedly 'scientific' socialism establishes a dichotomy that he would want to undermine. Against the monologism of 'actually existing' socialism in the Stalinist period he poses the popular utopia of laughter and carnival, dialogism that has taken to the streets. The other aspect of Marx's project revived in the Bakhtin 'circle' is apparent mainly in the polemical phase of the 1920s: it is his anti-systemic, critical, deconstructive way with the concepts of modern thought. Marx's deconstruction of the commodity is echoed in a deconstruction of that severest of all casualties of commodification as Bakhtin and his colleagues saw it: the sign. They do for linguistics and for poetics and stylistics what Marx had done for economics. What Lukács in 1923 calls the 'formalism' or the 'abstract and formal method' of political economy is replicated in the 'abstract objectivism' of Saussure's linguistics and in the famous 'formal method' in Russian literary studies.[5] In short, we find in works like Voloshinov's *Marxism and the Philosophy of Language* the prolegomena of a *Capital* of the 'superstructure'.

I

Perhaps the most direct route to an understanding of Bakhtin's specific anti-Hegelianism is through his pronouncements on the dialectic. A gnomic sentence from one of his later works provides a starting-point: 'Dialectics was born of dialogue so as to return again to dialogue on a higher level' (*MHS*, 162). What this seems to imply is that the classical speculative dialectic is itself the product of a dialectical process; it is the 'abstract product' which results when dialogue (in Bakhtin's strong internal – sense) is monologized by being located in a 'unique abstract consciousness', when its 'division of voices' is abolished in a single voice (*PDP*, 293; *N70–71*, 147). By staying there, however, we have only explicated the first stage of Bakhtin's critique, a preliminary re-situation of the dialectic within a process which it claims to transcend as that process's privileged metalanguage. We remain in this explication at the level of the signified. Moving to the level of the signifier – reading Bakhtin's sentence not *as* a sentence but as an utterance, not as exhaustible in a paraphrase but as an (inexhaustible) *answer* – we can see in its language nothing less than a *parody* of the language of the classical dialectic, bringing out the critical force of the (non-)concept of dialogism by granting dialogue priority. He blows apart the closure of the thesis–antithesis–synthesis model (the negation of the negation) by putting what for dialectics would be mere 'mediation' in the place of the thesis, so that it undergoes rather than effects the *Aufhebung*. Thus:

DIALOGUE DIALECTIC DIALOGISM ('synthesis')

What is 'restored' is not identity or self-coincidence but non-identity; the 'synthesis' is a term which undermines as an active force all synthesizing and homogenizing projects whatever. Bakhtin's mock synthesis is that which all institutional or conceptual syntheses endlessly posit themselves against. The philosophy of Hegel is from this perspective a kind of *felix culpa* of discourse, propelling dialogue-in-itself into the dialogue-for-itself which is dialogism. The logic of particular and universal is first of all reversed and then displaced altogether. That which lives unself-consciously outside itself encounters a unitary meaning on its inside – it acquires what Bakhtin calls in an early formulation an 'inner territory' – only to recoil from this discovery into a militant 'outsideness', an explicit politics of the boundary removed altogether from the logic and implicit politics of the binary (*PCMF*, 274). Thus:

OUTSIDE INSIDE BOUNDARY
Others as given Self Others for others . . .

In Bakhtin's philosophy there is a use of the language of rationality which is always at the same time a parodic displacement of that language, a dialogization of its monologism. Dialectics does not magically convert itself into an (or *the*) antagonist of metaphysics by taking on the attribute or assuming the 'content' of matter rather than spirit. It will remain a metaphysics unless and until it is truly radicalized in that self-parody of dialectics which has now issued in certain varieties of 'deconstruction'.

This radical politics of the boundary has its fullest elaboration, for Bakhtin, in the existential poetics of Dostoevsky. What the various existentialisms have in common is a protest against Being in general, a revolt of being-in-the-world against a metaphysics experienced as unfreedom, a disempowering tyranny of the essence. Now if Bakhtin's anti-philosophy is refracted through the tragic personalism of Dostoevsky it is nonetheless no more to be identified with the latter than with an optimistic collectivism imposed from above. Orthodox Marxism recognized only one route out of Hegel: that of so-called 'dialectical materialism' or *diamat*. Bakhtin asserts the right to dialogue with other post-Hegelian voices which do not implicate the thinker in the materialism–idealism binary and which help him to question the very *form* of the dialectic itself. Idealism is opposed not because it is a philosophy of the spirit but because it is the most authoritarian and totalitarian monologism imaginable. Spirit is opposed not because it is not matter but because it is one of the names of the identical subject–object, and to assign the role of identical subject–object to anything else (even the proletariat) is to remain within an identitarian or idealist problematic. Any systematic alternative to the latter sooner or later finds itself to be no alternative at all. There can be no 'dialogics' – to use a barbarous and falsifying term much in use now but with no basis whatever in Bakhtin. Indirection is not simply a response to the danger of direct assertion under Stalinism; it is an *internal* imperative of Bakhtin's thinking. Which is as much as to say: there are in Bakhtin only 'philosophy effects' generated by discourses that are not in themselves philosophical. The liminal discipline of translinguistics is not a philosophy – not even a 'philosophy of language' – but rather a discourse which signals certain philosophical bearings and has effects that might be called philosophical, while it is more directly preoccupied with other business: either polemicizing with

18

other disciplines of the sign or working on and within those special sites of dialogism called 'novel' and 'carnival'. Bakhtin's 'philosophy' is in this sense *strategic* rather than systematic, a matter of polemical or parodic glancing blows that avoid confronting systems with their elaborated antitheses or antidotes because of the complicities this entails. We are not surprised to find that the late 'experiments in philosophical analysis' never get beyond the stage of the note or the fragment. 'Every entry into the sphere of meaning is accomplished only through the gates of the chronotope': thus Bakhtin, concluding his last completed piece of writing (*FTC*, 258). Even abstract thought, he claims, is impossible without 'temporal-spatial expression': like Marx and Derrida (at least in Michael Ryan's construction of them) Bakhtin knows that theory is always situated in and exceeded by history and materiality.[6]

Some of Bakhtin's more 'materialist' readers might have a problem with the parenthesis that closes the sentence which we have taken as our starting-point, and which for the purposes of this analysis I have thus far suppressed. The full sentence actually reads: 'Dialectics was born of dialogue so as to return to dialogue at a higher level (a dialogue of *personalities*)' (*MHS*, 162). Now it is obvious that some Western canonizers of Bakhtin would seize on this parenthesis as a means of identifying him with a personalist 'philosophy'. Our answer to this should not be to excuse a late aberration in Bakhtin but rather to affirm the burden of his parenthesis by first of all reconstructing the context to which it plainly alludes – I mean the moment of the Dostoevsky book – and then showing how this emphasis on 'personalities' might be put to use anew in *our* context, and without any awkward apology.

I have already implied that Bakhtin's 'strategic' anti-philosophizing is inseparable from the positive hermeneutic of this great monograph, a hermeneutic which has as its negative obverse a critique of the instrumental rationality peculiar to modernity. What needs to be emphasized now is that this text marks the transition from the Bakhtin Circle's polemicizing and sociologizing of the 1920s to the politicizing and historicizing work of the 1930s – from the deconstruction of theories of signification which perpetuate the inside–outside binary in theory to an exploration of the forms and institutions which deconstruct it in practice. In the polemical work under other signatures than Bakhtin's own we have something like a sociolinguistics or a speech-act theory: translinguistics in this phase tends perhaps to take the sociopolitical space of discourse as given, whereas in the later phase it extends to an exploration of how hegemonies are organized, how the space of the sociopolitical 'real' is created. When the whole of Bakhtin's *actual* context was in creative flux – when the Russian Revolution still licensed a carnival of ideas – there is a tendency for the subject and the referent to be substantialized: in the text are inscribed 'relations between people', and 'extralinguistic reality' has the status of a homogenized transcendence. When this carnival is over, Bakhtin is driven to seek out sites and times where the play of signifiers is a manifest material force and when 'play' is itself the 'work' of history. Against the Formalists, for whom 'discourse in art' was the function of a cancelled sociality, Bakhtin and his colleagues rethought 'art' as an intensified sociality, an intensification of the immanent sociality of 'discourse in life'. If in the 1920s 'art' is thus assimilated to 'life', in the 1930s 'life' is assimilated to 'art': in the midst of 'ideology' Bakhtin conjures up (in Karl Mannheim's sense of these words) a 'utopia' of popular and novelistic deconstruction.[7]

It doesn't require much perspicacity to read the supersession of carnivalesque counterculture in a new official culture described in *Rabelais and his World* as an allegory of the betrayal of the revolution. Much more fundamental is the shift from the implicit homogeneity of a referent given before discourse to a referent understood as both irreducibly heterogeneous and issuing ceaselessly from the 'creative work' of discourse itself, in an active and collective making of the future. Discourse is never conceived as anything other than actively interventionist, but in the 1930s Bakhtin moves from a stress on the power of the utterance to 'resolve situations' to an almost hyperbolic affirmation of the power of popular assertion to turn the world upside down. Bakhtin's answer to the brutal abolition of popular politics under Stalinism is a reconstruction of the space of the sociopolitical as the realized and realizing self-activity of the 'people' – of 'historical becoming' as inseparable from powerful acts of meaning, acts which no 'power' can destroy without ultimately destroying itself.

Hindsight makes it possible for us to see the Dostoevsky book as the point of transition between these two phases: defined by its difference from both of them. Between the sociologizing imperative of his friends' polemical texts and the historicizing imperative of his own work on carnival and the novel, this book is the *locus classicus* of that existentializing imperative which we need to recognize – and affirm – as a perennial force in Bakhtin's thinking. By contrast with the aggressive assertion of an alternative objectivism to the 'abstract objectivism' of Saussurean linguistics and Formalist poetics, the book on Dostoevsky seems almost wilfully 'subjec-tivist'. Now from one perspective this could be seen as Bakhtin grasping and closely engaging with the problem of the subject which (as I have argued elsewhere) the Formalists had 'prematurely and undialectically' bracketed out, in a cancellation of subjectivity matching that cancellation of sociality already mentioned.[8] (The rampant phonocentrism of their theory of *skaz* is in this sense only the subject taking its revenge.) From another perspective, this text's (alleged) 'subjectivism' could equally be seen as a tactical return to Bakhtin's earlier meditation on the ethics and aesthetics of intersub-jectivity. If the polemics sought to contextualize the text (against Formalism), and if the later work on carnival textualizes the context (against Stalinism) – opening up the referent as a site of praxis – then the Dostoevsky book may be said to *textualize the subject*, against a composite opponent which includes 'idealism', its literary analogue in the homophonic novel[9] and their common root in the 'reification of man' under capitalism.

This, then, is the project of *Problems of Dostoevsky's Art*; and at first glance it seems somewhat quixotic and otherworldly to be proposing a definition of dialogism as 'a dialogue of *personalities*' in the first year of the First Five-Year Plan, arguing the epistemological merits of a kind of writing in which 'self-consciousness' is the 'dominant' when collectivization was already in train. Of course, Bakhtin's notion of the 'personality' has nothing whatever to do with the monadic individual of what Marxists would call 'bourgeois individualism'. Dostoevsky's 'profoundly personalized' world is also (Bakhtin insists) 'profoundly pluralistic': by 'personality' we are to understand the subject as a shifting function of intertextual boundaries (*PDP*, 26). Still, there is – as Ken Hirschkop has argued – a problem with the idea of a plurality of interacting consciousnesses, inasmuch as their interaction in the space of the text somewhat dubiously stands in for the truly objective space of the social itself. We can (on this view) only rescue Bakhtin from the charge of 'subjectivism' either by associating polyphony with carnival or by opposing to the humanist reading which sees behind the 'roles of real life' a 'certain irreducible freedom' a 'radical' reading which (for its part) sees the unfinalizability of the Dostoevskian 'person-ality' as an emblem of 'the ever-present possibility of change'.[10] Two points need to be made here. First, the link with carnival only becomes available in the edition of 1963. Second, unexceptionable as both this link and the alternative ('radical') reading may be, they are not necessary. Even in the 1929 edition of that work, the space of the text is not as falsifying of the social as Hirschkop makes it out to be: Dostoevsky's hero-ideologues are not all that unlike the subjects of a genuine Gramscian hegemony: 'philosophers' or potential author-functions whose 'common sense' must be rendered critical and self-critical by the dialogical agency of those professional authors of revolution called 'intellectuals'. At the very least we could say that there is a strong proto-political or quasi-political dimension to the Dostoevsky book, with polyphony shadowing forth the strategies and forms of subjectivity proper to a real politics of popular sovereignty.

The parallel with Gramsci can be carried further. The image that Bakhtin hits upon when trying to distinguish Dostoevsky's 'pluralistic' world from the 'unified, dialectically evolving spirit, understood in Hegelian terms' is an institutional metaphor that his Italian contemporary would have approved: namely, the church 'as a communion of unmerged souls, where sinners and righteous men come together' (*PDP*, 26–27). Gramsci's concept of the revolutionary party is not far removed from this catholic inclusiveness ascribed by Bakhtin to Dostoevskian polyphony. Gramsci's more general philosophical project – in which, centrally, metaphysics is redefined against vulgar-materialist orthodoxy as 'any systematic formulation that is put forward as an extra-historical truth, as an abstract universal outside of time and space'[11] – is very close to the specific anti-idealism of Bakhtin's text of 1929. (Bakhtin, moreover, would have had before him in the writing of Nikolai Bukharin the representative of orthodox materialism who is the object of Gramsci's critique.) A close look at the metaphors Bakhtin uses to give a sense of the relationship between author and hero in the homophonic novel leads us ineluctably to a homology between the poetics of the latter and the politics of absolute rule. Consider, for example, the claim that everything from the author's side which might have, 'as it were, sentenced' the hero functions in Dostoevsky not as a means of his 'finalization' but as 'the material of his self-consciousness'. Besides this forensic metaphor, there are recurring tropes of surveillance and rebellion: the Dostoevskian hero is not 'a being that can be spied on, defined, predicted apart from its own will, at second hand'; and he is in 'revolt' against 'his literary finalization' (*PDP*, 51, 58–59).

After 1929 the insistence on Dostoevsky's exceptionalism is played down and the word polyphony disappears from Bakhtin's vocabulary until the edition of 1963. Karl Radek's association of Dostoevsky with Proust and Joyce in 1934,[12] not to mention Lukacs's denunciation of two years before, would of course have made any heroization inadvisable. Bakhtin's recourse to generalizations about '*the* novel' springs, however, not so much from caution of this specific kind as from a more general logic of his politics of theory in the 1930s: it was inevitable that the dialogized 'voices' of Dostoevskian polyphony would become the dialogized 'social languages' of novelistic heteroglossia when his argument was not (overtly) with philosophies and novel types – or indeed with the reification of 'class society' – but (covertly) with the Stalinist state itself. The difference between this position and that of the Dostoevsky book is nonetheless in no sense the difference between a covert presence of the political and its overt absence: what after all unites them is the emphasis on the novel as an image of civil society, in Gramsci's (rather than Marx's) sense.[13] Polyphony stands for the ideal condition of civil society; homophony for its contamination by the *I–it* relations of the state. That this homology is not fanciful should be clear from the occasional excursions Bakhtin makes into the 'sociological' explanation of Dostoevskian polyphony in a text otherwise given over to its immanent 'formal' description. Dostoevsky's work is the novelistic correlative of the effect of capitalist relations upon the hitherto mutually deafened and blinded sectors of Russian civil society. Capitalism arrives with 'catastrophic suddenness' and breaks down the insulation of these 'diverse worlds and spheres', bringing them to self-knowledge through knowledge of each other, making their contradictory unity and interdependence a fact of consciousness (*PDP*, 19). The art of Dostoevsky is nothing less than the orchestration of these voices.

II

If we need any further proof of the political thrust of the Dostoevsky book, we need only turn to Anatoly Lunacharsky's (broadly favourable) review, written by the 'People's Commissar of Education' when Bakhtin was already in the Lubianka prison on his way to internal exile in Kazakhstan, and thereby starkly dramatizing the contrast between state repression and dialogue within civil society which is not only implicit in the book but actually brought into the open (to be sure, as a matter of 'history') in the review itself. Dostoevsky is presented by Lunacharsky as one of those 'great personalities' of nineteenth-century Russia who sought and tragically failed to organize the forces of civil society against the absolute state.[14] This 'first great petty-bourgeois writer in the history of our culture' not only reflected the confusion of his class but also served as its 'powerful and much-needed organizer'.[15] His project, within his fiction and without, was to detach the '"inner" understanding' of Orthodox religion from its 'outward forms' – in other words, to compel an institution compromised by its relation to the autocratic state into an institution of civil society from which that state might be opposed.[16] The church as a utopian 'coinherence of souls' provides him with the means to take his distance not only from the autocracy but also from any revolutionary-socialist solution. In Lunacharsky's reading of Dostoevsky-through-Bakhtin the writing is effectively construed as a positive gain conjured out of Dostoevsky's inevitable failure – inevitable not just because of his impotence as an individual, but also because he is an organic intellectual springing from a class with no 'historic mission' and little power to rescue Russian civil society from what Gramsci would later call its 'gelatinous' condition. It is also a reading which is not without a more sharply contemporary relevance than Bakhtin would have felt free to enforce. Lunacharsky ends his review with (among others) the following very striking observation: 'If we ourselves find no positive ideas in Dostoevsky we must remember that we are not as yet a majority in the country'.[17] In this formulation Lunacharsky makes the leap from 'Dostoevsky' as the name of an active intervention in civil society under the autocracy to 'Dostoevskyism' [*Dostoevshschina*] as a force within civil society under the Soviet state. The perspective held out here is one of 'proletarian' (properly, Bolshevik) hegemony as something to be fought for politically and dialogically in a situation where not only the 'vanguard' party but also the proletariat itself is a numerical minority. 'Dostoevskyism' is a material force within civil society which Lunacharsky seeks not to repress by administrative decree – in a move which would threaten the very survival of civil society itself – but to redeem (as it were) by promoting a critical inflection of its motifs, by acknowledging its hold over the other classes making up the 'people' and engaging it in critical dialogue.

Now I would not wish to suggest that Lunacharsky's case is identical with some supposedly Bakhtinian 'message' contained in the Dostoevsky book. Neither would I claim that 'Hegel' in that text is (as Fredric Jameson says it is in Louis Althusser) a code for 'Stalin'. What I am suggesting is that this powerful Soviet official's appraisal of Bakhtin–Dostoevsky is itself a political intervention within contemporary civil society; that it is predicated upon the permanence and value of this site of the dialogical negotiation of power; and that it brings out for us what is at stake when the name of Dostoevsky is invoked by Bakhtin (or anybody else) in 1929. Invoking that name in that year is not perhaps after all as perverse an act as it might have seemed. Beyond this, affirming Dostoevskian personalism as an 'ideology of the text' (rather than as the philosophy of Dostoevsky himself) is not inconsistent with that open-ended logic of the collective always in the process of becoming which is the dialectic in its non-speculative version. 'Polyphony' as a metaphor for that 'spiritual diversity' which is the 'dialogue of *personalities*' is admittedly wildly at odds with the kind of metaphor favoured by the contemporary Russian *avant-garde*. Formalism and Futurism take their metaphors from the economic base, in an aggressive de-theologization of aesthetics which (as we have seen) landed them in an ahistorical and abstract objectivism that saved them neither from the revenge of the subject nor from official denunciation. Bakhtin's metaphor is not only a musical one: it calls to mind (more specifically) a particular kind of ecclesiastical music and therefore by extension the church itself – that is to say, that part of the social totality which pre-revolutionary intellectuals like Dostoevsky sought to claim for civil society against the state.

Putting the Formalists' 'device' alongside 'polyphony', we can see that the more traditionalist of the two metaphors is by far the more politically astute, however unrevolutionary it might sound next to its modernist and productionist counterpart. Its great merit is that it identifies – against the complementary reifications of 'art' and the 'economy' – the real hegemonic battleground in any society undergoing revolutionary transformation, where sociality and subjectivity are forever born together. But 'polyphony' also has a philological meaning from the late nineteenth century, which Bakhtin (trained, like Gramsci, as an historical linguist) must surely have known: 'the symbolization of different vocal sounds by the same letter or character'.[18] The senses of phonemic-diversity-within-graphic-unity on the one hand and melodic-diversity-within-harmonic-unity on the other cross-fertilize (as it were) to produce a translinguistic concept of considerable power, in which the 'characters' of a certain kind of fiction are conceived as bearing within themselves the difference they have with respect to each other.

Such 'characters' – narratological rather than graphological – are of course precisely those dispersed author-functions Bakhtin calls 'personalities'. If I am to make good my claim that a 'radical' reading needs to affirm rather than apologize for this emphasis on the subject, then I must show not only that this subject is exhaustively textualized but also that its textualization has ethico-political and theoretical implications that challenge Western rationality. The Dostoevskian 'personality' is defined by Bakhtin as 'pure self-consciousness in its totality', polyphony being the kind of novelistic discourse in which such self-consciousness is the 'dominant of representation' (*PDP*, 48). In effect, this 'free' personality is a principle of radical immanence – or (better) a zone of absolute resistance to 'bad' transcendence, situated where no metalanguage or metanarrative can reach it. It is 'free' in the sense that it is only ever represented under the aspect of its own self-positing activity. Its work is like that of a black hole in discursive space, exerting so strong a gravitational pull upon all around it that it has always already drawn *into itself* all actual or potential 'final words' *about itself*. If the characters of the homophonic novel are not in this sense personalities, that is because they are merely empirical individuals from whom the 'direct power to mean' has been confiscated and monopolized by the 'author-monologist'. In a dialogue of personalities the power to mean is freely exercised on all sides, and the obverse of this thoroughgoing authenticity is the abolition of all idiosyncrasy. Bakhtin uses the concept of this 'consciousness for its own sake' to counter the monological or philosophical fiction of the unincarnated and unsituated idea, the idea which 'belongs to *no one*' and does not happen in time (*PDP*, 79). Homophony combines an empiricism of the character with an idealism of the author: the ideas of characters are mere psychological attributes (more or less erroneous, or at least non-affirmable), while those of the author alone are *meanings*. 'That which is individual' is not essential; conversely, that which is essential is not individual but rather *Bewusstsein überhaupt*, 'consciousness in general'. Or, as Bakhtin puts it in what is probably the shortest sentence he ever wrote: 'Only error individualizes' (*PDP*, 81). Truth and individuality are reconciled (can coexist) only on the side of the author: in the hero the power of an idea to mean is either negated by his individuality or only affirmed at the cost of the latter.

There is no paradox in saying that this extreme personalism is the very reverse of any subjectivism. Not to understand this is not to have understood that Bakhtin thinks by way of extremes: subjectivity thought of as pure immanence inverts itself into an immanent sociality; when everyone is absolutely an author, no one is absolutely in authority. If Bakhtin's metaphor-concepts are at odds with those of Formalism, it is nonetheless certain that he had already matched their extremist gestures in his own style of thinking. If he textualizes the subject (as I have suggested he does), he does so by giving the subject the same status as Formalism gives to the text: instead of the 'self-valuable word' freed from 'motivation' we have 'pure self-consciousness' freed from the heteronomy of 'character' and 'plot'. The (linguistic) signifier privileged by Formalism becomes the signifier *as actor* specialized to the task of signifying itself in the world and the world in itself. The result is something not unlike what Jameson calls the '"absolute formalism" of Marxism itself', with its 'dialectical and historical self-consciousness': in short, an absolute formalism whose other face is an absolute historicism, Gramsci's 'absolute humanism of history'.[19]

Listen to Gramsci himself, on the special stance of the Marxist philosopher: 'Consciousness full of contradictions, in which the philosopher himself, understood both individually and as an entire social group, not only grasps the contradictions, but posits himself as an element of the contradiction and elevates this element to a principle of knowledge and therefore of action'.[20] Bakhtin would find little to disagree with in this Gramscian summary of how the 'philosophy of praxis' refuses with its refusal of the Hegelian dialectic the 'single position outside of history' on which its system rests.[21] The philosopher of praxis and the polyphonic author have in common a continuing existential act of auto-situation – an ongoing self-positing which at once presupposes similar acts in others and opens a space for those others to empower themselves. The dialogue of intellectual and class is as much a dialogue of personalities as that of all the subjects (author included) in the polyphonic novel: both would define themselves against what Bakhtin calls the 'pedagogical dialogue' of idealism in which knowledge confronts ignorance unilaterally and unequally (*PDP*, 81).

III

Authenticity, historicity, legitimacy: it is the profound relationship that Bakhtin's thinking helps us to develop between these three terms – their transformation into each other, their dynamic homology so to speak – that unfits it for the purposes of that parochialism which the West seeks to pass off as universality. Authenticity is what the heroes of polyphony display supremely; polyphony is the interaction of authentic existents who resist in all their discourse the bad faith of objectivization. It is at the same time (at least in Dostoevsky) an exclusively synchronic interaction, its contradictions coexisting in textual space rather than unfolding in fictional time. Polyphony's association with synchrony is to be explained by its suspicion of diachrony as a dimension compromised by the latter's association with the classical dialectic. Diachrony fosters the illusion that the dialogue of personalities can be resolved in some higher unity. The resolute synchrony of polyphony not only offers a dimension in which authenticity and non-resolution can flourish; it is also the condition of a founding of historicity against that History which is only one of the more subtle guises of Being. The synchrony inhabited by the subjects of polyphony is a formal or textual allegory not of stasis but of perpetual possibility. This specific temporality of the *project* is the natural element of the unfinalizable hero, and it is bound up also with the narrative that is always enterable, in which everything is a pure instance of discourse, and in which the power of hypothesizing an end to the story is in no one subject's hands. The roles of author and hero stand in a relation of infinite asymptotic approach to each other, in a distinction which is always relative and never absolute. When there is nothing outside this pure immanence of consciousnesses there is by the same token nothing outside the pure immanence of history, nothing given from somewhere else in the sense of escaping that implication in narratives which is shared by representer and represented alike. Posed in directly sociopolitical terms, these issues of 'representation' become issues of 'legitimation'; the idioms of authenticity and historicity undergo translation as the perspective is opened up of a legitimacy which explicitly carries over into the realm of power their (already powerful) challenge to a dominant ontology and epistemology.

Now I am not suggesting that polyphony is to be precipitately re-read as a code for 'democracy': to do so would be equivalent to reading Dostoevsky as a realist of the English or Western European variety. Polyphony offers us a position from which Western humanism and universalism can at the very least be problematized – that is to say, seen in the light (or rather dark) of what they exclude or repress. It is the poetics of a politics that in Western Europe found fleeting expression in the insurgent stage of the 'bourgeois revolution', rather than the poetics (like realism) of an established 'bourgeois' order. Its bearings lie among those classes which have never ruled and which epitomize *revolt* rather than revolution: either the subaltern classes of the late pre-capitalist period who speak an antinomian language; or those intermediate classes of late capital whose language of crisis is one or other version of existentialism. Women under patriarchy, the global underclass of imperialism – any group which has reason to suspect Reason – will gravitate towards this idiom of revolt. Occupying the ground of Bakhtin–Dostoevsky, what we gain is not an alternative philosophical vision but a scepticism about the legitimacy of all victorious classes that do not listen to these marginalized voices, a sense of the complicity of enlightenment and (yes) secularization itself with the global hegemony of Europe. If the class whose 'historic mission' it is to end classes as such is not to become an author-monologist of history like its immediate forerunner, it will need to establish its legitimacy on the quite new basis of a complex dialogue with the discourses of groups for whom the tragedy of enlightenment is a matter of direct experience. In the Soviet Union in 1929 the refusal of a dialogue of personalities within civil society (that is, of groups or individuals with an equal power to mean) would lead to a forced collectivization of the economy and over it all a state which had effectively swallowed civil society and reduced it to a 'cult of the personality' of the leader himself.

Such a dialogue will not be the mere verbal accompaniment of an opportunistic alliance between a hegemonic (or hegemonizing) class and other constituencies, a tolerance of unpalatable idioms for the sake of the 'masses' they deliver into action. 'Unpalatable' in this case means unpalatable from the philosophical standpoint of a vulgar materialism or from the political standpoint of a 'workerism', given that the themes of these discourses are usually either religious or personalist or nationalist, or a combination of these three. Polyphony adumbrates a hegemonic style which gives these supposedly superseded languages their full weight. Religion is more than the mere epiphenomenon of a past mode of production – pre-capitalist, culpably 'pre-scientific', even 'objectively reactionary': third-world liberation theology is in our own time reinventing religion as a mode and code of popular assertion. Personalism as a post-Hegelian revolt against the category of the totality might have been caricatured by Marx in the early example of Max Stirner; in Dostoevsky (as Bakhtin points out), he is one of the prototypes of Raskolnikov (*PDP*, 90). It is Dostoevsky rather than Marx who must be our model in evaluating this tradition as it develops through Nietzsche to existentialism. If nationalism is irredeemably 'petty-bourgeois' and therefore always politically suspect for any narrowly instrumental-functional 'class analysis', it has indubitably also been an indispensable force in movements for liberation from colonialism and neo-colonialism – without which

even the organized working class would not get beyond 'corpo-
ratism' and 'trade-union consciousness'.

Indeed it is in the revolt of the colonized against their subalter-
nity that the dialogue of personalities has been most effectively
mobilized of late. Bakhtin's philosophizing is of the kind that finds
Dostoevsky's writing (in a Lévi-Straussian phrase) eminently 'good
to think with'; today's followers of Bakhtin would do well to 'think
with' the great living and ongoing narratives of decolonization,
whose supreme hero-ideologue must surely be Frantz Fanon. 'The
truth about the world, according to Dostoevsky, is inseparable from
the truth of the personality' (*PDP*, 78): what Bakhtin says of the
polyphonic novel's typical protagonist applies also to the writing of
Fanon: confession and generalization interpenetrate in a discursive
ambience where every uttered or imaginable 'final word' of the
colonizer about the colonized is answered, anticipated, matched,
faced and fought past. The effect is of guerrilla warfare in the realm
of thinking as Fanon exploits to the full the one respect in which the
balance of inequality in the colonial relationship lies in favour of
the colonized – in the intimate knowledge the latter has of his
master which the master can never reciprocate. Fanon's texts turn a
metropolitan idiom of revolt into a revolutionary force of the colonial
margin, a suspicion of the universal into something dangerously
uncontainable: a direct threat to those whose shyness about naming
themselves is most deeply underwritten by this epistemic
anonymity. These texts represent not 'the rational confrontation of
points of view' but, rather, 'the untidy affirmation of an original
idea propounded as an absolute'.[22] They set up a dialogism from
below which has nothing to do with the 'assimilated' elite, where
the initiative is wholly on the side of the imperial author-monologist. The relations of discourse and power which three centuries of
Western development have comprehensively and intricately mysti-
fied are scandalously exposed in a discourse that speaks of
counter-violence and counter-hegemony in the same breath. If the
violence of colonial conquest and the destruction of indigenous
cultures are bound up together – if the theft first of land and then of
et al. is accompanied not just contingently but internally and necessarily by a theft of the word – then so too must the people's
counter-assertion practically deconstruct the politico-metaphysical
opposition of 'peaceful' to 'violent' means of struggle. We are not
surprised to find in this discourse a politics of the boundary very
much like Bakhtin's, a critical relationship to Western philosophy
that is able to invoke as its worldly stimulus and materialization a

revolt of global proportions. In *Black Skin, White Masks* this anti-philosophizing takes the form of an autobiographical narrative which is at the same time an allegory (a sort of putative or potential history) of everybody in the colonized condition. It is unmistakably the writing of a person *in a situation*, apostrophizing friends and foes, casting backward and sideways glances as he takes his distance both from *négritude* and from a sympathetic metropolitan view which sees this antithesis to colonial racism as a mere phase to be dialectically transcended. What Fanon's writing insistently says to us is that a politics of the boundary is nothing if not *incarnated*: any exposition courts the danger of reducing this order of intensely engaged thinking to the bloodless categories of a metaphysics. If that is all one can say about it, that is because '*it*' is an inapposite pronoun in this context; because it demands to be spoken or written not 'about' but 'with', in solidarity rather than commentary. Such agonistic thinking always throws a merely cognitive consciousness into disarray. Fanon's whole output shows that the adumbration or institution of a Bakhtinian 'dialogue of *personalities*' is nothing less than a revolutionary act.

The question 'Who or what is Mikhail Bakhtin?' resolves itself into the question 'Where is he today?' Now that Fanon is dead, his project is most closely paralleled in the pedagogic writing of Paulo Freire – that Gramsci of the Third World for whom revolution is impossible without 'dialogical cultural action'[23] – and in the theatre of Augusto Boal, whose 'poetics of the oppressed' moves beyond a (Brechtian) poetics of the 'enlightened vanguard' to free the spectator into action, action which is a 'rehearsal of revolution'. In the work of these living teachers of liberation the discourse of 'high existentialism' has (as Jameson says of Fanon, who inspired both of them) 'fallen into the world'; its motifs have 'migrat[ed] outside philosophy departments altogether, into a more frightening landscape of praxis and terror'.[24] They are doing for the margins what Western Marxism sought to do for the revolutionary process in the metropolis – tracking the oppressor and exploiter down to the latter's last outposts in culture and in consciousness, inventing new ways of activating the self-articulation of the oppressed – and doing it moreover in writing that is, first and last, pragmatically oriented: like Bakhtin's writing, in short, in being only strategically philosophical and yet more devastating in their philosophical implications than any Western 'system'. It is a profound irony of our postmodern era that these genuine correlatives of Bakhtin's thought should both be found in the southern half of the American continent: while the liberal academics of that continent's northern *imperium* produce and reproduce themselves as intellectuals in misreadings of his work, Bakhtin himself lives in the fighting, praying, dialogizing, carnivalizing thinkers of the continental body's transgressive lower half.

2

AESTHETICS AND THE
AVANT-GARDE

> In this lies the profound distinctiveness of aesthetic
> form: it is my organically moving, evaluating, and
> meaning-giving activity, and at the same time it is the
> form of an event and its participant standing over
> against me (his individuality, the form of his body and
> soul).
>
> *(PCMF,* 315–16)

Bakhtin and Russian Formalism: the phrase signals a familiar
literary-theoretical *topos* of some thirty years ago,[1] elaborated (as
often as not) under the no longer tenable presupposition that
'Bakhtin' and 'Medvedev' were interchangeable proper names –
that the stridently polemical tone of the latter's critique of Viktor
Shklovsky and his colleagues was also in some sense Bakhtin's –
and in the absence of a (full) English translation of Bakhtin's own
earlier critique dating from 1924. We now know on the first score
that we were dupes of an opportunistic fiction forged by Soviet
semioticians anxious to legitimate their project by claiming kinship
with a supposedly 'Marxist' Bakhtin; and the incomplete translation that very few anglophones will in any case have read, buried
as it was in an obscure journal of Hispanic studies, has now been
replaced by a full English version.[2] Besides this, readers of English
who have no Russian now have the benefit of a translation of Pavel
Medvedev's revised version of *The Formal Method in Literary
Scholarship* to complete the story of the Bakhtin-inspired encounter
with Russia's twentieth-century critical *avant-garde*.[3] This revision
of 1934 is notably shorn of all positive proposals: any alternative to
formalism ran the risk of not squaring satisfactorily with the (by
then) official and monopolistic aesthetic of socialist realism. Purely

polemical, safe in the adversarial negativity of its formulations, purged of the offensive neo-Kantian heresy for which the 1928 text had been roundly denounced, *Formalism and the Formalists* is still more strident in tone – that is, still less like anything that could ever have been written by Bakhtin himself.

The fascination that the volume of 1928 held for Western and particularly English 'materialist' (that is, Marxist) critics is readily understandable. Wishing to take their distance not only from the older discourses of a homegrown 'liberal humanism' and of their own vulgarly sociologizing comrades but also from the latest in North American deconstruction (with a purchase upon 'textuality' as strong as it seemed to them historically enfeebled), they found in *The Formal Method* a text for their own time: Medvedev, after all, had before him a very similar configuration of adversaries to those they themselves faced. In its astonishing prefiguration of Pierre Macherey's *A Theory of Literary Production* it allowed them to be at once thoroughly socio-historical and thoroughly textual, and did so by dint of adding to the familiar (Althusserian) 'relative autonomy' of the ideological within the social totality an analogous and fully theorized autonomy – which, after the Formalists' habit, they sometimes called the 'specificity' – of the literary within 'ideology'.

I

It is time now, however, to tell another story for the beginning of the twenty-first century, in the wake of a pair of deeply (though obliquely) related historic failures: first, of the promises of the *avant-garde* in the face of repression in the East and of academicization or routinization in the West; second, of the *soi-disant* political 'vanguard' of the proletariat whose experiments in 'actually existing' socialism foundered at last in the 1990s (and not before time) in a grim mix of farce and tragedy. While these two vanguardist projects – of a charismatic cultural modernism, on the one hand, and of an aggressive economic and technological modernization, on the other – never related to each other openly except on terms of deep mutual suspicion, their subtextual two-way traffic forces upon those of us who live in the situation, following their common passing into history, a need to reassess everything we have ever said or read about them. Bakhtin is one of the names that we have most readily associated both with their temporary conjuncture in the 1920s and with their banishment beyond each other's borders a decade later. The new story we now need to tell will look not at how 'Bakhtin' moved beyond formalism into a 'Marxist' theory of the text – a ludicrous proposition in view of what we now know – but at how the movement which prompted the linguistic turn of his thinking simultaneously prepared him for the task of placing *all* vanguards where they belong: like some of the denizens of Dante's hell, everlastingly in each other's deeply unwelcome company, as heresies of a false emancipation, harbingers of a new and characteristically modern form of bondage.

To see this is to become aware of some extraordinary ironies: stories of profound complicity among overt antagonists that can perhaps only now be told. Stalinism's fear of Formalism is the paradoxical fear of a fiercely productionist social ethos for an aesthetic no less militantly productionist. Those who took their social engineering in the so-called 'infrastructure' to murderous lengths seemingly needed a mystificatory 'superstructure' arching over it. Formalism's metaphors of production were, after all, *too* modern, perhaps, for such cataclysmic socio-economic modernization. I would suggest that Bakhtin's critique of Russian Formalism is covertly a critique of the nascent Soviet Marxism that would go on to suppress Formalism itself. If he later inspired or sanctioned Medvedev's overtly Marxist polemic against Formalism, that is because no intervention could then *not* call itself Marxist. In the 1930s, when even that became impossible – the battle of ideas was too risky a game for anyone – his strategy became one of inventing his own modernism, locating it in a whole Western European early-modern tradition beginning with Rabelais, and steering well clear of any homegrown Russian examples. It was of course in this period that Medvedev was shot: an act of sectarian murder by the state ends the tale that began ten years earlier with Bakhtin's moving claim for the all-forgiving 'mercy' of art. This tragic outcome circuitously vindicates Bakhtin's attack on the 'material aesthetic' of Formalism – unjust as that may seem when we recall that the victim of this murder had striven so hard to accommodate the state line on art. By privileging the 'material' of 'verbal art' – that is, language conceived as the plastic, axiologically and semantically indifferent raw stuff of aesthetic production – Russian Formalism is almost a figure for the way those who professed (dialectical) 'materialism' went to work on the human material at their disposal. Pavel Medvedev went to his death thanks to the Faustian pact he had made with Soviet Marxism; Bakhtin outlived him, as he was also to outlive Voloshinov. Ironically, then, the movement whose very name was to become a state-sanctioned code word for the cultural equivalent of treason championed in its theory an aesthetic version of that same state's future brutality. For all the iconoclastic finesse of its textual readings, then, Formalism mimed in advance theoretically the very practice of the state that suppressed it. Bakhtin's 1924 encounter with the Formalists could only have strengthened his allegiance to the aesthetic as a poten- tially emancipatory category: he would not otherwise have tried in the work that followed to incarnate it in the historical phenomena of the novel and carnival. Early and late, he keeps faith with a conception of 'aesthetic activity' which has the same force in his writing as 'philosophy' does in Antonio Gramsci's; and, having made no diabolical pact, he survives.

Whilst Bakhtin might then have valued the Formalists insofar as they rejected the eclecticism of earlier criticism, he parts company with them in so far as this was done from the standpoint of a full- blown modernist anti-aesthetic. To refuse the aesthetic as they did was to imply *an* aesthetic nonetheless: no method is without an implicit theory. Bakhtin's strategy in 'The Problem of Content, Material, and Form in Verbal Art' is to show that Formalism's refusal to situate its poetics as a sectoral study within a 'general' or 'philosophical' aesthetics commits it willy-nilly to a perverse aesthetic of 'the material'. Language has not yet become for Bakhtin the home of that ineluctable dialogism which is (he is careful to say) 'almost' all of life; he takes it here at its Formalist face value, as mere phonic material comparable to paint or clay. It is important in any attempt to draw out of this early text its ethico-political rele- vance for our time that we should not play down the features of its earliness. As polemics go, for example, this early encounter with Formalism is not notably close, nor indeed notably dialogical: few names are cited of antagonists; no texts either; and there is no quotation of any length. These ordinary appurtenances of the polemicist's craft are indeed not only absent but consciously and loftily dismissed from the beginning as a 'superfluous ballast of citations and references', a sort of muddying of theory with history, a clogging of argument with unnecessary narrative (*PCMF*, 257). In terms that Bakhtin himself will later use, it is distinctly and tenden- tially 'single-voiced'; the voice of the other side is rendered only in the most distantly paraphrastic and third-person – we might call them 'arm's-length' – modes of indirect discourse, if it could be said to be rendered at all. In other words, the gulf between this essay's philosophical sophistication and its linguistic naivety is enacted in the very form and tone that it assumes: precociously magisterial, provocatively monological, without a hint of play.

Bracketing these considerations out, without ever quite forgetting them, we can now proceed with the substance of Bakhtin's argument. To divorce poetics from a theoretically elaborated aesthetics, Bakhtin holds, is to deny the more general specificity of the aesthetic over against the other – cognitive and ethical – domains that make up 'the unity of human culture' (*PCMF*, 259). By hypostasizing a method, giving it the pretension of theory, we isolate aesthetics from those established Kantian others to whose clear distinction late-nineteenth-century neo-Kantianism remained loyal even as it took them down into the investigation of the historical life-world, radically challenging the paradigmatic status of pure reason. Unfitted to see beyond the current *Methodenstreit*, we would be reducing art to the condition of a mute 'fact' among other facts equally dumb, emptying out the *value* by which alone all of the domains of culture can be said to have a kind of speech. Into the vacuum created by Formalist poetics at the general-aesthetic level there moves another discipline with no greater claim than poetics itself to occupy that space: namely, linguistics. The material aesthetics of verbal art is what is 'uncritically presupposed' when a poetics under the sway of criteria of positivist scientificity takes this 'auxiliary discipline' (*PCMF*, 261–62) as its methodological model, its hierarchical superior in the field of knowledge. As long as it confines itself to the 'technical aspects of artistic creation', it is without mischievous effects in theory; however, Formalism, for Bakhtin, knows no such confinement (*PCMF*, 263).

The most fundamental mischief is in the inability of 'material aesthetics' to found and clarify the (so to speak) eponymous category of Formalism: form itself. Understood as 'organized material', form cannot be seen for what it is: never the given; always the ever-posited-anew (*PCMF*, 264). Form is nothing apart from that tense relation of the author-contemplator to something which always exceeds the material that helps to realize it. Or, again: it is an effect of the active evaluation of that which is actualized, without at the same time ever being wholly exhausted, by the material. The upshot is a false exteriority, a collusion of the would-be objectivism of material-form with the subjectivism it seeks to renounce, inasmuch as the 'feeling' that it expels beyond theorization is thereby locked all the more firmly into the psyche, having nowhere else to go. Form must entertain a 'moment of content', in short; and no less in an 'objectless' art like music, from which an aesthetic of the intransitivity of form-as-material might seem to secure the ground for its predication across the whole terrain of art. Behind this case is an elementary category mistake, a confusion of 'content' with the propositionality or conceptuality which is only one of its modes. Music might indeed be generalized: not, however, as the paradigm of art's universal contentlessness, but rather as an extreme case of the hospitality all art offers to content that is other than cognitive.

The second mischief of material aesthetics, according to Bakhtin, is its failure to distinguish the object of aesthetic analysis from the mere 'givenness' of the completed work and from the 'compositional' activity of making it – more precisely, its failure both to bring that distinctiveness into consciousness and to give it first place in the hermeneutic itinerary. That object of analysis is 'aesthetic activity' itself, a primal reflexivity given before any actualization in material, an agonistics upon which Bakhtin confers the character of a calmly dynamic structure-as-structuring, and which he calls *architectonics*. Formalism errs in ignoring the 'appeased, self-sufficient being' of this truly aesthetic object of the work, instead identifying the aesthetic with its 'goal-directed' technicality (*PCMF*, 267). The famous (or notorious) self-referentiality of Formalism is, then, a *contradictio in adjecto*: a reflexivity of the inherently unreflexive, 'compositional' instrumentality raised to a higher power. Cognitive activity directed at the text sees there only a purposive rationality dedicated to purposelessness: means ominously personified, and endowed with the self-consciousness that properly belongs only to ends. Roman Jakobson was right, and in a profoundly Bakhtinian sense, when he called the 'device' the *hero* of the Formalist story of artistic meaning.[4] This perverse animation and autonomization of the instrumental turns the text into a little productionist utopia, a dream of freedom whose nightmarish obverse is a totally rationalized and administered world.

Only from its architectonic forms (as the forms of the aesthetic 'consummation' of a person or event) does the work acquire its individuality and sufficiency-unto-itself. These forms have no necessary correlation with genres: intriguingly, even the novel, which was to carry so much weight after Bakhtin's later turn to language, which was indeed to figure as the very incarnation of discursive reflexivity in history, is here deemed architectonically neutral. The novel is here so far from any special charge of cultural meaning within modernity that it is a merely 'compositional' form within the larger – and so much older as to be effectively transhistorical – architectonic category of 'epic consummation' (*PCMF*, 269).

Likewise, whilst drama is a set of technical devices which is indispensable to the manifestation of those modes of consummation called 'tragedy' or 'comedy', the latter are hierarchically higher than (logically prior to) the dramatization upon which they so absolutely depend. Formalism confounds confusion by 'dissolv[ing] architectonic forms in compositional forms' which have often themselves already been run together with the forms of language (*PCMF*, 270–71).

II

In the rest of the 1924 essay Bakhtin elaborates his own positive version of the concepts that Russian Formalism had provocatively (if altogether inadequately) problematized. The 'content' that Formalist insouciance had either banished or conflated with form is re-posed as a problem of our whole life-world of 'culture' and of the 'domains' that make it up. Culture as the medium of acts (rather than facts) constitutes a dimension which spatial metaphors can only falsify; it is traversed only by boundaries and is nothing beyond the intersection of those boundaries. Cultural acts must be imagined as living outgrowths of the boundaries upon which alone they thrive, and which they forsake at the perilous cost of their extinction. What cognitive acts find on hand, then, is not random and value-free matter but the value-laden precipitate of ethical action and aesthetic activity. Aesthetic activity in its turn has its being only in 'intense and active interdetermination' with a reality of cognition and action (*PCMF*, 275). Bakhtin gives this familiar Kantian scenario a twentieth-century neo-Kantian (we may say, with hindsight: proto-Bakhtinian) twist when he goes on to discriminate aesthetic from cognitive and ethical activity. There is absolutely no parity or symmetry or circular interaction between them: each is the two others' other, but aesthetic activity has a greater claim to be the other of cognition and action than *vice versa*. Cognition behaves as if nothing is 'already on hand' from those other tense cultural liminalities, living instead in its own narcissistic world of mirrors: what cognition cognizes stands to cognition in a relation of pure contingency, and it is cognized because cognition makes it transparently cognizable (*PCMF*, 276). Acknowledging no necessity or rationality that it has not itself conferred, cognition endlessly reinvents its purity on the negation of 'the preveniently encountered reality of actions and aesthetic vision' (*PCMF*, 277). The stubborn opacity that this work of pure reason encounters in its objects is understood as a problem for cognition rather than as the index of any inherent value in the object itself. In short, cognition is everything that the aesthetic is not. Art is marked by its 'kindness', its 'mercifulness'; it 'recognize[s] and remember[s] everything'; it 'divides' and 'abolishes' nothing (*PCMF*, 279). Art's 'intuitively uniting and consummating form descends upon [the] content' of cognition and action 'from outside' (*PCMF*, 282). Art is what can happen only when an essential aesthetic 'outsideness' embraces content conceived as the cognitive and ethical events of reality in all their (no less essential) 'weightiness' (*PCMF*, 278).

Now it is impossible for us to read the Bakhtin we have here other than through and against the Bakhtin he would become. That is to say, we note that the anti-hierarchical thinker of later years who championed the 'revolt of the hero' strongly inclines here to the pole of the author, and indeed cannot think of authorship (aesthetic activity) in anything other than benevolently hierarchical terms. Formalism's 'primitive' and 'nihilistic' democracy of 'the material' threatens to destroy with its critical guerrilla tactics that lovingly condescending exotopy which is (so to speak) the formal meta-meaning of every work of art. We note also that in berating Formalism for treating content as nothing more than a 'moment of form' Bakhtin at once concedes that there is a variety of art to which this formula might apply, and immediately consigns it to 'second-hand' status. In his middle period he will outdo the Formalists themselves in that universalization of parody and intertextuality which he here condemns, emerging as the avatar of the novel's 'autocritique of discourse' and of the virtual ubiquity of metafiction. Again, and conversely: when he writes in the same context that 'every artist is *the first artist*', he is universalizing as a condition of all true art an authorial aspiration to the Adamic that he will later specialize to poetry conceived as the antithesis of the novel's openly flaunted secondariness (*PCMF*, 284).

Our response to these superseded positions should not simply be to applaud the later Bakhtin for the turn his thought was so astonishingly soon to take, but rather to understand the essay of 1924 for what it is: a deeply engaged initial riposte to the challenge of a productionist aesthetic in the context of a turbulently modernizing Russia, from a young neo-Kantian who had taken leave of the philosophy of consciousness but still not made what now seems the inevitable next move. He may, that is, sound traditional to us in so far as he had not yet joined the twentieth-century quest for the lineaments of our *Dasein* in language; and yet this early work of his is surely to be valued none the less for its intuition of the variable but powerful freight that the aesthetic carries as a category of secular modernity. Any modernist anti-aesthetic runs the risk of losing the potential which an historically self-contextualizing aesthetics has to displace the modern dominance of epistemology and open the space not only for those ontological, phenomenological and hermeneutic projects that have transformed twentieth-century philosophy but also for the more praxis-oriented critical social science that was to establish itself between the wars. The brutalism of the Formalists seemed to throw out along with a discredited metaphysical aesthetics of the late nineteenth century the genuine and rich legacy that this mainly German tradition still had to offer. It has, then, to be said that Bakhtin has been vindicated by the decades that followed. It is also the case that through the deep changes which his own thinking was to undergo there remains this strong thread of commitment to an aesthetic horizon that preserves those dimensions of our living – its historicity, its creatureliness, its finitude – which were laid waste after the Cartesian *cogito* began doing its work. And so when (using an extraordinary, quasi-Christological metaphor) he tells us that in art the 'water' of cognition clarifies the heady 'wine of ethical tension and aesthetic consummation', but then goes on to insist that the cognitive only attracts the consummation of art in so far as it is rooted in 'event' and 'performed action', we are tempted to apply this view of the aesthetic to aesthetics itself: Bakhtin's own (necessarily cognitive) discourse upon art comes into the ken of our postmodern 'outside-ness' not in the sober neutrality of epistemological *askesis* but filled brim-full with the 'ethical tension' of a critical situation in history (*PCMF*, 287).

These observations may be taken further as we move to Bakhtin's discussion of 'material', the second of the concepts he attempts to re-posit against the Formalists. The science of the material of verbal art is linguistics, and it is with that art in particular and with that science in its current methodological state – and also with the appropriateness of the latter to the theorization of the former – that Bakhtin is here concerned. Bakhtin's judgement, shortly to be given a Marxist inflection by Voloshinov (and then echoed throughout Bakhtin's own later writing), is that linguistics is not yet fully the master of its object: 'scientifically, linguistics has not yet moved beyond the complex sentence' (*PCMF*, 293). For the art of the word (here specified as poetry; so far is Bakhtin from his legendary valorization of the novel), language as determined by

41

linguistics constitutes a merely 'technical moment'; at the same time, poetry as a discourse is distinct from all others in its recourse to *all* the possibilities of language (*PCMF*, 295). Like all of the arts, poetry is indissolubly wedded to the material it necessarily supersedes. What distinguishes poetry, then, is that it is the 'immanent overcoming' of language: the poet 'forces language, in the act of perfecting it linguistically, to surpass itself' (*PCMF*, 297). This violent sublation of the poetic signifier on its own ground is the subordinate moment illegitimately hypostasized by Formalism – sundered from that merciful consummation of the cognitive-ethical signified which it stages, and by which alone its violence is redeemed. Architectonic wholes arise as the quasi-miraculous transubstantiation of linguistic wholes; yet in emphasizing the 'auxiliary' nature of this 'material organization' we do so not to 'denigrate' it but to point to that which gives it 'meaning and life' (*PCMF*, 302).

This rigorous analytic separation of dimensions which can none the less not subsist apart in the finished work is replicated in Bakhtin's view of the discourses in which they are elaborated. Linguistics, as the discipline which offers to theorize this material, will best serve (and in turn be served by) poetics when their eclectic mingling has been supplanted by a strict division of labour which will ultimately be beneficial to both. The stringent reduction by which Formalism believed itself to have purged the work of all that was extra-aesthetic rests on a conflation of the aesthetic with the linguistic which will bedevil knowledge for as long as the disciplines devoted to them do not know the proper bounds of their competence. Bakhtin's objection is that the price of the linguistically oriented de-psychologization of the work in Formalist poetics is its 'empiricization'. We might add that Bakhtin's own (in the end highly creative) mistake is not simply that he identifies the study of language with linguistics as then constituted and can envisage nothing besides its future perfection along the lines of a value-free technicism – that he cannot, in short, imagine a theory of *discourse* or language-in-use (that, in 1924, is surely no inexcusable blindness); it is that he is guilty in his turn of a sweeping conflation: of linguistics with the sciences of the 'material' of arts other than the verbal. He himself in this very text describes linguistics as a 'human science'; yet at several points the 'bad' transcendentalism of his aesthetic optic is revealed in the way he speaks of this *Geisteswissenschaft* in the same breath as mathematics or acoustics or physics, as if they were unproblematically analogous. Bakhtin

seems in spite of himself to have fallen under the spell of the term
'material', which he uses of the Formalists' (implicit) aesthetic,
without realizing that he is using it quite differently from the
Formalists themselves: to signify the work's formal 'devices' at the
level of language, while they – in one of their more mischievous
binaries – used it of the device's 'motivating' content at the level of
theme. The otherwise fruitful transcendental reduction by which he
establishes the aesthetic as a category here displays its limits: in its
powerful presence, key distinctions evaporate; everything else is
relegated to the empirical, an aesthetically indifferent and neutral
realm of *things*.

Bakhtin's 'mistake' was creative, I would claim, in both a long-
term and a short-term sense. First, it was creative in that it was
motivated by that deep ethical commitment to the aesthetic of
which I have already spoken: it is a small myopia brought on by
genuine faith, a blindness which is negligible next to the insights
Bakhtin's whole argument yields for us now, a long way from its
point of origin. Disabused, we understand his forebodings.
Secondly, it is creative in that its incoherence is one outward sign of
a case taken to the brink of self-deconstruction, out of which in turn
a new case soon emerges. We might say that Bakhtin is here at his
most Husserlian, and that he learns from his own habit of (in an
Adornian phrase) proceeding by way of extremes the great lesson
of any reduction: its impossibility. From our own hermeneutic
vantage-point we can see the immanence – and imminence – of this
move in the space between Bakhtin's dismissive remarks on 'material' in the essay's third section and his closing and almost wholly
positive section on 'form'. Having elaborated the true (cognitive-
ethical) content of art and dismissed the false (linguistic)
form-as-content of the Formalists, he now presents in a largely non-
polemical idiom the sense that his aesthetic would give to their
favoured category. Anyone familiar with his 'Author and Hero in
Aesthetic Activity' of a few years before will at this point see what
Bakhtin is up to: the Formalist phenomenon has prompted him not
only to cling – as the very condition of saving the aesthetic in all its
critical and utopian force – to the binary opposition of form and
content, but also to correlate the two categories from his own
thinking that correlate most closely with the terms of that very
traditional dichotomy, which had in any case never been more than
superficially deconstructed by the Formalists themselves. If it now
becomes plain that 'form' for Bakhtin corresponds to the activity of
the author (in his extended meaning, which includes reader or

onlooker), 'content' as plainly belongs to the pole of the hero. Form, that is to say, is the realm of the other who consummates; content that of the self whose image (and the event of whose life) undergoes consummation.

Form, in a word, is authorship – authorship understood not empirically, as the agency of the originating and punctual act of producing the work, but transcendentally, as the condition of the possibility of aesthetic form in general. To understand this transcendental meaning of authorship is to see that it is absent from cognitive activity: real individuals write scientific works, but the works themselves are inwardly authorless in so far as the unity of their meanings is secured on the plane of the object and of reference. In aesthetic form (the phrase is effectively tautological) there is not only an activity but also the feeling of activity in a subject; it is the intensely felt activity of an axiological relation to content; in verbal art it is 'the feeling of generating the signifying word', of 'moving and assuming a position as a whole human being' (*PCMF*, 309). The unity and individuality engendered by form are reflexive rather than referent-oriented, 'the unity of an activity that returns to itself, finding itself anew' (*PCMF*, 310). It is as if Bakhtin is borrowing the motif of reflexivity so central to Formalist poetics and relocating it from the material of the empirical work to the form of the work conceived as a perennial potentiality of meaning. This *Ur*-reflexivity (as it were) is not an automatism in the material offered to passive perception but rather the activity by which the work's escape from material and from compositional form into the architectonic is ceaselessly re-effected. Form is, then, performance; not in the literal or secondary sense of playing or reading aloud, but in the sense of a primal, self-delighting drama of the making of meaning which confers upon everything semantic – even the most referential meaning – the feeling of a *choice*.

As if to enact the experience he is describing, Bakhtin's style here takes on that repetitive-accumulative rhythm, by turns quasi-erotic and mystical-ecstatic, which he had first deployed in 'Author and Hero' and would often return to in his later work, though never quite with this intensity. Never before, and seldom afterwards, would he signal so clearly his work's bearings within the line of internal critics of the German philosophical tradition (Young Hegelian, Kierkegaardian, Nietzschean) in whom the idiom of philosophy was notably at once resensualized and respiritualized. And appropriately enough: for the dematerialization of form – that is, the reduction with which he hopes both to replace and, more, consequently to carry through the Formalists' de-psychologizing reduction – entails not at all its rarefaction, but rather its *rebodying*. When Bakhtin writes that this authoring which *is* form is an 'activity of the entire human being, from head to foot' and that he enters into the event and stands over against its hero 'as one who breathes, moves, sees, hears, remembers, loves, and understands', we sense both a will to radicalize the claims of the aesthetic against the nihilism of the native Russian *avant-garde* and the strained hyperbole of a transcendental reduction taken to breaking point (*PCMF*, 316). No sooner has Bakhtin detached form from language than he provokes a crisis in his thinking by taking form precipitately towards the body and its life-world. The impossibility of reduction looms; and the rest of Bakhtin's work might then be seen as the revenge of language upon its consignment as 'material' to instrumentality in this early work. Polemic with the Formalists provokes Bakhtin into a sympathetic but none the less perilous overreaching of theoretical discourse. The hubris of his general aesthetics consists in overprotecting a category by scrupulous reduction and then overloading it, so that it threatens to swallow precisely that which has been so carefully bracketed out.

It is not only language that will later redress its relegation here by returning as discourse; the novel, too, will more than make up for its subordination in this early context, becoming that typical mature-Bakhtinian hybrid: a transcendental category with a vigorous historical life of its own, but without the need to defer to any higher instance of *Geist*. Here, we find not only that poetry is the paradigm of verbal art in general, but that lyric poetry in particular stands at one end of scale of possibilities, whose other and inferior end is occupied by the novel. As against this poetic kind in which the body is 'drawn into form' more completely than in any other, there is this prose genre where form as felt corporealization is so 'minimal' as to render its generation of meanings a virtually bodiless affair, a case of the aesthetic that only just qualifies for inclusion under that head (*PCMF*, 314). We can now see this move on Bakhtin's part as a sort of tempting of fate, an extremism of general aesthetics in respect of a particular genre that courts the danger of a revolt of the object against the metalanguage by which it is articulated. Ten years later, he is so far from this grudging admittance of the novel to the circle of art that he will begin 'Discourse in the Novel' with a critique of those accounts that characterize it as a 'rhetorical' genre, firmly asserting its 'artistic' status in a move which suggests that the category of art is still alive in his thinking, but with none of its earlier conceptual priority, with (as is the case here) little more than an heuristic force. For the rest, the aesthetic has withdrawn into a namelessness which might be interpreted as a policy of caution on Bakhtin's part, but could equally be seen as its new and richer life: as a reflexive potential now implicit everywhere in language-as-discourse, to which the novel points us as its artistic realization *par excellence*.

It is important to sum up what is at stake here. 'The Problem of Content, Material, and Form in Verbal Art' is worth our interest – even applause – for its strategic traditionalism, which can now be read as a function of two contingencies: its post-revolutionary Russian context and Bakhtin's own stage of intellectual development at that time. It is the outcome of a perhaps unique crossing of swords between two powerful early-twentieth-century positions: an audacious and unambiguous *avant-garde* assault on the institution of art, on the one hand, and, on the other hand, that most ambiguous of enlightenment categories in which art is now contained as a subordinate moment of modern subjectivity, now freed for a critical imagining of future community. Bakhtin is the direct heir to this potential internal counter-enlightenment within enlightenment discourse itself (of which Romantic discourse was the first realization: a doomed attempt to autonomize art without first undoing the aesthetic from within). Bakhtin's early neo-Kantianism is then one of the last attempts that will be made to launch this discourse into the world as a 'first philosophy' in the face of modernist practice and modernist critical methodology. The threat posed by modernism to the institution of art must not be allowed to threaten the category of the aesthetic; the exhilaration of that first revolt must stop short of its dangerous and by no means necessary corollary. Formalism in its 'sectarian belligerence' seemed to Bakhtin to exemplify precisely that arbitrary logic, and to exemplify it (what is more) in a situation where an analogous vanguardism in politics seemed ominously to back it up (*PCMF*, 273).

We might read the 1924 essay allegorically, if we wish: the plea for any modernist poetics first to set itself in the context of a 'philosophical aesthetics' would then have as its subtext an appeal for any revolutionary politics not to cut itself adrift from an appropriately modernized spirituality, an embracing legitimacy that radically reimagines community beyond the conflicts of the present. Bakhtin's discovery some time in the next few years of Dostoevsky's 'polyphonic' novel then falls into place as the upshot of a realization on his part that first philosophies of a transcendental kind not only are no longer to be tolerated under Soviet rule but also lack the charismatic power of the *avant-garde*. Bakhtin now strategically modernizes as he had before taken up a traditional stand against Formalism; if it is not 'art' or even 'verbal art' that is the site of his intervention, the essential terms of his aesthetics are none the less kept, though with an altered valency. The author-hero couple, that is to say, survives; but what interests him above all (because of its strong foothold in our modern life-world) is the version of that couple to be found in the quintessentially modern genre of the novel. He needs also to find somewhere discursively exemplified in the paradox of an immanent transcendence, and he finds it in the everyday language-in-use to which of all genres the novel is nearest. He needs, finally, to reconcile the idiom of 'consummation' with that of emancipation. Dostoevsky's fiction, with its unusually empowered heroes, is the perfect figure for the meeting of all of these needs. Meanwhile, his friend Pavel Medvedev was following another path.

III

The Formal Method in Literary Scholarship is not the definitive Bakhtinian answer to Russian Formalism, as many of us once supposed. It is simply the intervention of one member of the 'circle', which we do not need to force into commensurability with Bakhtin's own intervention of four years earlier. While Bakhtin himself, with his new concept of dialogism, raised dialogue from mere compositional or linguistic status to a sort of architectonics of the everyday – while he pursued a translinguistics of discourse conceived as always already rich with those emancipatory-consummatory possibilities that are supremely realized in novelistic polyphony – Medvedev entered, on what might have been thought the winning side, one of the still available dialogues of Soviet life at that time: that between Formalism and Marxism (or at least the Second International orthodoxy that went by that name). As an open polemic, with named antagonists and copious quotation from their writing, *The Formal Method* nowhere approaches the subtleties of 'hidden polemic' which Bakhtin celebrates as one among the many 'double-voiced' modes of the novel, and which constitutes the verbal dominant in that (proto-)modernist innovation he calls polyphonic. Subject as it was to plot closure by the state (which came very soon: around 1930), the dialogue entered by Medvedev's book had little prospect of breaking out of the sphere it occupied of the higher journalism and joining any 'great dialogue' stretching into semantic infinity. At the same time, placed alongside Bakhtin's somewhat distant encounter of 1924, *The Formal Method* stands out as being altogether at much closer quarters in the battle with its adversaries.

Medvedev, in short, is more open than either the Bakhtin of 1924 (or indeed the others on his own side in 1928) to taking on the colours of the position he opposes. Defending the higher ground of 'sociological poetics' as firmly as Bakhtin had defended the ground of 'general aesthetics' four years before – that much continuity we can acknowledge between the two interventions – Medvedev none the less shares at least some of the belligerence with which both he and Bakhtin reproach the Formalists themselves. 'Criticism of formalism', he may write, 'can and must be "immanent" in the best sense of the word' (*FMLS*, 37). He also hails the strength of his antagonists, locating it in their astuteness in choosing the ground of poetics as the 'specification' of the literary, and at the same time deploring the habit of 'polemical negation' which infects their way with texts as much as their way with foes and forebears in the critical and theoretical field (*FMLS*, 62). If anything, he is more generous in polemical concession than Bakhtin had been; and he is a long way from the outright denunciation (Lunacharsky) or patronage (Trotsky) or mechanically synthesizing proposals (Arvatov) of his fellow polemicists.[5] There is an attitude, even, of teaching the Formalists a lesson in the proper style and conduct of polemic. Now, in so far as Bakhtin himself had any hand in shaping this stance towards Formalism, we might see in it a backhanded acknowledgement of indebtedness for prompting the turn to language that he had so strongly resisted in 1924. Yet, for all this, it must be said that Medvedev inescapably adopts the tones of the cultural civil war that was Soviet intellectual life in the late 1920s. This bold move was to prove his undoing in the atmosphere of paranoia which was to overwhelm that once lively milieu in later years.

However that may be, it is perhaps just this tone of militancy combined with scholarly generosity to the other side that so endeared Medvedev's arguments to his anglophone Marxist readers fifty years after his book was first published, most of them by 1978 academics engaged in carrying the street insurgency of 1968 into the seminar room. Certain major Althusserian motifs seemed to be underwritten by Medvedev, and not surprisingly: as a (post-)structuralist Marxist project, Althusserianism was always likely to resonate with an attempt in 1928 to fashion a Marxist cultural theory in dialogue with a Formalism poised on the edge of its transmutation into structuralism, a turn implicitly proclaimed in the Jakobson–Tynyanov theses of that very year.[6] One such motif is the rigid opposition of the 'scientific' and the 'ideological'. Bakhtin's claim that the Formalists neglected aesthetic theory is expanded by Medvedev into the claim that they were essentially critical partisans of a literary movement; that they found(ed) their identity not in a principled inter-orientation with and against other (including Western European) players in the theoretical field, but in nothing more substantial than an anti-symbolist programme. Their openly pro-Futurist discourse is too close to its object to be scientific; it is 'not a part of scholarship but of literature itself' (*FMLS*, 57). The charge certainly holds with the likes of Viktor Shklovsky; and we might add that as Formalism shifted its attention from poetry to prose its methodology began largely to be driven analogously by an anti-realist polemic. But this is less important than the fact that Medvedev's strictures added force to the sharp Althusserian distinction between theory and criticism, and to the priority of the first over the second. Medvedev seemed, in short, to bring the authority of Bakhtin himself to the structuralist will to scientificity that is one face of Althusserian Marxism.

Another Althusserian motif seemingly echoed in Medvedev is the notion of the 'relative autonomy' of ideology or the 'superstructure'. Medvedev gives a fuller elaboration than anyone had before to the replication of this same relationship between the literary and the ideological. Where vulgar-Marxist accounts postulated an economic determination of the ideological and an ideological subsumption of the literary, Medvedev spoke the language of the latter's autonomy; where Formalism (in its early stage especially) isolated the literary from the other 'series' or 'systems', Medvedev firmly though subtly rearticulated it upon the ideological. Literature 'reflects and refracts the reflections and refractions of other ideological spheres'; or again: 'in its "content" literature reflects the whole of the ideological horizon of which it is itself a part' (*FMLS*, 16–17). This 'double orientation' whereby the literary uniquely and monadically contains the world by which it is simultaneously contained is not far from the Althusserian notion of the 'internal distantiation' of art within ideology, and moreover appeared to escape the isolationist (almost Formalist) expressions this idea often received in the earlier Althusser and Macherey.[7] The coincidence by which English translations of Medvedev and Macherey appeared in the same year helped to cement the connection between them and to underline the capacity of the earlier text to rectify the later. When, just a year later, a pathbreaking paper of 1974 by Macherey and Balibar also appeared for the first time in English, and seemed to render any such rectification unnecessary – so close had the Althusserian position then moved towards the Medvedevian – the two Marxist polemics seemed to be singing in unison across half a century.[8] If Medvedev had not been sensitively heard in 1928, he was being heard and applauded so warmly by those of his Western European successors battling (what looked like) the neo-formalism of deconstruction that many of them came to treat *The Formal Method* as a major theoretical intervention in its own right and to forget that (by their own criteria) it was only an inspired and exemplary piece of critical polemic.

In political terms, of course, Althusserianism was a Leninism of the most fundamentalist kind. There were Leninist texts on art, to be sure; but Leninism was overwhelmingly a theory and strategy of the seizure and holding of 'proletarian' power, not the basis of an aesthetics (in practice, of course, it amounted to a ruthless state terror from which Stalinism was to differ only in the scale of its brutality). Yet a post-1968 Western Marxism needed to theorize ungrudgingly – and with some of the flair of 1968 itself – the symbolic and affective resources of art, and the communist parties in particular, working under conditions of so-called 'bourgeois' democracy, needed the 'relative autonomy' of artists as partisans of the cause. The Althusserian aesthetic that a Medvedev supposedly ventriloquized by Bakhtin seemed to underwrite had, it must be said, a powerful pull among the great majority of self-styled 'materialist' critics. If it had this order of hegemony, that was because both cases allowed Western Marxism(s) to have it both ways: to marry the stern asceticism and secrecy of a vanguardist politics with something at least, however distant and dwindled, of the heady openness and the strong libidinal investment of a vanguardist aesthetics, the elitist cabal of one with the populist carnival of the other. We can now see, with Bakhtin's help – and this is the lasting insight of his essay of 1924 – that the very notion of a 'vanguardist aesthetic' is oxymoronic. Touching as it is that one of the more significant cultural dialogues of a Russia about to abolish civil society should speak so powerfully, and across so hideous a global tragedy, to Marxist intellectuals in the post-war Western *Öffentlichkeit*, it is hard not to see Bakhtin's aloofness from polemic in the late 1920s as offering not only survival for him in the short term but also a more durable and valuable lesson altogether.

This aloofness needs to be qualified just in so far as we affirm or deny Bakhtin's sponsorship of Medvedev's intervention. We will never know how far, if at all, the latter's writing task was self-imposed or delegated by another. That, however, Bakhtin has a presence in it, as an informing voice in the dialogue, there can be no doubt; and above all in the outlines it gives of what a positive alternative to Formalist poetics might be. The missing dimension in Formalism of general-aesthetic speculation is sketched in terms that Bakhtin probably inspired. Bakhtin's own earlier neo-Kantian aesthetic has a cameo part, not *in propria persona* but in the guise of his own mentor in these matters: the Marburg professor Hermann Cohen. For example, Medvedev's view of the literary as the elaboration of an already-elaborated (ideological) sign-material is generated in a simple terminological substitution of the word 'ideological' for Cohen's 'cognitive-ethical'. Medvedev effectively admits this debt to Cohen-*via*-Bakhtin even as he criticizes Cohen for his abstraction of these domains of culture (or dimensions of the text) from the materiality of their social being, his ignorance of 'the real existence which determines cognition and ethical evaluation' (*FMLS*, 24). We are not surprised, then, to find not only that it is exactly those more speculative and positive parts of the text of *The Formal Method* which betray a 'materialist' refunctioning of early-Bakhtinian or neo-Kantian positions, but also that it is exactly those parts that are suppressed in *Formalism and the Formalists*, to which we now turn.

However brave a gamble Medvedev's first anti-Formalist polemic had been, his rewriting of it six years later is the sad product of a cultural context altered out of all recognition. The context of his use in this book of the scriptory equivalent of an airbrush is largely one of the gross manipulation and extension of terms and of the criminalization of all debate that does not proceed from official premises to official conclusions, without true give and take, the fully weighted existence of another view having been banished by fiat beyond audibility. The major casualty of Stalinist semantics is the description 'formalism' itself: its upper-case version had had a specific application to a specific school of literary theory; its lower-case version is a confiscation of this term which generalizes it not only beyond literary theory but also beyond theory itself – in short, to the practice of art as such, to all the arts. So-called 'socialist realism' was proclaimed at the Soviet Writers' Congress in the year that *Formalism and the Formalists* was published.[9] 'Formalism' then became anything that did not conform to this single and unrefusable form bonded inextricably to the single and unrefusable content of 'Marxism–Leninism', inasmuch as anything outside this monopolistic definition must appear as arbitrary, 'mere' form, 'form' for its own sake. Where there is only one 'sake' or case – to inflect our English word towards its German cousin *Sache* – any technical means that does not defer to that 'sake' falls by the same token outside it, and in a 'phrasal regime' which reads 'outside' as 'against' and 'against' as (ultimately) 'guilty of treason'. 'Form', in other words, is an aesthetic code for the transcendental misdeed of any state of terror: difference. As Bakhtin himself had said in his Dostoevsky book, speaking of *Bewusstsein überhaupt*, or 'consciousness in general': under such a regime, 'only error individualizes'; all individuality is then error (*PDP*, 81).

One possible logic of this state of affairs is that difference must be represented as somehow unreal – either as unimaginable or as already defeated. It is in this latter spirit that Medvedev rewrites his polemic on Formalism: as a phenomenon of which we can only properly speak in the past tense. What is more, the freezing out of Formalism is represented as its 'collapse': as if the state had had nothing to do with its waning and it had merely crumbled either under its own self-contradiction or after the freely won triumph of the Habermasian better argument. The title of the revised volume is indicative in this respect: not only is the original subtitle, *An Introduction to Sociological Poetics*, omitted, in keeping with the expunging in the text itself of all positive proposals; the second element of the new main title points to the disintegration of Formalism as a coherent project into so many 'Formalists', individuals who are walking intellectual anachronisms within a consolidated 'Soviet reality'. And indeed the major addition to the text is a long conclusion headed 'The Collapse of Formalism', in which the three most prominent of its representatives are described as variously living out in their work the errors of what is now called the Formalist 'world view' or 'world outlook'.[10] Accused by Bakhtin in 1924 and then by Medvedev in 1928 of being a mere 'method' without even an overarching aesthetic theoretical frame – the title of 1928 points to this very limitation – the Formalists are now suddenly and quite inconsistently credited with a whole underpinning philosophy. It is not of course that the Formalists themselves have changed; simply that any metanarrative in monopolistic dominance will always see in even the most limited discourses outside its control the threat of a whole rival metanarrative. It cannot, in short, conceive of any discourse which is not as totalizing as its own.

In accordance with this logic, Medvedev removes every even mildly concessive reference to Formalism. Concession is now read as joining the other side; the 'immanent criticism' of *The Formal Method* led to 'a slippage into Formalist positions', and these positions are now associated with the very neo-Kantian aesthetics that had informed Bakhtin's 1924 critique.[11] In short, Medvedev explains the neo-Kantianism of his earlier polemic in terms not of Bakhtinian inspiration but of the contamination that follows from too close an engagement with the adversary. In the Manichaean universe of 'Marxism–Leninism' which Medvedev now decisively enters there are only two camps, to one or other of which everything historical must be assigned. Formalism is therefore – what else could it be? – 'bourgeois idealistic reaction on the literary front' which 'aspired to dictatorship' in literary theory.[12] The Stalinist line of 'intensified' class struggle under socialism is used to suggest that the 'class' character of Formalism has now been compelled openly to declare itself. Plekhanov, Engels and Lenin are adduced as authorities and judiciously quoted. The tactical sociologizing of late Formalism is nothing more than 'bourgeois sociologism' hostile to the category of class.[13] Medvedev brings his critique of Formalism up to date by discussing Formalist texts published since *The Formal Method*, including (in the case of Shklovsky and Tynyanov) their works of fiction, and exemplifying that elision whereby 'formalism' becomes a code for artistic heresy unproblematically correlated with 'idealism' in philosophy and 'bourgeois' class affiliation. When, finally, Medvedev concludes with a characterization of Formalism as 'a corpse stinking of decay', attempts to 'galvanize' which have 'far from ended', we are in the presence of Stalinist invective worthy of the *History of the Communist Party of the Soviet Union (Bolshevik)*.[14] The image speaks eloquently, again, of the totalitarian need to conjure up the paradoxical half-life or presence–absence of all enemies: alive enough to bolster by negation the identity of Bolshevism; dead enough to bear witness to its inherent strength and inevitable victory.

IV

We could end this story by concentrating on the ironic fates of individuals: the Shklovsky who is denounced in *Formalism and the Formalists* lived on to become a neighbour of Bakhtin's in Moscow in the last years of their lives; the writer of that denunciation was shot; Bakhtin himself, having eschewed polemic, was exiled for religious observance, not for his writing. The lesson would seem to be that it was safer to follow a project that left orthodoxy alone – neither overtly contradicting it nor quite embracing it, nor opportunistically wearing its clothes – than to call oneself Marxist: to do so is to lay oneself open to shifts in the party line, to find that one's loyalty is one day construed as only a more subtle form of treachery, and to learn too late that it is in truth more hazardous to take on the Marxist label than not to wear it at all. Bakhtin and Medvedev represent, respectively, those two options available to intellectuals in the early Stalin period. We have no more right to see Bakhtin's strategy as a merely skin-saving self-elevation above politics than we have to see Medvedev's descent into cultural politics as an equal but opposite falling off: as anything other than a brave attempt to reform that realm from inside, perhaps in the far-sighted (if tragically mistaken) belief that it constituted a model for a wider public sphere of the future. At least we could surmise that of the Medvedev of 1928; 1934 is another matter altogether. Bakhtin found sustenance elsewhere, no doubt, in the privacy of his banishment. The 'aesthetic' thread in his writing is, even in its anonymity after 1924, the secular and ecumenical version of that continuing and always spiritual dimension: the means, perhaps, of its junction with the modern, and certainly indispensable to us as we try to make sense of the tragic story which wove the vanguardisms of aesthetics and politics at once conflictually and complicitly together in the early part of this century, and of which Medvedev's death is only one episode.

Alternatively, we might instead tentatively personify *discourses* and look at *their* varied fortunes. Thus we could see Formalism, defeated in Russia, journeying westward to Prague.[15] There – as structuralism – it becomes a cultural theory under Saussurean influence, and is academicized, only to move still further west after the Second World War. Surfacing in Paris thirty years later, it finds itself once again in an atmosphere of insurrection, and is coaxed by our twin vanguardisms (friends again for a while) out of the academy. The legacy of structuralism in the context of this ultimately failed junction of vanguards is of course *post*-structuralism, which we might call that self-interrogating moment of the modernist critique of modernity which follows the withdrawal from the streets. The shift may be summed up in slogans: when it became clear that 'Workers of the world, unite!' and 'Under the paving-stones, the beach' were not after all going to chime together and sublate art in life, the banner of radicalism passed into the hands of those for whom the watchword was either Derrida's 'There is nothing beyond the text' or Althusser's 'Philosophy is the class struggle in theory'.

Now while Bakhtin could not of course ever have literally foreseen these outcomes, his critique of 1924 (beyond and in spite of its evident shortcomings) strikes the strong note of his distance from those aggressive modernisms – among them, and above all, those oxymoronic 'productionist aesthetics' like that of Russian Formalism – which ironically open the space for the very forms of rationality and routinization that they start out to contest. Using Weberian terms, we may say that Bakhtin divined in the charismatic force of that early Formalism of the 'device' the outlines of a typically modern logic, one which would issue before very long in a proto-structuralist theoretical discourse rich in metaphors that connote bureaucracy. The project that begins with 'the resurrection of the word' ends with 'literary functions' and the 'system of systems'. Bakhtin could not be expected to say (with Russell Berman, some sixty years later) that 'the commonly held assumption that innovative aesthetic activity is or ought to be a carrier of an anti-bureaucratic potential must be scrutinized'; still less might we expect him to say in 1924, less tentatively, that the 'aesthetic revolutionism' of the historical *avant-garde* 'itself contributed significantly to bureaucratic power'.[16] What we can say is that between the aesthetic and political vanguards of the early Soviet period there is a relationship of parallelism and (as it were) mutual parody that was livable until they both underwent routinization; then the literally bureaucratized politics of the one could no longer accommodate the metaphorically bureaucratized poetics of the other, if only because the latter reminded the former of its own charismatic and emancipatory repressed. If the Bakhtin of 1924 still speaks to us now, that is not because he specifically foresaw any of this, but because his anti-modernism of that time was free of the backward-looking reflexes of a Lukács and never became a mere oppositional partisanship. Instead, he held tenaciously and even quixotically on to the category of the aesthetic, radicalizing its claims to the point of self-undoing and ceasing to speak of it only when he had found it in the very forms of life themselves.

3

SYNTAX AND ITS SUBVERSION

How is this to be connected with the overriding, creative role of fantasy in language? Is a member of the proletariat such a fantasizer, then? Surely Lorck had something else in mind. He probably means that the proletariat will bring with it new forms of socioverbal intercourse, new forms of verbal interaction of speakers, and a whole new world of social intonations and accents. It will also bring with it a new linguistic truth. Probably that or something like it was what Lorck had in mind when he made his assertion. But there is no reflection of this in his theory. As for fantasizing, a bourgeois is no worse a hand at it than a proletarian, and has more spare time for it, to boot.

(*MPL*, 154)

My epigraph above finds Bakhtin's friend Valentin Voloshinov in a relatively relaxed discursive mood, freely fashioning a response to a suggestion from a 'bourgeois' German philologist that the French language be radically proletarianized. The full implication of my reason for quoting it will need to wait until much later in this chapter: I will content myself for now with pointing out the rich transnational negotiation that is in play when, in the early twentieth century, a Russian not only quotes a German on the condition of French, but also tries to enter the German's mind and ventriloquize the unspoken subtext of his call for linguistic revolution in another part of Western Europe. In the meantime, I will begin my major argument with another quotation – this time on the theme of quotation itself.

I

> Reported speech is speech within speech, utterance within utterance, and at the same time also *speech about speech, utterance about utterance.*
>
> (*MPL*, 115)

It seems fitting to begin a study of the Bakhtinian view of 'reporting' with a quotation 'about' quotation, allowing that quotation to frame what follows rather than be framed by it, bringing about an infinite regress of citation. Part III of *Marxism and the Philosophy of Language*, where Voloshinov comes down from the heights of philological polemic to focus upon this particular stylistic problem, has itself been treated as if it were the most abjectly subordinated kind of pedagogic quotation – the 'for example', the instantiated sentence illustrating the rules of grammar for the novice in a new language – rather than what it is or can be made to be: an active modifier of its own frame, and the prolific generator of themes that will dominate the later work of Bakhtin himself. Linguists and stylisticians have (with one notable exception in Brian McHale) largely ignored its pathbreaking typologies; Marxist readers have tended to invoke the broader arguments of the whole book and implicitly consigned its more empirical peroration to the status of a dispensable technicality.[1] Seasoned readers of the work produced by or in dialogue with Bakhtin should, however, know that the passage to Bakhtin's most productive general insights in history and theory runs directly from just such minute particulars as these, if only we take the trouble to enter fully into them. Or, to put it another way: without our full exploratory and meditative consideration, they will remain 'mere' technicalities.

The cue for a foregrounding of this 'supplement' to the main argument comes from Voloshinov himself, when he insists in his opening remarks that 'what had appeared a limited and secondary phenomenon actually has meaning of fundamental importance for the whole field of study'. 'So-called *reported speech*' will be rescued from secondariness in order that its 'whole hermeneutic power' may be 'disclosed' (*MPL*, 112). With this phenomenon of discourse Voloshinov is able to install himself on the border between grammar and style, thereby making another border crossable by Bakhtin in the Dostoevsky book of the same year: that between linguistics and translinguistics, where the opposition of grammatical codification (privileged over style by the Saussureans) and stylistic creativity (privileged over grammar by the Vosslerites) no longer operates. If he does not ever quite cross the latter border, he certainly attacks the border between grammar and style at its most vulnerable point by isolating within the general phenomenon of reporting the particular case that had already modified the old classical binary of *oratio recta* and *oratio obliqua* with its scandalously hybrid syntax. 'Free indirect discourse' (*style indirect libre*: henceforth, for brevity's sake, FID) could never act deconstructively against the grammatical categories upon which it is wholly parasitic, which define it as intermediate and which are still residually operative when Voloshinov rechristens it as 'quasi-direct discourse' (QDD). What this syntactic hybrid does is to push grammar to the limit of its competence: FID might be defined as all that grammar can 'see' of dialogism, which it registers only as the semantic ambiguity of certain sentences in narrative contexts, missing altogether the dialogical relations that organize meaning in wholes that are 'lower' or 'higher' in the linguistic hierarchy than the sentence – in single words, or in whole texts. The challenge of FID to linguistics is analogous to that posed by the novel to traditional poetics, inasmuch as the latter only 'sees' a stabilized generic form and not the whole field of 'novelistic discourse' or 'novelization' which antedates or exceeds the novel as narrowly demarcated. Bakhtin was to make this point only later; Voloshinov is content to tease out the difficulties a linguistic stylistics must inevitably have with a syntactic pattern that will always elude all the refinement of description that is lavished upon it.

We have by no means done with FID in these brief formulations; we will see later that its misleading description does not relegate it to immateriality. Voloshinov's rethinking of the problem of 'reported speech' in general begins from the premiss that in the realm of discourse 'within' or 'alongside' is always 'about', where *about* signifies not (necessarily or only) the fixing and finalizing formulae of a metalanguage but any kind of active relationship between discursive instances. Juxtaposition, in short, is always evaluation; *montage* is never anything other than (at least the potentiality of) dialogue; the co-presence or coextension of two or more utterances generates active understanding, actual or virtual *answering*. 'Commentary' and 'retort' do not need to be manifested semantically or thematically: they are inscribed in the *forms* of reporting, in (as it were) micro-generic acts of presentation. Reporting makes overt the process of 'inner-speech reception' of 'another's utterance', while its standard patterns are only the provisional 'grammaticalization' of the 'tendencies in understanding and evaluating' that are dominant in an epoch and in a particular culture or society (*MPL*, 118). (Inadequate though grammar may be in the theory of discourse, its codifications help those who are writing the history of a national language from below to find their sociopolitical bearings.) Traditional accounts of quoting focus exclusively upon the inner features of the quoted instance and ignore completely this active interrelation or 'inter-orientation' of the reported speech and the 'reporting context'.

It is when Voloshinov goes on to specify the 'two basic directions' in which this relationship can move, and to map these onto a schematic history of reporting in the European languages, that we find him once again anticipating Bakhtin on the novel. Borrowing the terminology of the art historian Wölfflin – analogue in his field, according to Pavel Medvedev, of the Vosslerites in linguistics – Voloshinov proposes a distinction between a 'linear' style of quoting, in which the boundaries separating the reporting and the reported are scrupulously respected, and the 'pictorial' style, in which those boundaries are programmatically transgressed. Tzvetan Todorov points out the seemingly exact 'fit' between this opposition and that elaborated at great length by Bakhtin in his notion of a 'stylistic line' in the novel for which heteroglossia is always 'outside' and engaged 'from above', and another line which goes down into heteroglossia and takes this diversity of social languages into itself.[2] The difference lies in the chronological mapping: whereas for Voloshinov linearity dominates until the end of the eighteenth century and pictoriality dominates the two centuries since, Bakhtin's two 'lines' are not so much consecutive as concurrent, coexisting even in antiquity and fusing early in the nineteenth century.

Now if this is not the mere inconsistency or revision that it might seem, that is because the two versions of the 'same' opposition are in truth the stages of a deconstruction: a problem of Bakhtinism becomes an opportunity, a blindness carries within itself an insight. Voloshinov's couple is a metaphor taken from the theory and history of another semiotic system (the visual arts) to illuminate a bifurcation which is predicated over the whole system of written discourse – plainly canonical in the linear case, implicitly non-canonical in the pictorial. Or rather: with (linear) 'dogmatism' his terms suggest discourse in general, and in particular rhetoric; with (pictorial) 'individualism' his terms suggest literary discourse, and in particular the novel. Almost parenthetically he notes certain wayward exceptions. The pictorial style 'characterizes the Renaissance (especially in the French language)' – is Voloshinov thinking perhaps of Rabelais? – and it is there also in the 'low genres' under neo-classicist hegemony in the seventeenth century (Jean de la Fontaine, supposed 'father' of FID, is the example cited) (*MPL*, 121). In Bakhtin these deviations join so great a multitude of others as to become a new norm in 'the novel', which is both the name of a practice of writing and the name of the move which carries through the deconstruction of the linear/pictorial binary. The dogmatisms of 'reporting' would not be 'themselves' if there were not pictorialisms to which they were always already dynamically and inwardly related, even if this relation is only one of unilateral and occluded exclusion. Linearity and pictoriality exist indeed only to be undone by the phenomenon that (in a first move) they so helpfully clarify: any instance of the linear is kept in being by the absence of the pictorial, by, so to speak, its *negative citation*.

The heuristic value of the distinction is not of course threatened by this undoing which takes place when Bakhtin begins to 'think with' the novel and allow that genre-which-is-not-a-genre to wield its full subversive force in theory. Voloshinov himself offers weighty empirical instances of the other kind of exception – not the pictorialism that earlier qualified linear dominance, but the linearity that persists today in 'judicial language' and 'political rhetoric' after the pictorial style has become the dominant in 'verbal art' (*MPL*, 123). These rhetorical languages of the state, with their 'acute awareness of property rights to words', stand in sharp contrast to a field of writing in which the common ownership of the word is taken to extremes (*MPL*, 122). For if in the realist text the boundaries of the reported speech were breached from the authorial side, in the modernist or proto-modernist text they are breached in the opposite direction: 'The verbal dominant', Voloshinov writes, 'may shift to the reported speech, which in that case becomes more forceful and more active than the authorial context framing it' (*MPL*, 121). Other speech assumes priority; authorial speech begins to experience itself *as other*: its objectivity and authority dissolve in a subjectivity with no greater purchase upon truth than the subjectivity of the quoted. We are not surprised to find Dostoevsky cited as a Russian example of this 'relativistic individualism' in the novelistic handling of 'other' speech, given that Bakhtin was to launch publicly in the same year the properly translinguistic concept of 'polyphony' for those cases where the discourse is so radically dialogized as to 'decompose' not only the local objectivity of authorial discourse but also that whole dimension of 'motivating' monological paraphrase called 'plot'. The stylistic metaphor-concept of pictoriality cannot take us into this polyphonic universe because it carries within itself too many residues of an unexamined aesthetic of representation. A 'pictorial style' which confers such autonomy upon the pictured, which makes interchangeable the pictured and the picturing, has already ceased to be a 'style'. However sternly Voloshinov's categories might confront a linguistic stylistics with its limits, their own limits are exposed when the active relation to which they draw attention is no longer unilateral. They are the categories of a peculiarly critical and self-conscious and sociolinguistically oriented theory of *parole*, but not yet (quite) the categories of a translinguistics.

How then – if it is seen to be superseded by Bakhtin almost simultaneously – is Voloshinov's project in Part III of *Marxism and the Philosophy of Language* to be justified? It would be hard to justify if the launching of a translinguistics were to have the immediate effect of reducing the descriptions of linguistics to the status of powerless and bodiless illusions. The project has its justification in the fact that the linguistically (syntactically) specified patterns of 'reporting' are themselves material forces with real effects not only in the reception of discourse but also in its very production – are, that is to say, themselves pedagogically inspired agents of monologism which need to be challenged if not *on* then at least *not far from* their own ground. In so far as translinguistics proper has already left this ground, it needs perhaps to be complemented by the kind of dissident stylistics practised by Voloshinov here. Chapter 3 of *Marxism and the Philosophy of Language* therefore takes us from the schematic pan-European diachrony of chapter 2– from the general phenomenon of quoting within discourse in general – to a minutely discriminated synchronic specification of the 'modifications' of indirect and direct discourse in literary (mainly novelistic) contexts in the Russian language. This typology both retains the traditional bifurcation and at the same time problematizes it in a preliminary way that seems innocently 'empirical' but has profound theoretical implications. Linearity and pictoriality might seem from the perspective of common sense to correspond to the classical grammatical patterns of indirect and direct discourse, respectively. Voloshinov implicitly rescues us from this supposition, and from the delusions of grammar itself, which might indeed suggest the reverse: that the syntactic unification of quoting and quoted in indirect discourse signals a breach of their mutual boundaries, while their syntactic independence in direct discourse corresponds to a strict policing of those boundaries. Instead, the linear and pictorial styles are taken to be the extremities of a continuum spanning direct and indirect discourse alike: a repertoire of possibilities (as it were) variously realized in the European languages. There is also no question here of 'deriving' one pattern from the other by rules of transformation and projecting this derivation hypothetically onto history. By discussing indirect discourse first, Voloshinov goes some way towards undermining notions of its secondariness; direct discourse is no more original than indirect. It is also no less secondary, in the sense that it is always a signification of speech and never its 'real' *presence*. Voloshinov's transitional project moves in all these ways *within* grammatical descriptions but *against* the mystifications they can generate. Its relationship to a fully elaborated translinguistics is one of preparation and complementarity.

When it comes to the distinction of patterns and their modifications, Voloshinov forsakes grammatical criteria altogether for others that we can only call (in an adaptation of the terminology of Michael Gregory) the criteria of *writing-as-differential-hearing*.[3] Indirect discourse 'hears' analytically; it is characterized by the syntactic ironing-out of 'formally' signified emotive-affective features and their transposition into 'content'. Imperative, interrogative and exclamatory utterances must submit to the syntax of the declarative sentence – often supplemented by a periphrasis which appears to be obligatory where those second-person 'addressing' nouns known as vocatives are involved. 'Analysis is the heart and soul of indirect discourse': does this mean that the essence of direct discourse is *synthesis*? (*MPL*, 129). Voloshinov resists this move (it seems) as much out of a suspicion of such antinomies as out of a sense that the nuanced empirical richness of this pattern itself escapes exhaustive analysis. We can perhaps only say that in direct discourse 'the analytical transmission of someone's speech' has *not* taken place, that a fiction of ventriloquizing has replaced a fiction of analysing (*MPL*, 128). Indirect stands to direct discourse as speech which has been manifestly acted upon to speech which has been manifestly *acted out*. At the same time: if the acting-out of ventriloquism is as 'active' as the acting-upon of analysis, then the latter might be said to be as 'enactive' as the former. The effectivity of the feint, the materiality of the mimed, is common to both.

The modifications of indirect discourse – the 'directions' taken by the analysis – themselves have an analytic neatness: relative linearity is 'referent-analysing', while relative pictoriality is 'texture-analysing'. Referential analysis depersonalizes speech in so far as it 'simply does not "hear" or take in whatever there is in [the] utterance that is without thematic significance' (*MPL*, 130). Its attention is directed not to the referent in its strict sense (that is, the name given by linguistics to the extra-linguistic) but rather to the signified: indirect discourse of this kind is paraphrastic, taking liberties with the message's stylistic autonomy in order the more completely to respect its semantic autonomy. It is ruthlessly reductive of expressive intonation and *anacolouthon*; 'understood' syntactic or logical relationships are spelled out with recognized lexical connectives; ataxis is compelled into parataxis and parataxis is eased towards hypotaxis. The respect paid to the signified in this modification is matched only by the respect paid to the signifier in textural analysis. This starkly contrasting type 'incorporates into indirect discourse words and locutions that characterize the subjective and stylistic physiognomy of the message viewed as expression' (*MPL*, 131). The signifiers of speech are 'made strange'; so deflected from the transparency of their first-order signifieds as to produce both a particularized (individual or typical) image of the speaker and an authorial attitude – of 'irony, humour, and so on' – towards that image (*MPL*, 131). The signifiers signify first and foremost a speaking subject under the evaluation of a writing subject, and only obliquely serve that speaker's putatively 'original' intentions.

Now it might be objected that my Saussurean idiom of 'signifier' and 'signified' misleadingly subtilizes a distinction which, when all is said and done, revives uncritically the form–content binary that even the Formalists had partially deconstructed.[4] If it is not deconstructed here, Voloshinov at least puts it into dialectical and historical motion. Deeply as the two 'directions' diverge (he insists), they also continually converge in the process of analysis of other speech that governs both, in what I have called a common 'action-upon': we are amateur logicians in so far as our transmission of speech analyses the signified, amateur stylisticians insofar it analyses the signifier. The pattern of indirect discourse exposes the underlying continuity of linearity and pictoriality, and beyond this the continuity of whole epochs otherwise so discontinuous with each other. Or again: Voloshinov helps us to see all binaries of the form–content variety as products of (what we might call) the analytic attitude. Their polar terms are only mischievous if we treat them as absolutes rather than as emphases within a common analytic perspective. The analytic attitude itself is only to be reprobated when (as, for instance, in structuralism) it believes its particular order of rationality to be the only rational and human attitude. Voloshinov's own discourse on indirect discourse is 'indirect' in this attitudinal rather than abstractly grammatical sense; it is a tactically structuralist idiom which takes its character from the phenomenon that it discusses and also knows that it does not have a monopoly on truth.

Nothing of this 'analytic neatness' (as I have called it) is to be found in the discussion of direct discourse and *its* modifications. As we would expect, a certain undecidable ambiguity haunts Voloshinov's attempt at a typology, giving his discourse a decidedly 'post-structuralist' cast. It is not simply that the pictorial style is given priority over the linear, overturning the order of discussion of indirect discourse – though that shift should not be lost on us. Within pictoriality itself the emphasis is first explicitly put upon the type in which authorial 'objectivity' is 'decomposed' by other speech, and then almost immediately the whole distinction between this and the opposite type is called into question. There is no 'sharp dividing line' between them; there is often 'a reciprocity of effect'. In 'pre-set direct discourse', where 'the basic themes of the impending direct discourse are anticipated by the context and are coloured by the author's intonations', it is the context itself that 'almost always' ends up reading like other speech (*MPL*, 134). A 'realist' pictoriality carries within itself the constant potential of a self-undoing 'modernist' pictoriality. Dostoevsky is of course Voloshinov's decisive exemplification, just as Nikolai Gogol is (predictably) his example of a 'particularized direct discourse' where this potential is relatively speaking *un*realized, where 'the authorial context . . . is so constructed that the traits the author used to define a character cast heavy shadows on his directly reported speech' (*MPL*, 134). Speech that is quoted in this way for its 'characterological significance' or 'picturesqueness' or its 'time-and-place typicality' is discourse that a Bakhtinian translinguistics (in *Problems of Dostoevsky's Poetics*) will call 'objectivized': an object language of rich particularity more or less successfully subordinated to an authorial metalanguage (*MPL*, 134). Voloshinov seems, however, to imply that even this type is less a matter of straightforward dominance than the provisional outcome of a continuing battle against the inherent dialogism of language, and that when either type is extensively used – when the narrative is conducted 'exclusively within the purview of the hero himself, not only within its dimensions of time and space but also in its system of values and intonations' – the result is an 'anticipated and disseminated reported speech' which demands a category of its own (*MPL*, 135). Hidden everywhere in the narrative, non-attributed but implicitly attributable other speech keeps breaking out into the fully attributed direct speech of the hero. Such global (rather than merely local) 'pre-setting' constitutes a radical 'speech interference' in which 'differently oriented' speech-acts meet and clash within a single construction. It goes without saying that it is precisely this textual and narrative phenomenon identified by Voloshinov's dissident stylistics that translinguistics will predicate across the whole of discourse under the name of dialogism.

Such 'interference' is the essence of so-called 'free indirect discourse'. Voloshinov's reference to this form as 'quasi-direct' must not be taken to imply that it is another (the fourth) modification of the direct-discourse pattern: it is only a 'syntactically standardized' form of interference which might occur empirically anywhere in any instance of the pictorial modifications. Two points need to be made about FID as a stylistic concept. First, it takes account only of what happens within the confines of the narrative context, without regard to that differential relationship between narrative and formally quoted speech on which the modifications themselves are based. Secondly, FID is what happens when interference is not a matter of a word here or a locution there but affects the very construction of sentences in the narrative – when, in short, interference comes to the notice of *langue* and falls under the latter's jurisdiction. FID is inaccurate as a description because it foregrounds the superficial (abstract-grammatical) kinship of the form with indirect discourse – its sharing of the same tense and person with the latter – while ignoring altogether those more radically definitive *qualities of the whole utterance* that it shares with direct discourse: intact intonation, emotive-affective features, 'mood' and the like. It is no accident that this description founded upon affinities in the realm of *langue* should have been coined by Charles Bally, a pupil of Saussure's; Voloshinov's borrowing from the Vosslerite Gertraud Lerch is what comes of attending to the form in all its rawness and concreteness as a phenomenon of *parole*.

If interference (or dialogism to some degree) is the defining characteristic of the pictorial modifications of direct discourse, its linear modifications are characterized by an absence of interference, 'a parallelism of intonations' between ventriloquist and ventriloquized (*MPL*, 138). In 'rhetorical' and 'substituted' direct discourse the author *speaks for* the hero, 'says in his stead what the hero might or should have said' (*MPL*, 138). This empathetic authorial soliloquizing is – to judge by the examples Voloshinov adduces from Pushkin – a sort of poetic and monological equivalent of the novelistic dialogism which it sometimes outwardly resembles. The correlation of the two 'directions' of the pictorial style in direct discourse with (respectively) realism and modernism is here completed by the implicit association of linearity in this pattern with Romanticism. To correlate these styles with 'poetry' and 'prose' would, however, be mistaken: FID/QDD is to be found in narrative poetry (one of Voloshinov's two Russian examples is from Alexander Pushkin), and linear direct discourse has its place in prose. Charles Dickens's anonymous narrator in *Bleak House* provides a notable English example, with his impassioned addresses to authority and his acts of urgent identification with characters in critical scenes. The historic present of the narrative is the diegetic element from which these mimetic passages seem 'naturally' to emerge; what we have is not so much a narrative in the traditional sense as the permanent possibility of such hortatory or empathetic interventions – *histoire* always ready to burst into *discours*.[5] It is characteristic of anglophone stylistics that it should invent for this phenomenon the description 'free direct discourse', as if direct discourse of this kind, without quotation marks or character-attribution (and *within* the narrative), were nothing more than an interesting transformation of FID.[6] The usefulness of the category can be measured by its conflation of the cited and patently linear instances from Dickens with the 'interior monologue' of Joyce's *Ulysses*, which could hardly be further removed from linearity. In that text the 'interference' is so absolute as to make the distinction of interfered-with and interfering undecidable.

II

Part III of *Marxism and the Philosophy of Language* ends with a chapter entitled 'Quasi-direct Discourse in French, German and Russian'. To give this stylistically defined hybrid pattern a chapter to itself is not at all to reify or fethishize such linguistic-stylistic categories; it is to acknowledge that such definition – such clear syntactic crystallization coupled with such manifest disarray among the experts when it comes to *naming* it – signals obliquely a broad mutation within Western discourse whose ideological significance needs to be extricated from stylistic mystification, and that such mystifying categories are 'material' enough (thanks to the power of the very pedagogy that transmits them) to have a life of their own. Beyond this, there is, in the terms of Voloshinov's chapter heading, an index of the will to resume and bring to an exemplary focus the main lines of the polemic against the schools of Saussure and Vossler that finds expression in Part II of his book. The intersection of 'French' and 'German' voices in the 'single construction' which is Voloshinov's text achieves formal closure in a discussion of the formal patterning of just such dialogical utterances; the two cultural voices through which a modernizing Russia found itself meet precisely on the ground of a theorization of such interlocutory meetings. To an already complex transaction – Bakhtin in dialogue with Voloshinov in dialogue with two Western European discourses that differentially misrecognize a dialogical phenomenon – our own discussion adds still further complexity, bringing as it does an 'English' cultural voice and another history to bear upon the positions established with and against those histories and voices that (as Erich Auerbach points out) were so powerfully fertilizing in the Russia of the late nineteenth and early twentieth centuries.[7] The emphasis in what now follows will be on the implications of Voloshinov's argument for English writing and on what is revealed of his text's 'political unconscious' when this defamiliarizing perspective is self-consciously adopted.

Among the many attractions of FID/QDD as the closing *topos* for a polemic of this kind is the fact that it was the subject of a celebrated scholarly exchange between Voloshinov's two antagonists which took place in the pages of the *Germanisch-romanische Monatsschrift* at a time of heightened tension between the major European powers, on the eve of the First World War. His installation of the project of a 'Marxist philosophy of language' in the space defined by the mutual antagonism of his Western antagonists might almost be said to answer Lenin's famous call of 1914 for socialists to exploit the 'imperialist' war in order to bring about the downfall of 'capitalist class rule': there is perhaps a more than passing resemblance between the strategy of Voloshinov's revolution in the theory of discourse and the Leninist political strategy for social revolution in Europe and the East.

The history of FID/QDD is a history of lags and deferred realizations. Emerging as a deliberate novelistic practice in the context of the late eighteenth-century crisis in language, the form only came to be theorized in the context of the next major crisis in representation a century later. When the Geneva linguist Charles Bally launched the polemic in 1912, then, he was not only entering a field opened up within German philology some fifteen years before; he was party to a belatedness of European dimensions which should speak volumes to any astute student of cultural modernity and its uneven, crisis-ridden development. In 1897 Adolf Tobler had isolated a style of 'reporting' which cut across the classical patterns and (in a formulation which hardly advances anybody's knowledge) called it a 'peculiar mixture' (*eigentümliche Mischung*) of both. Two years later, Theodor Kalepky moved on from this crude syncretism to a full sense of the pattern's novelty and autonomy in the description 'veiled speech' (*verschleierte Rede*). Where Tobler identified a mere sum of two patterns, Kalepky at least recognizes that it is a coincidence of two voices – that of the author and that of the character. Voloshinov parts company with Kalepky, however, when the latter assigns an active role to the message emitted by the grammar of sentences. Grammatical form, with its tenses and pronouns, tells us it is the author speaking; content or context signals the character's speech: 'the point of the device consists in guessing who the speaker is' (*MPL*, 143). The Bakhtinian answer to this dilemma is that it is a mystification of linguistic stylistics from which only the postulate of two 'differently oriented' voices speaking at once can offer an escape. Bally's Saussurean riposte predictably puts Kalepky into reverse by revivifying the abstract patterns: *style indirect libre* is a late result of the gradual attenuation of classical indirect discourse, a matter first of elided conjunctions and then of 'verbs of saying' or 'speech tags' falling away. The synchronic analysis which complements this diachronic account of the form is (for us, now) even more recognizably Saussurean, and it points up the anomalous status of a stylistics growing out of a linguistics of this kind. Pure FID/QDD is not strictly a 'linguistic form' but rather 'a figure of thought: in linguistic forms the articulation of signifier upon signified is regular, properly systemic; figures of thought violate this regularity and are illogical from the standpoint of language' (*MPL*, 145). Stylistics is the inventory of what is left after linguistics has completed the drastic reduction which sets up *langue* as its object, and FID/QDD is one of the more egregious instances of such linguistic 'noise'. The stylistics of forms like FID/QDD – perhaps indeed all stylistics – is in effect the teratology of language. In a passage not quoted by Voloshinov, Bally writes of the 'grammatical monstrosities' that are produced by the 'contamination' of the form, as when its characteristic use of the *imparfait* corrupts the epic preterite of unequivocally diegetic sentences that find themselves in its neighbourhood.[8]

In the months before the outbreak of war the polemic intensified, with a response from Kalepky in 1913 and two more responses from the Vosslerite side in 1914 itself. The Munich lecturer Eugen

Lerch volunteered yet another description: *Rede als Tatsache*, or 'speech as fact'. Speech becomes fact in the sense that its content appears to have the stamp of authorial authority; mimesis, in short, has the full force of diegesis. If of all forms this is the most vividly mimetic, that is because it optimally combines the weight of authority with its manifest absence. From a Bakhtinian perspective this move is a retrogression from Kalepky inasmuch as it replaces his at least provisionally dialogical authorial mask with a monological trick of total disappearance. Of more lasting influence was the intervention of Etienne Lorck, who launched the Vosslerite tendency (endorsed, as we have seen, by Voloshinov) to assimilate the form to direct rather than indirect discourse. His other importance is as the inventor, seven years later, of the still standard German description *erlebte Rede*, or 'experienced speech' – a description already anticipated in 1914 when he writes that the author 'inwardly experiences' what the character putatively experiences. Lorck represents *Sprachseelenforschung* taken to the point of hyperbole: normality and priority are conferred upon everything in language that the Geneva school thought secondary and deviant. The form is monologized as it was in Lerch; but, unlike his fellow Vosslerite, Lorck is concerned solely with its subjective dimension and not at all with any validating authority of 'fact'. Sheer subjectivity-for-its-own-sake springs from authorial empathy with the character and elicits the same from the reader. *Erlebte Rede* is what Gregory would later call discourse 'written to be read as if overheard'; it happens to have been heard by a second person but would be utterly out of place in any communication to a third person.[9] The third-person pronouns function not for the benefit of a third party but immediately for the writing and reading subjects, and even the preterite is interpreted as the tense of the author's 'having-heard'. The author's fantasy hears the character speaking; the reader's fantasy replicates this hearing. In this form we have *in nuce* the very creativity of language itself, at once the source and antithesis of all the 'finished, inert products' of the intellect.

This account of the polemic has emphasized the diametrical opposition of the sides, their almost wilfully antithetical identities. As important for our purposes is the asymmetry in Voloshinov's exposition of their cases, both quantitatively and qualitatively speaking. The greater length devoted to the Vosslerite party can be explained by the greater number of its protagonists and contributions and their continued activity after the interruption of the war. What is then arresting is the difference in quality between the two renderings – a difference for which Voloshinov's own categories of reporting may provide the terms. Bally's case is 'analytically' transmitted, and with a strongly linear tendency: insistent attributions keep it at arm's length, so to speak. Conversely, the other side is more or less quasi-directly ventriloquized, with a tendency towards the pictorial style. Attributions are fewer and further between, and in the instance of Gertraud Lerch (praised for her diachronic understanding of the form) disappear almost completely. This intense 'speech interference' generates an ambiguous endorsement of Vosslerite positions which breaks through and beyond the closure of Voloshinov's formal critique; indeed the criticism has an energy which is plainly determined-from-within (as Bakhtin himself would say) by the free rein already given to that 'other speech' and its dominant theme of the *energeia* of language.

The value of the Vosslerite case for Voloshinov is in its foregrounding of the speaking subject rather than the system and syntax, and in its notion of language as belonging to 'culture' rather than 'nature'. Where that case errs is in its attempt to explain the generation of language by means of the speaking subject, accounting causally for language by appeal to one of its *effects*. Far from merely being expressed by language, the 'inner subjective personality' is itself only 'an expressed or inwardly impelled word', which like all words is thoroughly worldly, inseparable from the interaction of 'producers'. Its undoubtedly special status as 'one of the most important and profound themes' of language should not tempt us into believing that it is more than a theme of language – that it is somehow the latter's generative source (*MPL*, 153). Now if this critique is familiar enough today, if it is nowadays the stock-in-trade of post-structuralist accounts, that is no strange coincidence: Robert Young has drawn attention to the direct influence of Bakhtinian ideas on these accounts and to the crucial role of Julia Kristeva in this transaction.[10] What has not so far been noticed is that in this neglected supplement to the main polemic of *Marxism and the Philosophy of Language* there are inscribed the elements at least of a typically Kristevan extension and elaboration of those ideas. To be more precise: Voloshinov's close engagement with a pattern of pseudo-quotation that is at once marginalized by the Saussureans and fetishized by the Vosslerites brings him into a political and psychological space where even he would have been surprised to find himself, a space not only beyond the complicity of those dichotomized cases but also somewhat askew to the overt allegiances of his own text. The main polemic strongly implies that his own position is a (dialectical?) synthesis of 'abstract objectivism' and 'individualistic subjectivism' – presumably an 'objectivism' which is 'concrete' and 'social'. The supplement to the polemic cuts across this symmetry and finality in the much warmer discursive hospitality we have seen it offering to the 'subjectivist' argument; the slogan of 'objectivism' becomes ever fainter as its place is taken by a politics of discourse which is (in a strictly non-essentialist sense) more 'feminine'.

Once this perspective has been admitted, its ramifications are virtually endless, and can only be hinted at here. We could begin by noting how the debate about the status of this dubiously nameable form of quoting enforces a swapping of those essentializing national-linguistic stereotypes that might stamp French as feminine and German as masculine: on the francophone side *style indirect libre* is consigned to an irrationality beyond the pale of language, while for the German theorists what makes *erlebte Rede* the epitome of the creative essence of language is precisely its flouting of diegetic and syntactic reason. The dissidence of what I have called Voloshinov's dissident stylistics now takes on a more complexly overdetermined character: it appears not simply as a matter of Marxist versus 'bourgeois' theorizations but also as a certain construction of Russian as a site of fluid non-identity which is both ground and transgression of those more clarified linguistic identities. This comes through in Voloshinov's reminder to his first readers that their (Russian) language does not admit of the clear division of quoting patterns that is to be found in French and German. Russian is 'weak' in its development of indirect discourse and above all in the linear modifications; conversely its strength is in the more ambiguous of the pictorial modifications of direct discourse. Its lack of *consecutio temporum* so runs direct and indirect discourse together as to make all reported speech in Russian sound in foreign ears like a variant of a single quasi-direct pattern (*MPL*, 132). Indeed the examples given by Boris Uspensky of '*nesob-stvenno-priamaia rech*' in his *A Poetics of Composition* suggest that 'quasi-direct discourse' is a far wider category in Russian usage than the very specific foreign phenomenon with which it is supposed to correlate, embracing as it does kinds of quoting which would seem to non-Russians mere colloquial illiteracies.[11] If it is not exactly the norm in Russian, quasi-direct discourse in this broad sense is neither so plainly deviant nor so plainly a matter of 'artistic' refinement. 'Russian' in Voloshinov's text becomes in all these ways the name of a discursive flux where the confident distinction of norm and deviation is profoundly shaken, along with other binary oppositions. It is perhaps not coincidental that Voloshinov – and Russian stylistic terminology down to the present – should settle, among the welter of foreign terms on offer, for the nomenclature of Gertraud Lerch, the only feminine voice among the Vosslerites.

We can now begin to see how this pendant to Voloshinov's main argument actively modifies its frame. It is not at all a matter of dogmatic closure in Parts I and II being qualified in Part III by a pragmatic openness. The general polemic against 'bourgeois' linguistics is after all a model of the kind of immanent critique exemplified by Medvedev the year before in his book about the Formalists; while the supplement itself is, as we will see, subject to a closing retraction. Rather, the conception of language as (in Kristeva's terms) heterogeneous 'signifying process' which the whole text enforces is differently inflected in its postscript: there is a shift from macro- to micro-perspectives and from one interface to another; from the general articulation of the 'symbolic' and sociality to the pressure of the 'semiotic' within and against the symbolic in a particular 'signifying practice'. Also, instead of 'language' and its 'philosophy' the issue is now one of languages and their theoretical self-images – of their different distributions of what Kristeva calls 'the relation between unity and process' within the speaking subject, or at least the differential privileging of these instances in the homespun auto-theorizations of the European national vernaculars.[12] The particularization extends from space to time: Voloshinov's review of the 1897–1914 polemic around FID/QDD cannot but bring into view a conjuncture of crisis in which all unities – of the state no less than of the sign – came to be relativized. No ideology in history can have enjoyed so short a span between consolidation and crisis than the liberalism which in the late nineteenth century found its hegemony threatened from without and within by the growth of socialism and feminism. The women's struggle 'introduces into the heart of symbolism and sociality the echo of the woman's unsaid': Kristeva's formulation of this 'rhythm that cannot be named'[13] might be applied to the phenomenon of *signifiance*, which occurs in the signifying practice of fiction when the intonations of an (infinite) other make themselves heard in the structure of sentences, and which can also only be problematically named.[14]

Naming this syntactic hybrid has indeed a sociopolitical dimension, which now becomes visible. *Style indirect libre* might be seen as an analogue of the citizen under the grand condescension of the modern state, in a moment when the European polities were widening the franchise to take in women and the working class. Marginal, irrational, they none the less have a place in the sociosymbolic order, enjoying the 'freedom' of being represented 'indirectly'. *Parole* is the civil society of language; the system of *langue* plays the state's part in distantly acknowledging the denizens of this unruly space, without which it would not exist. For its part, *erlebte Rede* speaks rather of that 'petty-bourgeois' protest which comes not so much from below as from in between, unstably poised between the great political options of left and right. The readiness to speak of the political which distinguishes this tendency from those whose intellectual production underwrites a mature 'bourgeois' order is noted by Voloshinov when he praises the Vosslerites for 'teas[ing] and worr[ying] the ideological nerve in language', and then (by way of illustration) quotes the term's inventor on the 'inertness and intellectualist sclerosis of French': 'There is only one possibility for its rejuvenation: the proletariat must take over command of the word from the bourgeoisie'. This statement is fascinating enough; even more so is Voloshinov's response, which is quoted as the epigraph to this chapter, and to which I invite the reader to turn back (*MPL*, 154). Nowhere else does Voloshinov violate so creatively the decorum of scholarly discourse; the passage reads almost like a passage from a novel – an authorial speculation, somewhat rhetorically oriented, as to the subtext of the enigmatic speech of a character whose motives he chooses only partly to understand. Voloshinov refracts his own tentative propositions through a reconstruction of the inner speech that may have accompanied Lorck's overt remark, modulating in one sentence from indirect to quasi-direct pseudo-quotation when the most extravagant claim is made: 'It will also bring with it a new linguistic truth' (*MPL*, 154). 'Hypothetical' adverbials ('surely', 'probably') produce a sense of the ongoing making of sense, of thinking aloud. The result is a dialogism with vertiginous possibilities of meaning: as our author debates the compatibility of a proletarian renewal of language with the Lorckian *Leitmotiv* of 'fantasy', bringing the forces of history and of the psyche together, so the values of 'inside' and 'outside' are inverted and redistributed. The perspective is opened up, at least potentially, of that theorization of subjectivity which feminist theory has shown to be a crucial political and therapeutic task but which the conjunctural necessity of proving one's robust masculine 'objectivism' closed off at this date.

III

What does all this have to say to anyone working in the field of writing in English? My account of the complex cross-cultural transaction that is Voloshinov on reported speech has of course already been deeply and inwardly constituted by just such an occupational and cultural placing; it remains only to make this investment explicit in a note on FID/QDD in English writing and anglophone stylistics. The first thing to be noted is a belatedness in theory more acute than any to be found in German or French scholarship: before the 1950s a silence either of agnosticism or ignorance (or both) prevails; the form was buried in grammatical manuals written by foreigners like Otto Jespersen, and it had no place whatever in all the copious discussions of 'point of view' that flowed steadily from their Jamesian source through the 1920s and 1930s and beyond.[15] Once noticed, it is discussed in terms that are predictably eclectic: a translation of the Saussurean description is used in accounts that borrow their categories indifferently from traditional grammar and from neo-Firthian linguistics (that is, when they aren't simply appealing to a naive pragmatics of communication, as in the claim that FID/QDD has the edge on its direct and indirect rivals in so far as it felicitously combines 'dramatic immediacy' in quotation with an 'economy' of narrative means and a 'smooth' transition from authorial to 'other' discourse and back again). Paradoxically – but, within the legendary peculiarity of English history, quite explicably – there goes with this belatedness in theory an earliness in practice, English fiction being the first to make seemingly conscious and extensive use of the form not only for characters' overt speech but also for their inner speech, thus laying the ground for its later (modernist) status as the latter's privileged vehicle. German and francophone stylistics had long recognized this earliness: Bally's pupil Marguerite Lips, in her monograph of 1926, and the German scholar Lisa Glauser, in 1949, concur in identifying Jane Austen's novels as the site of this mutation.[16] The first English monograph on 'free indirect speech', written by a Germanist who uncritically repeats this claim, only appeared in 1977.[17]

Now the truth is that Austen is only first in the field in the specific sense defined above – in consistency of use, and use across the border dividing spoken from unspoken speech. Henry Fielding sporadically uses a somewhat formalized and 'tagged' variety of FID/QDD for overt speech a good half-century before Austen, and in 1778 Fanny Burney's heroine in her epistolary novel *Evelina* is made to report her interlocutor's speech in a classically 'free' style. Burney's practice would seem to be both (dia)logically and historically transitional, intermediate between comic fiction's occasional epic-authorial (often ironic) hearing of overt speech and sentimental fiction's early experiments with ways of empathetically *over*hearing the inner speech of its central characters. The point is not, as stylisticians needlessly insist, that the notation of inner speech in FID/QDD is technically impossible and anyway unnecessary in a 'first-person' narrative like *Evelina*. Rather, comic fiction provides the syntactic precedent for a 'subjective' hearing of spoken speech which answers to the ambient 'subjectivity' of a novel in letters.

This inner-speech hearing of an interlocutor in its turn licenses the move made ten years later in Mary Wollstonecraft's 'third-person' narrative *Mary, A Fiction*, where some of the earliest instances of characters' inner speech in FID/QDD are to be found. When Austen then uses the form for both orders of speech, she does so not in a vacuum but as the heir to a rapid transformation in the modes of scriptory (over)hearing in a moment of revolutionary crisis. The syntax of a pseudo-subjective hearing of objective speech deriving from comic fiction (Burney) lends itself to the pseudo-objective hearing of subjective speech in the (radicalized) fiction of sensibility (Wollstonecraft). In other words, there is from the beginning an 'inner-speech' dimension to our form which facilitated its passage from the hearing to the heard and is perhaps never wholly lost. Austen's move on from this recycling inversion is to run both functions together, thereby exemplifying in the particular field of quotation Bakhtin's more general claim that the two great 'stylistic lines' of the European novel fuse in the early nineteenth century. However, there is much more at stake here than the mere confirmation of a literary-historical generalization. If Austen's precedents were to find themselves on opposite sides of the polarized ideological divide in 1789, their stylistic innovations coexist (unequally) in her writing under a strongly reasserted and comprehensively ironizing authorial authority. On the one hand, this is the very image of confident gentry rule: just as that class's title to the land was absolute – not even the feudal ruling class could claim that – so is the territory of the sign in Austen's novels subject in the end to the Law. On the other hand, we must also register a long-term advance: the novel in the late eighteenth century is transformed by a woman who reworks the work of two other women, and at the centre of this transformation is a form which crystallizes in a syntactic routine the power of the unsaid to undermine syntactic rationality.

There can be no doubt, then, as to where this form comes from: whatever its later fortunes, it first appears not as a Flaubertian sophistication of style but as a spontaneous resource of at least one woman fighter in that great battleground of class and gender that recent work has decisively shown the eighteenth-century English novel to have been.[18] Wollstonecraft's flouting in her audacious plots of what Jane Spencer calls the 'terms of acceptance' of woman writers at this time has its linguistic correlative in this violation of authorial syntax. To Austen falls the task of establishing it as a device – civilizing it, as it were, removing it from the field of a radical sexual politics. Its vitality in her writing is a function, first, of the air of political and libidinal scandal that clings to it from the radical years, and, secondly, of the narrow social range of her characters whose speech it is called upon to mimic. When in the later nineteenth century these conditions no longer obtain – as, for example, in the high-Victorian realism of George Eliot, with its liberal tolerance of subaltern discourses and its sympathetic sociology of moral and political error – FID/QDD survives, but in a certain dilution. In Eliot, it must battle with the monologism of those linear 'rhetorical' modes of 'speaking for' the inarticulate which it superficially resembles; or it intricately traces the evasions of a developed moral pathology of 'egoism'; or, again, it dramatizes the ambiguities of 'custom' in its refraction of a communal voice with just enough intact idiom to signify a picturesque parochialism. In Dickens, it functions almost always as it did in eighteenth-century comic fiction, as a means of miming overt speech. Only one among many conduits of social heteroglossia in his writing, it characteristically carnivalizes official occasions and discourses by exploiting the fact that two quotidian styles share its syntax: a populist variant of the form is born as faint echoes of the neutrality of journalistic reporting of legal proceedings intersect with much louder echoes of the broadly ironic 'cross-talk' or by-play in a music-hall double-act.

What unites these otherwise disparate liberal and populist uses of the form is the openly rhetorical strategies it is made to serve – a rhetoric (typically) of passionately understated intimate talk in Eliot's case, a rhetoric of emphatic public speaking in Dickens's, with the direction of the dialogical 'interference' moving in both cases tendentially from author to character. A later fiction will not only reverse this direction but also renounce any such 'voice' for what Voloshinov calls the 'voice-defying complexity of intonational structures that are so characteristic for modern literature' (*MPL*,

156). No longer either a device or a strategy, FID/QDD becomes in some modernist novels a *principle* of organization: the moment of its first theorization is also the moment when its decisive association with inner speech coincides with the movement of other speech into priority. No longer reducible to the polarized aesthetic effects of either sympathy or irony – whether distributed differentially across a range of characters or shifting from one to the other as the protagonist grows away from or towards the authorial position – FID/QDD is no longer subject to what the Russian Formalists called 'motivation'. Or, to put it another way: novels come to be written in which pseudo-quoted inner speech is the dominant not (or not only) quantitatively but (also) qualitatively, dissolving space and time into (single or multiple, attributable or non-attributable) acts of perception and retrospection.

The 'author' does not – *pace* the ideologues of modernism – 'disappear', supplanting the earlier postures of lyric fusion and ironic distance with an impossible, unimaginable, God-like neutrality. The writing subject is, rather, destabilized, becoming little more than an after-image of that stable authority which the old polar effects are now seen to have at once implied and presupposed. This practice of writing in which FID/QDD is thus egregiously empowered and foregrounded not only outstrips the pioneering theorizations of the form that are coeval with it; it also almost immediately supersedes itself. In anglophone writing this self-supersession of the form can be seen in process in the work of James Joyce: it is as if its success in imposing its syntax of the infinite 'other' upon the very narrative logic of a text is at the same time an exposure of its limitations. Its compromise with the epic preterite and third person becomes redundant when its battle with that particular version of the logic of identity and non-contradiction has been won. Non-identity and contradiction assert themselves in the flagrant ataxis of an inner speech directly quoted (the misnamed 'interior monologue') and in the accompanying heterogeneity of cultural voices, would-be absolute contexts that are only ever contexts for each other. This self-surpassing of FID/QDD is by no means inevitable, as the case of Henry James so clearly attests. His alternative to the Joycean process is a strategy of naturalization which appeals to a specular unity of point of view and motivates the form in the global event of consciousness conceived as that of the artist or near-artist. It is perhaps no coincidence that *A Portrait of the Artist as a Young Man* – the Joyce text which takes our form to its ultimate potential – should be (a parody of) a *Künstlerroman*; neither should we be surprised that the move beyond *Ulysses*, where it is only one among many other liberated possibilities of language, should be to a text which makes indistinguishable from each other the twin infinities of inside and outside, of heteroglossia and the unconscious.

Any investigation of free indirect discourse in the late twentieth century will inevitably have the character of an archaeology. What this stylistically specialized archaeology of literary signifying practices reveals is a certain continuity between realism and (early) modernism, a shift of function beneath an exterior not all that radically altered. The decisive break is elsewhere and later: we can only speak of modernism when postmodernism is already imminent, when that new function overreaches and thereby abolishes itself. Despairing of finding any consistency of function where this form is concerned – across the length of a text, across the whole extent of a signed output, let alone across time – McHale's very comprehensive study has suggested a 'meta-function': FID/QDD is *an index of the literary itself*, one of the situationally defined varieties of language.[19] Suggestive as it is, this latter-day Formalist proposition invites the well-known general Bakhtinian critique of that case, inasmuch as it not only hypostasizes and essentializes the literary but also fixes the form at that early-modernist moment of naturalized dominance which I have characterized above. Beyond this, a Bakhtinian perspective shows this issue of FID/QDD's 'function' to be a pseudo-question. To that practical supersession of the form which comes to a concentrated focus in Joyce there corresponds another (theoretical) supersession – that of Voloshinov's sociological stylistics by the Bakhtinian translinguistics which, as I argued earlier, it both complements and prepares. Along with all other linguistically defined categories, FID/QDD has no place in the earliest and most purist version of that new discipline: the famous table of prose elements in *Problems of Dostoevsky's Poetics*. Indeed it is not to be found anywhere in that whole text. When it does appear, in 'Discourse in the Novel' some five years later, it is under the overarching rubric of 'Heteroglossia in the Novel' and then only as an implicit subheading under one of that section's own more explicit subheadings. The heteroglot intertext has various points of entry into and routes of traversal across the novelistic text – 'comic style', 'the posited author', 'the language used by characters', 'incorporated genres' – and *nesobstvenno-priamaia rech'* concludes a discussion of the technical possibilities for realizing the language of characters. Quasi-direct discourse not only orders the inner speech of characters and brings about its merging with the author's context; it also preserves what indirect discourse would efface: the 'inability [of inner speech] to exhaust itself in words' (*DN*, 319). In short, its syntax is the conduit of a psychic heteroglossia which takes us to the very edge of the sayable – to one of those boundaries on which, according to Bakhtin himself, all discourse 'lives'.

IV

Twenty-five years later we find Bakhtin returning fleetingly to QDD, wondering why its dialogism and its place in the spectrum of 'forms of hidden, semi-hidden, and diffused speech of another' are still not properly understood (*PT*, 121). These brief references are perhaps less germane than a still later passage where translinguistics makes what must rank as its most daring leap of generalization, predicating over the whole of linguistic modernity an infinitely graded or shaded irony: a ubiquity of voices which only speak 'with reservations' and in mimicry of other voices. All modern European languages are more or less secularized and democratized; all are in their structures defined against the unconditional 'proclamatory' voice of patriarchal and sacerdotal authority. The liberated heir to these authorities is that figure who is nonetheless ambiguously bound to them as their professional ironist: 'the writer, simply the writer' (*NM70–71*, 132). QDD is not cited by name, but as a syntactic pattern which codifies semantic ambiguity it would plainly belong within the diachronic development Bakhtin is here tracing and, to judge by his strongly positive tone, applauding. The specialized history of *parole* that is sketched in Voloshinov's periodization of 'reporting' tendencies – that passage from single-voiced linearity to double-voiced pictoriality – is here daringly rewritten as a history of *langue* itself, or at least (since the latter can only be thought in a bracketing of diachrony) of *langage*. We might be led to believe that Voloshinov also welcomes this development – that is, until we reach the last paragraph of *Marxism and the Philosophy of Language*. QDD and other 'extreme forms' of the pictorial style are symptoms of a 'crucial turning-point in the social vicissitudes of the utterance' and are to be explained by the *'general, far-reaching subjectivization of the ideological word-utterance'*. He goes on:

> No longer is it a monument, nor even a document, of a substantive ideational position; it makes itself felt only as the expression of an adventitious, subjective state. Typifying

and individualizing coatings of the utterance have reached such an intense degree of differentiation in the linguistic consciousness that they have completely overshadowed and relativized an utterance's ideational core, the responsible social position implemented in it. The utterance has virtually ceased to be an object for serious ideational consideration. The categorical word, the word 'from one's own mouth', the *declaratory* word remains alive only in scientific writings. In all other fields of verbal-ideological creativity, what predominates is not the 'outright' but the 'contrived' word. All verbal activity in these cases amounts to piecing together 'other person's words' and 'words seemingly from other persons' .... All this bespeaks an alarming instability and uncertainty of ideological word. Verbal expression in literature, rhetoric, philosophy, and humanistic studies has become the realm of 'opinions', of out and out opinions and even the paramount feature of these opinions is not *what* actually is 'opined' in them but *how* – in what individual or typical way – the opining is done. This stage in the vicissitudes of the word in present-day bourgeois Europe and here in the Soviet Union (in our case, up to very recent times) can be characterized as the stage of *transformation of the word into a thing*, the stage of *depression in the thematic value of the word*. The ideologues of this process, both here and in Western Europe, are the formalistic movements in poetics, linguistics, and philosophy of language. One hardly need mention here what the underlying social factors explaining this process are, and one hardly need repeat Lorck's well-founded assertion as to the only ways whereby a revival of the ideological word can come about – the word with its theme intact, the word permeated with confident and categorical social value judgement, the word that really means and takes responsibility for what it says (*MPL*, 158–59).

How are we to take this closing statement? I find myself in the position of Voloshinov himself before Lorck's 'well-founded statement' about the proletarian renewal of language. Is this the cautious retraction that it seems? Is it, as Todorov suggests, a 'denunciation' of the phenomenon that Bakhtin was to applaud some forty years later?[20] The timespan surely makes a difference: Bakhtin is concerned with a whole epochal development, occupying centuries of post-mediaeval history; Voloshinov with a topical or conjunctural situation, only the latest phase of that long development. Even if we refuse Todorov's identification of Voloshinov with Bakhtin, our knowledge is scarcely advanced by referring these sharply different evaluative accents to some personal difference between two members of the Bakhtin 'school'. Neither is it (much) advanced by noting that the denunciation was written for immediate publication at the beginning of the Stalin period, while the applause appears in a piece of private speculation written well after that phase of Soviet history had ended. This paragraph's bearings and effects in the cultural politics of 1929 are complex enough even at the level of conscious polemical intent; it is far more than a safe reiteration of current sloganizing. The branding of the 'formalistic movements' as ideologues of the reification of the word is clearly meant to align Voloshinov's polemic with Medvedev's *The Formal Method in Literary Scholarship* of the year before. In doing so, it must inevitably also align itself with the tactical indirection of that assault: if the 1927 polemic against Freud had used a frontal attack to cover a rearguard action against behaviourism, the 1928 polemic against Formalism uses the same tactic against 'sociologism'. The polemic that ends with this paragraph shares with those other immanent critiques a dimension of self-criticism that is formative rather than a mere formality. All of them adumbrate in their very styles of argument a 'Marxism' which is not a dogmatics but a movable theoretical feast which must be enjoyed in the company of strong antagonists.

The ambiguities of Voloshinov's concluding paragraph proliferate when we move to the level of its (political) unconscious. We then realize that the subjectivization and reification which it condemns – and which in any case only dubiously cohere as diagnoses – are the codes for a reflexivity which is not so much outside his text as within it: *Marxism and the Philosophy of Language* turns upon the discursive epidemic of 'formalism' in the modern world in a desperate escape from the turning *in* upon itself that its 'supplement' has forced upon it.

4

CHRONOTOPICITY AND CONCEPTUALITY

> The work and the world represented in it enter the real world and enrich it, and the real world enters the work and its world as part of the process of its creation, as well as part of its subsequent life, in a continual renewing of the work through the creative perception of listeners and readers. Of course this process of change is itself chronotopic: it occurs first and foremost in the historically developing social world, but without ever losing contact with changing historical space. We might even speak of a special *creative* chronotope inside which this exchange between work and life occurs, and which constitutes the distinctive life of the work.
>
> (*FTC*, 254)

Chronotope, 'time–space': Bakhtin's neologism is even more of a stranger to us than 'dialogism'; the latter is at least in the dictionary. Perhaps that is why, at least in anglophone contexts, it has not been given the welcome accorded to that category or to 'carnival', a phenomenon from the margins which is licensed now in our studies no less than on our streets (in both cases with unobtrusive policing). We think we know where we are with 'novel' – naming as it does that generic upstart which made good, and which is somehow peculiarly ours as heirs to its 'great (English) tradition' – only to find that this home ground becomes slippery and that Bakhtin means disturbingly more by that term than we could have guessed. Yet if this other thoroughly strange term which is meant to name the 'gateway' (*FTC*, 258) to all meaning stands somewhat forbiddingly over the entrance to the field it opens up, isn't its very provocative oddness the first move of any understanding: namely, the defamiliarization of what is so familiar as not to be noticed? The Heideggerian sense in which Greek is the language of philosophy has little to do with the accident of history by which that national culture, rather than some other, nurtured the first philosophers.[1] Because its classical variety is no longer spoken by anyone anywhere, Greek participates in that paradoxically illuminating opacity offered by the *universally* unfamiliar; and because the compound 'chronotope' shares in this non-contingent strangeness, it is not compromised by a recent revisionist critique showing Greece to be the mere conduit of currents that flowed from another continent – strange to the point of 'darkness' for modern Europeans – where our species itself began.[2]

I

However inviting it may be to follow the vertiginously global and epochal tangent suggested by that last sentence of mine, we must concern ourselves with matters rather more rooted in one particular continent – Europe – and in a particular time: the early twentieth century. Proceeding in this spirit, we might begin by saying that the project Bakhtin had in mind in his work of the late 1930s and early 1940s is best named and made sense of by means of a somewhat leaden and uninspiring phrase that occurs both in the title of the *Bildungsroman* fragment and again in the title of his thesis on Rabelais: 'the history of realism'. This history, it seems, is at one level what all these works are variously trying to write. I want to suggest in this chapter that there is far more at stake here than a dry academic literary historiography reconciling a key slogan of Stalinist aesthetics with what some commentators (Caryl Emerson and Gary Saul Morson, notably) would claim is Bakhtin's implicit preference for the novelistic canon of the nineteenth century.[3] This notion of Bakhtin as narrating the prehistory of an achieved and finished and exemplary form of writing puts him in intellectual company he most assuredly would not want to keep. In the course of a complex 'hidden polemic' with identifiable antagonists, I would argue, Bakhtin subtly turns a whole currency of unsubtle slogans against their own official uses, and the upshot is a reading (in a very specific and critical historical moment) of the whole project of European modernity, a reading which speaks directly to the debates of *our* time. Situating Bakhtin's essays in this international context will help us to see that the concept of the chronotope is itself best understood chronotopically: that it never quite throws off the marks of the time–space of its origins; that its own chrono-topicity is ineluctably part of its meaning.

Bakhtin defines the chronotope as 'the intrinsic connectedness of temporal and spatial relationships that are artistically expressed in literature' (*FTC*, 84). He seems, though, to imply that *all* discourse is chronotopic insofar as it must somehow thematize its own inescapable conditions, and that 'abstract thought' is the function of a repressed but still inwardly determining chronotopicity. 'Literature' is then what we have when the 'inseparability of space and time' is positively foregrounded in a fusion of their indices 'into one carefully thought-out, concrete whole'. Time 'thickens, takes on flesh, becomes artistically visible'; space for its part 'becomes charged and responsive to the movements of time, plot and history' (*FTC*, 84). This complex in which the two perennial and ubiquitous dimensions of all our saying and doing signify each other defines not only 'genre and generic distinctions' but also the 'image of man in literature' (*FTC*, 85). Bakhtin follows these themes through a more or less diachronically ordered typology of chrono-topes, beginning with the abstract space and static time of the Greek romance and ending not so much with a type as with a work in a class of its own, one which in compelling these vertical dimen-sions into the common horizontal of historical becoming marks the beginning of the modern world: François Rabelais's *Gargantua and Pantagruel*. All other chronotopes take their place between these extremes as constituents of a long generic memory which all later novels selectively recall and revivify. Now this formidably scholarly excursus will daunt all readers less well read than Bakhtin himself; it also unfortunately has the effect of blunting the challenge that the chronotope essay offers to our ways of thinking about much else besides narratives of everyday life in prose. To begin to uncover this challenge we need to look at its relationship to 'Discourse in the Novel', the essay of the same period with which it most plainly asks to be paired.

'Forms of Time and of the Chronotope in the Novel' dates from 1937–38 (with a postscript of 1973) and seems at first simply to function as a complement to the essay of 1934–35, matching that work's study of the textuality of novelistic language with a study of the referentiality of novelistic narrative, a stylistics of the novel with a compatible semantics, an anti-poetics (in Russian Formalist parlance) of the *syuzhet* with an anti-poetics of the *fabula*. All of these distinctions rest, though, on a form–content antinomy and on an opposition between reference and self-reference that 'Discourse' has already undone: a dialogism which was only a principle of 'style', which (that is to say) did not organize the whole semantics of the utterance, would be little more than dialogue in the sub-Bakhtinian, merely technical or 'compositional' sense. Even the Formalist couple cited above is unsatisfactory: if crucial distinctions are not to be flattened out, we would have to add that these aspects of the literary work relate to each other as paraphrasable to unpara-phrasable – finite to infinite – the later essay concerning itself with the relation to a putative 'referent' of a relatively stable repertoire of narrative signifieds that the linguistic signifiers of an unbounded novelistic dialogism have historically portended. In other words, this gaze that goes from signified to referent and back in the chronotope essay is deeply and inwardly determined by the gaze from signified to signifier and back in the essay on dialogism. Indeed the two gazes seem to be of the same order, bringing us round in a circle which is not vicious but beneficently hermeneutic. What they reveal, moreover, is that a certain reflexivity character-izes both articulations: both the novel's dialogism and its chronotopicity partake of a certain self-reference that clings to all signification and all reference whatever. If the novel as dialogue, in Bakhtin's strong sense, is the name for discourse as autocritique – that is, discourse in its critically self-signifying mode – then the novel as narrative is discourse thematizing its own ineluctable situ-ation in space and time. To tell a story is to dramatize the spatial difference and temporal deferral thanks to which telling is at once made both necessary and possible. Chronotopic analysis insists that the story's particulars only signify in so far as they have always already established in the most general way the spatio-temporal worldliness of the world.

Far from being opposed, then, referentiality and reflexivity dissolve into each other: that is what these two great essays, taken together, would seem to suggest.[4] To see the Soviet Writers' Congress of 1934 as prompting in Bakhtin an impulse to correct the potential or residual 'formalism' of 'Discourse in the Novel' with the 'realism' seemingly underwritten by 'Forms of Time' is, then, to miss the way the latter answers a reflexivity at the level of the speech-act with a reflexivity at the level of the spoken-about. It is also not to see how this later essay is a strategic move enabling Bakhtin to engage on common ground with the strongest body of Marxist writing on the novel then available: that which bears the signature of Georg Lukács. Bakhtin counters Lukács's conception of the novel as most wholly itself when it is most 'epic' not only by pointedly leaving that oldest among genres out of the novel's stock of chronotopic prototypes, but also by insisting that the novel is nothing if not always chronotopically *diverse*. To assimilate the novel to epic narration is to confine it within a single chronotope, one that Bakhtin was to describe in his address to the Gorky Institute in 1941 without ever using the word itself. The temporality of epic is monochronic, an 'absolute past of national beginnings and peak times' hierarchically higher than the present, from which it is utterly cut off (*EN*, 15). We cannot speak of *a* chronotope unless there is at least one other to choose; *the* chronotope (of epic) cannot exist inasmuch as it would not know itself apart from others – or indeed any other time apart from its own. Chronotopicity being inseparable conceptually from the empirical multiplicity of chronotopes, and from the actuality of choice between them, an 'epic chronotope' would be an historical *contradictio in adjecto* – merely a conceptual anachronism. The epic poet has as little choice in the 'temporal co-ordinates' (*EN*, 11) of his narration as his hero has in the realm of meanings and values. When Bakhtin writes, then, about the novel's 'generic heterogeneity', that phrase has a specific polemical resonance which could only come to be heard when his implied interlocutor was no longer able to answer (*FTC*, 85). We scarcely need to enforce the parallel with Bertolt Brecht's claims for the 'range and variety of realist modes of writing' in his famous essays 'against Lukács's: if the date had not been 1938, the Hungarian exile living in Moscow might just have learned of these objections that were being formulated at almost the same time in Svendborg and Savelovo.[5]

Bakhtin would no doubt never have polemicized in this way if his interests had not coincided with what Fredric Jameson describes as Lukács's 'lifelong meditation on narrative, on its basic structures, its relationship to the reality it expresses, and its epistemological value when compared with other, more abstract and philosophical modes of understanding'.[6] The chronotope is the concept by means of which Bakhtin poses narrativity against conceptuality itself, while contesting (without, to be sure, any overt display of contention) the monopoly of Lukácsian 'epic' narrativity. Conversely, the contestation of Lukács on this ground helps to explain the relationship to each other – the conjunctural rationale, as it were – of all the known and extant writings of Bakhtin in this phase, including the *Bildungsroman* fragment. For whatever the ambiguities of his relationship to Stalinism, Lukács was at this time not only claiming Stalinism's official literary mode as the rightful successor to a tradition in the novel described and valorized as 'realist' in so far as it approximated a (needless to say, impossible) reinvention of the epic; he was also writing of an 'ever-rising tendency to the epic' in a new 'socialist' reality where the people 'acquire the characteristics of epic heroes'. 'Socialist realism' had only to 'reflect' this reality for that reinvention to be realized. If the 'proletarian' novel with its 'positive hero' could not – and would not wish to – revive 'the formal elements or the subject matter of the older epic', it would none the less (Lukács implies) be predicated upon analogous historical conditions, and would therefore carry the same epistemological and axiological weight as the latter.[7] Bakhtin's later response to this notion that the narrative of the communist future would return on a (presumably 'dialectically') higher level to the narrative of the distant premodern past was to stress the necessary relation of the novel to the *present*, and to do so against the contrastive background of a genre in which for posterity pastness is taken to the second power, the epic point of view being always already oriented towards the past. In 1936–38 he confines himself to undermining the (by then Marxist) Lukács by realizing some strongly antithetical motifs from *The Theory of the Novel*. Shorn by its own means of its outward Hegelianizing, radicalized by the removal of a dialectic which its own premises constantly threaten, Lukács's great essay of 1920 projects the novel as a perpetual reinvention not of the epic but of itself. Unlike other genres, 'whose existence resides within the finished form', the novel 'appears as something in the process of becoming'.[8] It is that order of narrative which thematizes its own reflexivity, mirroring its search for meaning in the quest of its problematic hero, its ceaseless becoming in the latter's striving. Its truth to life lies in its irony; only in the 'self-recognition' and 'self-abolition' of its necessary subjectivity is the contingency of its world transcended and that immanence of meaning in life which is true concreteness fleetingly revealed.[9] In *The Theory of the Novel* the novel appears as both the first existentialist and the first formalist: finding its essence only in the freedom of its constant self-reinvention, it connotes the real only in its constant introversion. Whilst we are 'in' this dimension of Lukács's text – where, we might argue, a quasi-formalist textuality crosses with a quasi-existentialist ethics and ontology – there is neither nostalgia for a lost totality nor prospect of the epic's dialectical return. Bakhtin's achievement in these texts is to have revived these scandalously modernist motifs under the rubric of 'realism' (Brecht, we recall, used a similar code) and to have done so in the context of a breadth of literary-historical scholarship that Lukács himself could hardly have matched. Indeed we might read Bakhtin's work of 1936–41 as his version of the 'series of concrete historical monographs' which in Jameson's view is implied by the schematic typology of *The Theory of the Novel* – as, in short, a realization of the possibilities Lukács opens but never follows up in his later development.[10] The last short paragraph on Dostoevsky was the cue for Bakhtin's first monograph; his other major works display the logic of a working back from that point through the Renaissance and Middle Ages to a classical antiquity far more concretely and sociopolitically specified than that celebrated in Lukács's rhapsodic first paragraph, which begins: 'Happy are those ages when the starry sky is the map of all possible paths – ages whose paths are illuminated by the light of the stars'.[11]

If there is no comparable privileging of epic fullness in Bakhtin, that is partly because of the perspectives he sets up: the ten chapters of the chronotope essay consider antiquity only in a backward glance from the Hellenistic period, whilst modernity is considered only in intermittent glances forward from a history beginning then and ending in the Renaissance. This strategy works to neutralize any idea of a punctual and once-for-all fall from epic plenitude: what we have is a novelistic memory in which all chronotopes are always potentially revivable, rather than a history only of departed things. Bakhtin wastes no time in undoing the Lukácsian antinomy of 'abstract' and 'concrete' which conceptually founds the familiar Lukácsian story of the fall of Western narrative. The subject of his first chapter is determined as much by this theoretical imperative as by any chronological priority: in the highly schematic narrative of Greek romance, with its interchangeable spaces and reversible times, we are shown that abstraction is itself chronotopically generated. Its 'mathematical' logic of events (*FTC*, 97), the evident arbitrariness of its narrative signs, might almost be said to prefigure the structuralist mode of analysis that it plainly invites. (Bakhtin is here, unsurprisingly, as close as he will ever get to Vladimir Propp or Claude Lévi-Strauss.) The obverse of the dominance of the paradigm in this genre is the paradigm's dependence upon the syntagm for its very existence: Bakhtin uses the limiting case of the Greek romance to enforce the point that all 'abstraction' and all 'concreteness' may be resolved into the common matrix of an integral chronotopicity.

Bakhtin implies that the abstractness of this Hellenistic genre – an effective emptiness of time matched by an extraterritoriality in its characteristically alien space – is the price it pays for its great advance over epic and tragedy. This decisive novelty is its invention of the 'private person', the individual whose private life is (in the Formalist sense) the *motivation* of 'social and political events' rather than depending solely upon those events for its meaning – even if he or she 'behaves, on the surface, like a public man' (*FTC*, 108–09). Where, then, does the novel derive what for Bakhtin later comes to define it: namely, its construction of time as the dimension of change? The answer is: in the pre-novelistic 'biographical forms', which offer a prototype of a genuinely historical time with their image of 'an individual who passes through the course of a whole life', and which (as witness Plato's *Apology*) antedate the Greek romance by several centuries (*FTC*, 130). It is in this discussion that Bakhtin not only most patently approaches early-Lukácsian territory but also comes closest to identifying his antagonist. If (classical) Greece in both Bakhtin and Lukács is the name for a state in which interiority and exteriority are not known apart from each other, then we should add that the likeness between them ends precisely at this point. Bakhtin's version of this story not only invests much less in its literal truth; it also so qualifies the simplicity and absolutism of Lukács's story as virtually to deconstruct itself; in short, it is plain that he thinks of his version as overcoming the de-realized abstraction that he finds in Lukács. Empirical differences in their accounts open out, then, into divergences which are far from academic. Consider the place each of them accords to philosophy: like all other post-epic forms, philosophy for Lukács is a 'symptom of the rift between "inside" and "outside"';[12] for Bakhtin the Platonic texts he cites are precisely examples of a 'wholeness' anterior to this rift. With the exteriority of all self-consciousness, with the individual 'open on all sides', there could as yet be no distinction between biography and autobiography (*FTC*, 132). 'Biographical time' has its being not in a private space but in the unqualified publicity of the *agora*: the public square is coextensive with the whole of the public sphere, where 'all the most elevated categories, from that of the state to that of revealed truth, were realized concretely and fully incarnated, made visible and given a face' (*FTC*, 132). It is this direct reality of an utterly comprehensive public sphere – this space where no category was bloodless, where the metaphysical had not come to know itself from the sociopolitical, where what could not be seen and heard could not be thought – that Bakhtin substitutes for Lukács's 'epic', and in case we should miss the polemical pointedness of his argument Bakhtin actually appears to quote Lukács in a striking parenthesis: 'this utter exteriority of the individual did not exist in empty space ("under a starry sky, on the bare earth") but rather in an organic human collective, "in the folk"' (*FTC*, 135).

II

The folk: that concept of a specific historical space of the collective, which here makes its debut in Bakhtin's writing, will become the *Leitmotiv* of the work of 1936–41. Its peculiar force will be lost – it will itself seem a somewhat suspect occupant of the 'empty space' of theory – unless we reinsert it in Bakhtin's own historical space, in another dialogue which runs parallel with his dialogue with Lukács, and in which his partner is Maxim Gorky. Indeed Bakhtin can be seen to be skilfully enlisting Gorkian motifs against Lukács, correcting the expatriate communist critic with the Soviet writer's formidable authority. Gorky's address to the Writers' Congress of 1934 provides him with the terms both for the radical reading of the early Lukács that we have just been examining and for a populist alternative to the later Lukács's valorization of a high-bourgeois 'critical realism'. The preoccupations of that speech clearly underlie the rest of the chronotope essay from this point on, as a glance even at the chapter headings will show. Under the sign of 'folklore', Gorky argues the 'realism' of mythology: 'abstract thought' is the thinking of the 'solitary man' in a 'later period'; 'materialist thought' is implicit in those much earlier 'unwritten compositions of the people' to which 'the processes of labour and the sum total of phenomena in the social life of ancient man inevitably gave rise'. The 'hidden motive' of 'ancient fancy' is always 'the striving of men to lighten their labour'.[13] Bakhtin's eager embrace of these essentially Viconian themes (to which Gorky only gives a *marxisant* inflection) could be cynically explained by a general need to conform, and perhaps also by a more particular circumstance: his intention of submitting his doctoral dissertation on Rabelais to the institute named after Gorky himself. Gorky had, after all, cited *Gargantua and Pantagruel* in this very speech of 1934 as one of those 'great works' upon which the culture of the 'folk' has 'again and again had a definite influence'.[14] The simplicity of this explanation is immediately qualified when we note that the tendency of the Rabelais book is not only to detach the Gorkian emphasis on folklore as the common source of literary realism and philosophical materialism from its subordination to Stalinism, but also cunningly to turn it against the latter. If in Gorky the gigantism of popular mythology assorts with the hyperbole of Stalinist rhetoric and iconography – a style indeed much in evidence at the Congress itself – in Bakhtin it is by contrast ludic and parodic, directed against orthodoxy and authority. Bakhtin rectifies the fetishization of technology and productivity which is a major effect of Gorky's celebration of the folk and their 'toil' by emphasizing alongside the battle with an intransigent nature that other battle of the popular classes against an official culture. Taking his cue from Gorky's notion of the people's 'collective body' as 'distinguished by a conscious-ness of its own immortality and an assurance of its triumph over all hostile forces',[15] he adds to the epistemological value of this ineluctably material practice of theirs a combatively ethico-political dimension which Stalinism would of course play down: as impor-tant a 'creator of all ideas'[16] as the people's unremitting labour is their resounding *laughter*.

Folklore, it might be argued, plays in Bakhtin's discourse the same part as the category of *epic* does in Lukács's, and with the same effects; they are (on this view) merely interchangeable names for the same fiction of 'originary' plenitude. That this is not the case should be clear from my account of the complex three-way transac-tion in which this category is generated: Bakhtin's 'fully exteriorized individual' (*FTC*, 136) is implicated in an unfinalized and unfinalizable process rather than frozen in the finality of an ancient genre or a superseded polity – cannot ever disappear, never having properly come into being in the first place. In later writing we find 'experiments' in 're-establishing' this individual who is only ever a shifting function of the space and time of the face-to-face collective. The 'most remarkable' of these was made by Rabelais; another, 'on an entirely different basis', was made by Goethe (*FTC*, 136). Bakhtin's two monographs of this period now fall into place as detailed explorations of a narrativity which can challenge the binary oppositions of conceptuality without having to look over one shoulder at its prelapsarian childhood in the epic. 'Forms of Time' provides the broad historical and theoretical context of these more focused investigations, setting up the chronotope as a concept in its own right, telling a story about stories which treats all cate-gories in an almost Nietzschean way not as the fatal effects of a single original fall from immanence but as ever-repeated effects of the abstract or the conceptual produced by ever-repeated stories. It is perhaps not too much to say that this most general account of narrative in Bakhtin does for phylogeny what psychoanalysis had done for ontogeny.

Against Lukács's notion of a pristine epic innocence, then, Bakhtin poses a version of the childhood of Western narrative which is, we might say – and the Freudian allusion will later prove apposite in other ways – polymorphously perverse.[17] His emphasis on the forms of ancient narrative hypothesizes an alternative and plural infancy for the novel, which he then sees not only as carrying this heterogeneity into the future but also as safeguarding the historical gains it has made possible. Bakhtin in these pages lays bare the elements which will later coalesce in that vision of historical becoming and of utopia which is the defining consciousness of modernity. If the category of history as we have come to understand it is not yet thinkable in the ancient genres, any more than the fully private individual whose interiority is a marginality or dissidence valued for itself – motivating rather than needing to be motivated – they are in no sense dispensable: without their differing yet complementary spaces and times and images of the human, that development would not have taken place. Their value is also in calling to mind an age in which the forms of narrative and the forms of 'abstract thought' overlapped or were close bedfellows, profoundly influencing each other. Bakhtin retraces the novel's uncertain early steps, its epistemological gains which may involve losses but never the absolute loss of a once-for-all (Lukácsian) fall. He returns to ancient kinds of narrativity which are not epic and examines them from the standpoint of what they do not (yet) deliver, but which they may now be seen as enabling – that is, from the standpoint of a future in the Renaissance and Rabelais which is now (along with antiquity) part of our own past.

We have seen how the Greek romance invents the (quasi-)private person at the cost of de-materializing space in a generalized alienness and time in a static reversibility. Ancient biography conversely dynamizes time but at the cost of submission to the Aristotelian entelechy: the end of a character is identical with its first cause; time is therefore merely the time of the actualization of a potential that was always there in the first place. It is only in the 'adventure novel of everyday life' (*FTC*, 111), exemplified in *Satyricon* and *The Golden Ass*, that an irreversible and non-teleological time is invented, along with a human image more fully private than the romance could offer. The idea of development is here figured in the motif of *metamorphosis* that this form of written narrative shares with the 'popular folklore' that is one of its sources and with Greek cosmogony. This development is not, however, a continuous horizontal: a life is presented as definitively shaped by its moments of crisis, moments in which the individual 'becomes other than what he was' (*FTC*, 115). Early-Christian saints' lives, with their sequence of sin followed by rebirth and blessedness, belong to this type. Time makes its mark on an individual who is only subject to chance in so far as he or she has willed a guilty life; space is a concrete, everyday, native space of the road. The obverse of these decisive advances upon the stasis-abstraction of the romance is a construction of the world of everyday life as a static axis of 'social heterogeneity' without 'social contradictions' at right angles (as it were) to the dynamic horizontal of the protagonist (*FTC*, 129).

Bakhtin values this genre above all for its clarifying anticipation of two much later moves which are the European novel's decisive contribution to modernity. First, in the metamorphosis there is the prototype of an open-ended becoming which will later be extended beyond the protagonist to take in the everyday world he or she only observes without being able to modify – will, in short, mark the inception of 'history'. Secondly, the perspective of the third party who (thanks to this same metamorphosis) eavesdrops upon the 'secrets of everyday life' (*FTC*, 122) will shift from a peripheral to a central position – will be released from the secondary status of 'motivation' into the freedom and priority of an independent authorial perspective. The epistemological privilege of a socially subordinated outsider like 'the servant who goes from one master to the other' (*FTC*, 124) then at last comes into its own. Bizarre though it may sound, Apuleius's ass is the forerunner of the intimate publicity of the memoir or the epistolary novel. Historicity and private experience are thus born together in the transformation of a narrative dominated precisely by the motif of transformation. The strong implication of Bakhtin's argument is that the novel derives its force not from a nostalgia for a state where inside and outside did not yet exist in separation, but rather from its active and ceaseless negotiation of the border between interiority and exteriority.

Modern narrative's immediate forebear gets rather less space than these earlier forms in Bakhtin's story. If antiquity is represented in his narrative of narrativity not by the epic but by certain rather later and 'lower' prose genres, feudality is represented by a much briefer account of both the 'high' and 'low' verse genres of that epoch. Bakhtin seems here to be cementing his consensus with Gorky, who had claimed in his address that 'the influence of feudal literature was never particularly great'.[18] Equally, he seems to be deepening his dissent from Lukács by implying that the older narrative form on which the modern European novel (negatively) structures itself is its immediate antecedent in the chivalric romance rather than its distant forebear in the epic of antiquity. This reinvented epic whole of the Middle Ages is already in transition to the novel, 'on the boundary' between the two genres (FTC, 154). What is then striking is that Bakhtin plays down the ruling-class origins of the romance – its status as, in Gorky's terms, 'a creation of the feudal nobility', its ideological mystifications – and emphasizes instead its 'unique' and almost modernist chronotope, its status as a kind of latter-day epic of the quotidian marvellous.[19] (That surrealist phrase is not without authorial warranty: Bakhtin himself cites surrealism as a twentieth-century re-emergence of the romance's 'subjective playing' with space and time (FTC, 155).) Mediaeval romance is viewed not from without, from the standpoint of a later 'realism' which is its demystification, but from within, in terms of its own quasi-oneiric logic of events. This 'peculiar distortion of temporal perspectives characteristic of dreams' is what sets the romance apart from all the ancient genres, including the epic, whose 'glorified' hero and 'fullness' it otherwise more or less completely replicates (FTC, 153–54). Its heroes are everywhere at home in the spaces of its miraculous normality; they belong moreover to a 'storehouse of images' (FTC, 153) which, unlike the local mythology of the epic, crosses all national borders.

How far this last point is polemically directed against the chauvinist tendency in Soviet 'socialist realism' or against the rise of fascism in Europe – or indeed against their complicity, soon to be sealed geopolitically in the Molotov–Ribbentrop pact – we can only speculate: Bakhtin might well have been seeking to rescue romance from its confiscation for Nazi cultural ends, through the medium of Wagner's music. The more general argument about a dreamlike hyperbole and spatio-temporal elasticity in the romance chronotope has, if anything, more profound implications for the politics of theory. The novel of modernity is not only not fixated upon a distant genre whose time is an unreachable absolute past; it is more closely and perhaps not always wholly negatively engaged with a genre of the epoch just preceding its own, whose way with time is like nothing so much as the free play of the individual (Freudian) unconscious – just as its heroes, we might add, are represented as being archetypes of the latter's (collective) Jungian counterpart. This signal departure from the canons of verisimilitude is not denounced, any more than it is applauded. In one possible reading, Bakhtin covers himself by associating a reprehensibly 'formalist' distortion of the real with feudal society; in another reading, he merely assigns chivalric romance its place in the novel's generic memory as a resource it will later draw upon. Given a strong populist and future-oriented cast, it is treated in those aspects that bring it closest to 'folklore and fairy tales' from the 'pre-class' world, on the one hand, and to Rabelais, on the other: 'hyperbolization' (FTC, 154) of space and time will, after all, be a key element in Bakhtin's later account of *Gargantua and Pantagruel*. The contemporary reference may well be quite pointed: 'socialist realism' ought to borrow as freely from the 'bourgeois' writing it seeks to replace as the 'grotesque realism' of the early-modern period did from the romance it parodied; no style is irredeemably ideologically tainted by its earlier uses. When Bakhtin goes on to discuss the *Divine Comedy* as a 'special' work 'on the boundary line *between* two epochs' (FTC, 158), and when he then concludes by assimilating Dante's work to Dostoevsky's, there can be no mistaking the implied analogy between two historical moments of transition. The relationship between Dante and his successors, including Rabelais, is the relationship of free and open participation in the same global project that Bakhtin would like to see between late-feudal Russia's great proto-modernist and the new writing of the (putatively) 'socialist' order.

Whilst the difference between chivalric romance and works like the *Divine Comedy* might only have been hinted at by Bakhtin, it deserves nonetheless to be spelled out if we are to take the full force of his argument about its importance for the future of narrative. The romance, with its horizontal plane of magical events, brackets out – takes as read, in more than one sense *underwrites* – the otherworldly vertical of feudal ideology; in Dante's poem, by contrast, that vertical is not only *within* the work rather than outside it: it is its very organizing principle. Everything time separates is here ranged in an eternal synchrony, in a paradoxical chronotope of the omni-temporal. Unlike 'feudal ideology' in its other inscriptions, however, this global and dominant verticality must subsist alongside local and subordinate horizontals of narrative that branch out from it at right angles, their human images 'full of historical potential', 'strain[ing] with the whole of [their] being toward participation in historical events'. Anticipating Erich Auerbach a decade later – their common source is probably a passage in Hegel's *Aesthetics* – Bakhtin sees the 'extraordinary tension' of Dante's world as arising from the way the vertical 'compresses within itself the horizontal, which powerfully thrusts itself forward' (FTC, 157–58).[20] History first comes to know itself in these tense tangents to the soaring

Gothic perpendicular of Eternity. The Rabelaisian move which undermines feudal ideology by privileging a thoroughly worldly horizontality oriented upon the future is already imminent, already as it were negatively proposed, in the *Divine Comedy*.

The Rabelaisian chronotope represents the elemental chronotopicity of folklore become self-conscious – aware of the verticality that effects its sublimation, semanticizing all of time and space even as it spatio-temporalizes all meaning, capable of meeting the high genres of late feudality on their own ground. It would be fitted for none of these tasks without the catalytic force of the 'low' genres of that epoch, and in particular of the chronotope that surrounds their characteristic figures of the rogue, clown and fool. With these masks, yet another Gorkian *topos* is echoed by Bakhtin. According to Gorky, the diminution of the heroes of the feudal ruling class coincides with the emergence of these ' "simpletons" of folklore' as heroes of full stature who 'acquired boldness to ridicule their masters, and without doubt contributed to the growth of that state of feeling which, in the first half of the sixteenth century, found its expression in the ideas of the "Taborites" and the peasant wars against the knights'.[21] Bakhtin complements Gorky's broad genetic account of the rise of these canny subordinates with his own much fuller account of their specific functions in the novel. Their chronotope is that of the public square: that space which he will later call 'carnival' and which, unlike its ancient correlative, is not only not coextensive with the public sphere but also in every respect defined against the latter, as (so to speak) its negative image. These professional maskers generalize the role temporarily assumed by the ancient hero of 'everyday adventure'. As nature's antinomians, they claim the 'right to be 'other' in this world, the right not to make common cause with any single one of the existing categories that life makes available' (*FTC*, 159). Their scandalous effectiveness as others to the dominant conceptuality lies in their prior and constitutive inner otherness, their otherness to themselves. At once laughing and laughed at, they complete the circle of laughter by laughing first and last at themselves; transformed with their entry into writing, they transform that writing in their turn. Bakhtin shows how the various authorial positions *vis-à-vis* the novel's invented world and its implied reader – positions that have now become automatized, that we now take for granted – are the work of an early and deep-going carnivalization of the written forms of narrative. The clown and the fool help to overcome this problematic freedom of a genre unprecedented in history in not having an 'immanent position for the author', and they do so by offering a prototype of the person who, being 'in life but not of it', can 'reflect private life and make it public' (*FTC*, 161). Bakhtin seems here to be transferring to the context of the author Lukács's derivation of the novel hero from the types of madman or criminal; he also anticipates Auerbach's general argument in *Mimesis* in a fascinating parenthetical claim that these figures are the product of a metamorphosis of a ruler or god whose best-known instance is the story of the Incarnation and Passion of Christ. This might prompt in us the reflection that, whilst realism has come in a much later aesthetics of narrative to be counterposed to allegory, in its beginnings it owes everything to a thoroughgoing existential allegorization of the 'entire human image' (*FTC*, 161), a saturation of the human with meanings that had hitherto been associated with the divine. At the heart of realism, then, there is this heresy – or renewing miracle, depending upon one's point of view – of an integral and utterly creatural allegory. Thanks to the inverse privilege that is granted to its characteristic figures of 'not understanding' (*FTC*, 164) what is conceptualized or institutionalized, the novel is (Christlike) able to offer its ethico-political challenge to all false pharisaical spirituality, and the corollary of this challenge is a redemption of the 'healthy "natural" functions' of the body from the bestiality to which mediaeval dogma had consigned them (*FTC*, 162). In the picaresque novel from the sixteenth century onwards the space of the native high road is used for just this kind of epiphanic exposure; in the influential example of *Don Quixote* the romance chronotope is parodied and hybridized by this chronotope of the road. At a later date, but in a lineal development from this last move, a 'pure "natural" subjectivity' (*FTC*, 164) is invented through the mask of the Sternean eccentric, that practitioner of comic-parodic byplay who inhabits the more restricted (if no less culturally creative) 'theatrical space' of the *entr'acte* (*FTC*, 163). The exteriority of Pantagruelism and the interiority of Shandyism are deeply connected and mutually complementary.

III

We need to spell out how much is at stake in these positions that Bakhtin takes, if they are to be more than merely interesting observations on European literary history. By tracing the great epistemological and cultural discoveries that crystallize in novelistic discourse to the carnivalesque and 'folkloric' chronotope inhabited by clown and fool, he is able precisely to uncover what a narrowly literary historiography has occluded. If 'folklore' in Bakhtin is the name for – and hypothetical site of – a chronotopicity of all doing and thinking that is manifest though not yet conscious, 'Rabelais' is a shorthand for the ceaseless incarnation of meanings and values along a spatio-temporal horizontal, a direct proportionality of worth to size in the worldly here and now (*FTC*, 167). Chronotopicity militant wrenches apart what 'feudal' discourse brings together, brings together what it sundered: ordinary contexts evaporate in a potentially infinite context portended by these extraordinary meetings. To the strongly affirmed spatio-temporality of the world there corresponds the equally strongly affirmed corporeality of the body, and this correspondence is signified by their interpenetration. Meaning is generated in a logic of the concrete, in simultaneities and coextensions. All the bodily functions appear in *Gargantua and Pantagruel* as so many 'series' which are 'at times parallel to each other and at times intersect each other' (*FTC*, 170). Bakhtin uses Rabelais to 'think' a world of existential parataxis, where the human body signifies universally by drawing all signifiers to itself. It is almost as if he were trying single-handedly to make good the absence in Russian history of a 'Renaissance' or 'Rabelaisian' moment, and to supply the goods of an epochal shift that his own national culture had never had in practice – or, rather, had had only vicariously, in versions imported from those classicizing cultures by means of which the rising social elites of early-modern Europe had sought to consolidate their power. Bakhtin's analysis of this explosive work has a hermeneutic energy and a prolix, inventorial tendency that reminds us of nobody so much as Rabelais himself. It is easy to see this hyperbole of Bakhtin's case as an infection caught from the very Stalinist discourse he opposed. It can also be seen as a symptom of the strain of the task of epochal redemption he here takes on, a task beyond the power of any individual to carry out, let alone anyone as obscure as he then was, in the least auspicious of all places and times.

Three propositions would seem to sum up the thrust of this chapter so far: first, that Bakhtin's cultural preferences might be described as modernist rather than realist, or at least as rendering that distinction less than absolute, a matter of tact and of context; second, that modernism is less a negation of realism than a reminder of its beginnings in a humanized allegory with the strongest of ethico-political charges; third, that Bakhtin is by these means de-classicizing the much longer and broader story of modernity itself, emphasizing its birth crisis and the early unity of its now-separated discoveries – in short, narrating its history anew and from below. These three threads of Bakhtin's textual fabric are not in fact separable: give the case made for Rabelais as European modernity's midwife a slight twist and you have a defence of the whole contemporary practice of European modernism. A 'socialist realism' which modelled itself upon Rabelais rather than Homer could hardly define itself so absolutely against (say) James Joyce; indeed anyone taking Bakhtin's account of *Gargantua and Pantagruel* truly to heart could not consistently baulk at *Ulysses* or at the Joycean 'Work in Progress' that was just then, in the late 1930s, coming to an end. The other side of Joyce's Rabelaisian materialization of language is a semanticization of the body that is no less Rabelaisian in its inventorial thoroughness. Bakhtin helps us to read the work of Joyce in the spirit of those alternative readings which were coming through in the early 1980s, and which stress the 'politics' of Joyce's 'style'.[22] In the long view that Bakhtin offers us, a text like *Ulysses* appears less as innovation than as a revival of the early assertiveness of the 'low' genres raised by Rabelais into a concrete universalism: its celebrated 'textuality' is inseparable from a chronotopicity at once global and radical.

This submission of all categories to a logic of the spatio-temporal had been not so much lost as reduced or made invisible, first with the novel's subordination under classicism, and then (in the nineteenth century) within an ideology of literature which canonized the novel at the cost of binding it the more firmly to the abstract universalism of the unsituated and purely thinking modern subject. Although this now canonical 'realism' shares with its 'grotesque' (Bakhtin) or 'fantastic' (Gorky) realist forerunner in Rabelais an affirmation of the body and its world against an alienating social order – and this is after all what justifies Lukács and other Marxists in calling such 'bourgeois' writing 'critical' – neither of these two constituents of Bakhtin's hypothetical 'ancient complex' is able to signify in its own right, in a mutual overstepping of boundaries. Bakhtin nowhere mentions Joyce, but his case here provides the terms for a strong defence of the latter's work. If to break, as Joyce very patently does, with the moralized spatio-temporality of what Bakhtin calls the (nineteenth-century) 'idyllic' chronotope – and to re-establish thereby a revitalized chronotopicity – is to be 'modernist', then modernism is surely no longer to be denounced for its anti-realism, and the Stalinist aesthetic is shown up in all its narrowness and historical shortsightedness. And so it is that when we read Samuel Beckett writing in 1929 that Joyce reduces 'various expressive media to their primitive economic directness' and fuses 'these primal essences into an assimilated medium for the exteriorization of thought', we could be forgiven for thinking that these words were Bakhtin's on Rabelais.[23] Bakhtin's unique feat is, then (without knowing it, and however odd this may sound), to have reconciled the terms used by Gorky on an occasion notorious for its anathematization of modernism with those used by Beckett in the volume he co-wrote under the self-parodic title *Our Exagmination round his Factification for Incamination of 'Work in Progress'* just five years before.

Bringing the voice of Joyce into the dialogue which is the chronotope essay may be an act of critical licence. There is, however, another (Western, late-modern) voice in it which is as plainly already there as those of Gorky and Lukács: that of Sigmund Freud. Allusions to Freudian theory, and in particular to the so-called metapsychology, are too evident to be missed. Like Herbert Marcuse twenty years later (though of course not openly, and far less programmatically), Bakhtin 'historicizes' what Freud seems to 'biologize': the Rabelaisian chronotope is, on one level, nothing less than a phylogenetic 'return of the repressed'. As if to provoke this association, Bakhtin repeatedly writes of the repressive modification of the 'gross realities of the ancient complex' (*FTC*, 213) in modern religious or philosophical or literary discourses as the work of their 'sublimation'. Folklore would on this view effectively be the unconscious of the European social order – more or less wholly repressed from the rise of 'class' society, though helpfully returning to energize the forces that effected the passage of feudality into modernity. Bakhtin might have taken his cue from Freud himself, who had suggested on more than one occasion that analogues of 'unconscious ideation' are 'to be found in folklore, and in popular myths, legends, linguistic idioms, proverbial wisdom, and current jokes to a more complete extent than in dreams'.[24] We might argue that this illustrative Freudian parenthesis moves in Bakhtin to centre-stage, that it becomes with him, as it were, the whole story.

However that may be, Bakhtin's emphasis on the 'sexual element' in the pre-class 'matrix' is certainly provocative. Whilst insisting (against Freudianism) that 'it would be particularly wrong' to give that element 'primacy', he challenges the puritanism of Stalinist ideology in even mentioning it at all. Freud's Eros and Thanatos have their Bakhtinian counterparts. Sexuality assumes the 'sublimated form' of love; death in turn loses its link with sexuality;

all elements lose their articulation upon 'communal labour'. Pre-Rabelaisian sublimation is mainly religious; with high modernity its contexts are secular, literary, philosophical. Michel Foucault's critique of the 'repressive hypothesis' – his claim that modern discourses not so much 'multiplied' as 'rarefied' sexuality – might encourage us to reformulate this difference between epochs (as indeed Bakhtin himself might have done had he also considered medical and other scientific discourses).[25] The critique seems, though, to carry less weight when we reflect that Foucauldian analysis is itself profoundly chronotopic, and when we reckon up the worth of other insights that Bakhtin's refunctioning of a Freudian motif makes possible.

Finally, let us consider the implications of Bakhtin's case for the problem of *metaphor*. When we take our stand in the space of an autonomous chronotopicity, a new relationship appears between metaphoricity and conceptuality; seeming opposites converge. Like Beckett on Vico and Joyce in the *Exagmination*, Bakhtin understands all metaphor to be a sublimation of originally chronotopic thinking – a degeneration, in other words, of a primal narrativity. Now it is tempting to think of chronotopicity as essentially metonymic, until we realize that both members of the Jakobsonian polarity depend for their definition upon logical relations, so that contiguity (the basis of metonymy) is in truth no more concrete than similarity (the basis of metaphor). Conceptuality is the abstract relational dimension of the semantic hypertrophy which historically accompanied the dystrophy of the lived breadth and inclusiveness of Bakhtin's 'ancient complex'. Or again: conceptuality is the vapour that is given off in the process of rarefying that complex's already disparate elements into metaphor. 'Where there is already a hierarchy of classes', Bakhtin argues, the only thinkable unity of the manifold of experience is 'abstract calendaric' time; concreteness becomes an effect only of 'individual life-sequences', whilst 'what is held in common becomes maximally abstract' (*FTC*, 214–15). In the first of these developments a once strong chronotopicity survives in the dim allusive recollection of its (literary) signifiers; in the other (philosophical) member of the fateful bifurcation there are gathered the ghostly signifieds which are the cost of this forfeited autonomy – products of a will to transcend all corporeality and spatio-temporality altogether.

If the 'ancient complex' knows no metaphoricity as such – the richness of metaphor being, as we have seen, bought at the cost of the poverty of its motifs as real constituents of the life of the collective – then for Bakhtin we have the beginnings (at once the archetype and the antithesis) of all later metaphoricity in the extended or Homeric similes of classical epic. Approximating Auerbach on *figura*, Bakhtin says of such similes that in them '[a]n image selected for comparison is worth just as much as the other member of the comparison', and that the latter is 'a dual episode, a digression' with its own measure of semantic autonomy (*FTC*, 218).[26] That is to say: meaning is generated in the interaction of two independently signifying narratives, and in the resultant metaphoricity-narrativity the hierarchy that ordinarily raises 'tenor' over 'vehicle' has not yet come into being; narrativity is at no point forsaken for something else. Pushing these brief hints of Bakhtin's rather further, we might register a last anti-Lukácsian resonance here. When we place the stress upon the sheer narrative extension of such similes, their fore-shadowing of later written narrative forms comes clearly into view. Among these, the novel might then be seen as the lively offspring of the epic's digressive margins rather than an attempt at the recovery of its (unrecoverable) totality. Realism would thus be the effect that is produced when an extended and dynamic metaphor of this kind, in creating its 'own' chronotope, breaks the epic's monopoly and *inaugurates chronotopicity itself*. Having freed itself from the solip-sistic temporality of epic monochrony, it strives towards its own optimal literalization: a *real*ization (or 'set' towards the referential) whose ultimate but necessarily forever unreachable horizon is the folkloric matrix. This formal imperative always activates at least some of the contents of that matrix; equally, and just as surely, it entails in the phase of high modernity their 'idyllic' rarefaction. The upshot is a 'literary' discourse which knows its (residual) concrete-ness in contrast with a 'conceptual' discourse which is nothing more or less than the extreme case of (cultural) sublimation.

If it is then objected that anyone who hypothesizes a strong chronotopicity of the distant past risks investing too much in a narrative of origins, a defence of Bakhtin is nonetheless possible. He is surely fully aware that in projecting this complex as a state which historically undergoes disintegration he is reversing the real order of our knowledge; that we can only know the unity of that complex through and by means of the concepts–metaphors which are the product of its breakdown. Like Julia Kristeva's 'semiotic *chora*' (or indeed Jean-Jacques Rousseau's 'state of nature'), Bakhtin's folkloric matrix is a 'theoretical supposition' which 'exists in prac-tice only within the symbolic'.[27] 'Folklore' does not signify some (Lukácsian) immediate unity of subject and object; itself already a signifying practice, it enters writing and acquires self-consciousness as the carnivalesque; in a further transposition, the carnivalesque enters the high-modern signifying system of literature in the tamed guise of the idyllic chronotope. Reading between the lines of the works of that chronotope, we can reconstruct this unfinishable journey. Chronotopic analysis is nothing more than another incarnation of chronotopicity itself, as provisional as its forerunners; it takes its place alongside those other late-modern self-situating and historicizing orders of thinking and writing that seek to effect a return to the concrete by infusing abstract thought with the highest degree of historical self-consciousness.

IV

It is time to draw all of this together. Against the whole Aristotelian and Cartesian tradition in which time is thought apart from space and both apart from value, Bakhtin poses what he calls 'the single great event that is life' (*FTC*, 211). In the work of this phase the modern project is reimagined in its most combative and popular-utopian moments, along a line that generally elevates artists over philosophers. If the Renaissance *is* Rabelais, the enlightenment is epitomized in a Goethe for whom the world was always an emerging *event*, who could '*see time*' in 'the spatial whole of the world' (*BSHR*, 25). We would not expect the modernism of Bakhtin's thinking in the Soviet Union of the late 1930s to have gone along with open polemical support for contemporary *avant-garde* aesthetic practice (as that of the Formalists had been bound to Futurism, or as Ernst Bloch was then backing the Expressionists). And it is no loss that it did not do so: Bakhtin's modernist critique of modernity – in its way every bit as radical as that of Theodor Adorno and Max Horkheimer – is achieved in the Rabelais book by the simple and yet astonishingly creative gesture of projecting the story of the European *avant-garde* back into the continent's past. What Peter Bürger has seen as that movement's doomed will to sublate art in life is imagined as having happened: carnival is the name Bakhtin gives to this perpetual possibility.[28] Bakhtin offers secularized modernity an alternative icon: the closed classical body was then serving the iconography not of emancipation but of the century's colluding authoritarianisms; only in the grotesque body open on all sides to the world could modernity's tragically arrested narrative of emancipation move forward.

Read with the other late writings, the 'Concluding Remarks' added in 1973 to the chronotope essay help us to see *Rabelais and*

His World as the last heroic throw of the modernist Bakhtin. The passage from those 'Remarks' that I have used as the epigraph to this chapter not only perfectly catches the strikingly lower key of the late-Bakhtinian voice; it also helps us to modify the terms in which I began by distinguishing the project of 'Forms of Time' from that of its sister essay, and which threaten us with the conservative alternative to the *avant-gardist* will to sublation. In speaking of its 'gaze that goes from signified to referent and back' I was in peril of implying a self-standing and unified 'reality' which the whole essay puts into question. For if discourse's relation to reality is interventionist, reality's reciprocating relation to discourse is (so to speak) *interpenetrationist*: to invoke the concept of the chronotope is to conceive the world and the work as separated by a 'categorical boundary' that is there only to invite its own overstepping in both directions – as 'resist[ing] fusion' and yet as always dynamically alive within each other. Fortuitously (if felicitously) assonating and alliterating in their English translation, *work* and *world* are woven by Bakhtin in this passage into a chiastic verbal pattern which forsakes the idiom of punctual sublation for one of infinitely recurring and renewing 'exchange'. Every Aristotelian 'law of thought' is violated by this conception of each as standing to the other in a relation of mutual indwelling; but it is, in the end, what every informed use of Bakhtin's least-understood category asks us to do.

To conclude, then: the Bakhtin who breaks his silence in these and other notes made after the war and the death of Stalin is a Bakhtin who has soberly recognized the hubris of the 'carnival sense of the world' in the face of carnage on a world scale. Instead of reading the modern as a matter of revolutionary breaks and acts of forgetting of the past ('one ridicules in order to forget', he had once written (*EN*, 23)), Bakhtin emphasizes in the concept of 'great time' the long memory of genres and the immortality of all meanings. Now more concerned with the threat of a dogma of relativism than with exposing the relativity in dogmatism, he re-inflects his earlier themes of 'answerability' and 'outsideness'. The story he had once told of modernity as permanent revolution – a story in which first the novel and then carnival were the heroes – is not cancelled. It simply becomes one of the many stories we might at any time tell from the absolute position (or positional absolute) of our unique place in the present, the 'creative chronotope' of our own global here and now.

5

THE NOVEL AND ITS
OTHERS

Only the mythical Adam, who approached a virginal
and as yet verbally unqualified world with the first
word, could really have escaped from start to finish
this dialogical inter-orientation with the alien word
that occurs in the object. Concrete historical human
discourse does not have this privilege: it can deviate
from such inter-orientation only on a conditional basis
and only to a certain degree.

(*DN*, 279).

'The novel' in the work of Mikhail Bakhtin is at once an empirical
phenomenon and a transcendental category. It is not only a fact of
literary history: it is also the rubric under which Bakhtin wishes us
to think about the forms of sociality and subjectivity that belong to
everyday life and to modernity. One of the ways in which he
detaches the novel from its banal phenomenal familiarity and
enforces its anti-generic non-self-identity is by contrast with the
forms of writing which are – or at least have been – 'genres' in the
proper sense: the older, canonical, classical or (as he puts it)
'straightforward' genres of poetry and drama. These forms have not
of course been superseded by the novel upstart in their midst: they
live on, transformed, bereft of their original innocence. Bakhtin
veers between an insistence on their categorical difference from the
novel and a case for their historical interaction, a power struggle
among forms in which the novel always calls the shots. The test of
Bakhtin's concepts lies here, as elsewhere, in confronting them with
that to which (usually for very good conjunctural or strategic
reasons) they accord only a secondary or instrumental theorization.
This means two (complementary) things: first, examining certain

manifest exceptions to the monologism of the older genres; secondly, showing that the old forms are not just a convenience of Bakhtin's thinking but inwardly constitutive of it, intimations of the absolute that live in the closest intimacy with its far more developed and overt celebration of relativity. In the scattered remarks he makes on these generic others of the novel we can trace the outlines of an idea whose importance to our experience of being human may be measured by the number of obituaries it has prompted and yet still refuses to go away: that of God.[1] The upshot will be a Bakhtin who may be strange to some but who none the less has much to say to sociopolitical scenarios such as that of South Africa in the process of transformation, as I hope to show in my conclusion.

I

We might begin by observing that for Bakhtin the novel stands to the other genres as the textuality of incarnation to the textuality of transcendence. There are strong hints in the Dostoevsky book of a homology between the authorial position in the polyphonic novel and the mediating figure of Christ, the 'highest and most authoritative orientation' perceived as 'another authentic human being and his voice' (*PDP*, 97).[2] There are equally strong hints in 'Discourse in the Novel' (see the epigraph above) that the task of the poet is an impossible approximation to the figure of Adam. Whilst the prose word foregrounds the difficult drama of arriving at its object, the word in poetry seeks a direct relation with an object conceived as 'virginally full and inexhaustible' (*DN*, 278), behaving for all the world as if it had not had to struggle with other words in order to reach the latter. Every word in poetry strives ideally towards the status of the first word ever uttered, uniquely and primally naming alien things while acknowledging no alien words. The epic thematizes this putative condition of the poetic word by encoding the values of 'best' and 'highest' in the 'first', in a narrative of beginnings. Poetry, in short, names a postlapsarian impossibility: language living wholly inside itself; a language of the Name and the Same. The historicity and social specificity that are so sensitively and minutely registered by novelistic prose escape poetry altogether, whose temporality is that of the epoch rather than the moment. True, in periods of change in 'literary poetic language' a certain hybridization may take place – poetry might admit the Other into itself – but the outcome is an instant codification, rather like the Saussurean *langue* which opens itself momentarily to take in change from the world of *parole* and diachrony, reshuffling its internal relations only to close ranks again immediately afterwards.

Now of course in all this I am using the somewhat qualified case Bakhtin makes in 1934–35, where he confronts the novel's generic others more directly and extensively than before, and where he is describing not the actual status of all poetic discourse but only 'the extreme to which poetic genres aspire' (*DN*, 287). (Neither does he in any sense equate poetry with 'writing in verse': Alexander Pushkin's poem *Eugene Onegin*, for example, is so thoroughly novelized as to render its verse form a matter of indifference, a mere technicality. In 1940 he was to analyse it as a novel.) In 'Discourse in the Novel' he finds a way of insisting on a categorical distinction between novel and poetry which none the less avoids the trap of seeming to assign an essence to poetry which is only contingently modifiable, as he was to do in the typology of prose discourses in *Problems of Dostoevsky's Poetics*. There, poetry is relegated to a brief afterword and is summarily characterized as requiring 'the uniformity of all discourses, their reduction to a common denominator' (*PDP*, 200). This typology is (perhaps like all taxonomic projects) dominated by a functional rather than a genetic perspective, very much in keeping both with the character of the whole book and with its subject, whose novelistic imagination has, Bakhtin claims, a synchronic rather than a diachronic cast. Even as it breaks with the old hierarchy of traditional poetics, it is in this residual way haunted by the shadow of the classical division of kinds which runs all the way from Plato and Diomedes to Hegel and Lukács. In this ahistorical schema, epic, lyric and drama realize and thereby exhaust three logical possibilities founded in the 'compositional' presence or absence (speech or silence) of author and/or characters: in the lyric only the poet speaks; in drama only the characters speak; in epic both speak. Bakhtin here seeks to overthrow the monopoly of the classical kinds by a sort of parody of their triadic division, rejecting it as a valid division of the verbal arts of European modernity and remapping a version of it onto the field of prose. Thus his first 'type' is directly authorial discourse; his second is the 'objectivized' speech of characters; and in the third type Bakhtin unveils his (or rather the novel's) special discovery: 'double-voiced' discourse', in which author and other speak together in the sense of *with each other at the same time*. Far from being a mechanical sum of the first two types, the third embodies a counter-logic in which, as Julia Kristeva would put it, their 0–1 interval is challenged by that of 0–2 in priority.[3] Where this discourse of the other-in-dominance is itself the 'dominant' of a text, dissolving the logic of plot, flouting and outliving all resolutions, we have novelistic polyphony.

In the attempt to account theoretically for the novel's dialogism, then, Bakhtin's earliest move is one of dialogizing the very triad by which the monological forms of writing are demarcated, putting in the place where the epic 'should' be the discourse type most closely identified with the novel. A radical semantic ambiguity crossing author with other reigns where epic homophony would place the referential transparency of 'one's own' speech over the referential opacity of 'somebody else's', an omniscient metalanguage over an oblivious object language. The corollary of Bakhtin's theorization of the novel in a parodic internalization of the old classical threesome is a further implicit move whereby epic is first subsumed under the more general head of the poetic, then lumped together with drama, and both finally counterposed to the novel. If this new and recognizably modern triad of genres seems to be a simple correlative of the 1929 typology of prose discourses – with poetry and drama and novel, in that order, as generic reflexes of the three intra-novelistic types – then it must be said that such simplicity is qualified even in that earlier text. The summary definition of poetry quoted above adds that the poetic word 'can either be discourse of the first type, or can belong to certain weakened varieties of the other types' (*PDP*, 200). By poetic speech of the second type Bakhtin would seem to mean the forms that in the English tradition are known as the epistle or the complaint – that is to say, recognized canonical forms in which a speaker other than the straightforwardly lyrical 'I' is represented as speaking, and which are among the forerunners of the nineteenth-century 'dramatic monologue'. With the third type Bakhtin is more specific, even proffering illustrations: the '"prosaic" lyric' of 'weakened' dialogism is exemplified in 'Heine, Barbier, some works of Nekrasov and others' (*PDP*, 200). In 1926 his friend Valentin Voloshinov (also citing Heine) had instanced a cognate type of 'lyric irony' which violates that 'unhesitating confidence in the sympathy of the listeners' which is 'the fundamental condition of lyric intonation' (*MPL*, 113). The later Bakhtin would doubtless ascribe this inwardly anti-lyrical lyric to the work of 'novelization' in the late eighteenth and early nineteenth centuries, and we might add that the lineage thus begun issues in the poetry of the various European modernisms.

Of William Blake's *Songs of Innocence and of Experience*, arguably the earliest English examples of this generic anomaly, I shall have more to say later in this chapter. My present purpose is to situate the change in Bakhtin's understanding of the poetic that takes place between the Dostoevsky book and 'Discourse in the Novel' within a more general shift in his theory of discourse from *forms* to *forces*, from 'types' within structures to 'lines' within histories. In short, his 'sociological poetics' is re-inflected, with a stronger stress on the adjective than on the noun within that phrase. Whatever the problems involved in this shift – and Bakhtin's undertheorization of the institutional dimension of these forms that he now frees from their static functional definition has been discussed elsewhere – its interest for us here is the greater exposure of the novel to its generic others that this shift brings in its train.[4] A whole chapter in this book-length essay is headed 'Discourse in Poetry and Discourse in the Novel', and this issue refuses to be thus confined, spilling over as it does into the next, headed 'Heteroglossia in the Novel'. As the novel is more fully exposed to its others, and as the genres are linked in relations of analogy and participation to particular social forces, so certain highly productive complexities and incoherences which had been repressed by the schematism of a taxonomic imperative come to light. The typology of 1929 had, as we have seen, somewhat rhetorically and decorously dialogized the logical schema of traditional poetics; the essay of 1934–35 is in a different theoretical style altogether. Carrying forward the typology's firm refusal of purely linguistic categories (its 'translinguistics'), 'Discourse in the Novel' signals by its very repetitious prolixity a dialogism of theory less reined in by system, more in touch with its own unconscious.

The concept of the poetic is extended in two ways. First, looking at poetry's ideological effects, Bakhtin insists on its complicity in the project of linguistic and sociopolitical unification. Secondly, looking at its formal features, he both specifies in more detail the status of the poetic word (its would-be unconditionality) and critically refashions from the translinguistic standpoint some of the established categories of poetic analysis (rhythm, image, symbol). It is from a difference in the tone of these two elaborations that we become aware of an ambiguity in Bakhtin's thinking about the poetic, an ambiguity which – far from threatening that thinking with collapse, as it would any systematic or monological conceptual edifice – actually opens it up further, taking us into some highly engaged ethical and theologico-political reflections that were inapposite (perhaps quite inchoate as conscious themes) in the Russia of the mid-1930s, but whose moment may now have come.

Consider: when Bakhtin writes that 'the poet is a poet in so far as he accepts the idea of a unitary and singular language and a unitary, monologically sealed-off utterance' (*DN*, 296), he makes poetry out to be an accomplice in the cultural centralization and linguistic standardization that historically created the modern European polities. The poetic genres are the prime literary agents of that sociopolitical unity which is never given but always a matter of struggle from above, always *posited against* the actual heteroglot stratification of language. The intonation in these passages is militant and polemical, its intention demystifying. When, however, Bakhtin turns to the characteristics of the poetic word that fit it for this ideological instrumentality a modulation takes place in his tone. These genres in which 'the natural dialogization of the word is not put to artistic use' – which mimic the project they subserve in so far as they do not abolish dialogism (an impossibility) but rather 'suspend' it by 'convention' – attract to themselves a description that we would otherwise associate with his valorization of carnival: 'utopian' (*DN*, 284, 288). Popular they certainly are not; nonetheless they represent that ideal of a 'utopian philosophy of genres', a 'language of the gods' (*DN*, 331). Poetic monologism may be bound up with a project that subordinates the individual to the state; novelistic dialogism may by the same token be understood as a metaphor for the subject in civil society constituted by multiple intersecting identities and positionalities; but any language that places itself in a ventriloquial relation to God can only be an instrument of the centralizing state by a continuing political effort of insulation and a deliberate monopoly over its use. The 'hierarchical relations' which poetic and other monologisms seek to set up between stratified and (potentially) mutually dialogizing languages can always be translated into 'contradictory relations'.[5] The history of heretical and antinomian sects within Christianity has shown that part of this process will be the transvaluation of the idea of God, its refunctioning away from hierarchy and submission and towards community and struggle. No notion is more powerful than this personification of the unconditional, yet none is more at the mercy of conditions.

Bakhtin does not, of course, 'say' all this; I am not paraphrasing. Rather, I am trying to show that Bakhtin in this moment of his thinking is more Nietzschean than we, or even perhaps he, might have supposed; that the 'linguistic and stylistic worlds' which he opposes as Edenic to Babelic, or as Ptolemaic to Galilean – these are his terms – are no more to be counterposed as (cognitively speaking) false to true or (ethically speaking) bad to good than those Apollonian and Dionysian principles which they so insistently recall. Bakhtin follows Nietzsche in his conception of epic as a 'wholly Apollonian' genre, and he would not dissent with the latter's identification of its perennial Dionysian other in the 'uneven and irregular imagery' of folk song: we are not after all surprised at these echoes of *The Birth of Tragedy* in someone who had been a pupil of the Polish Nietzschean classical scholar Tadeusz Zielinski.[6] What is more interestingly at stake here is the theoretical standing of the poetic word, which we might see as Bakhtin's equivalent of the Apollonian *principium individuationis*. For Nietzsche, that principle may well show its repressive side when 'Apollonian forces' constitute 'a perpetual military encampment' against the 'titanic and barbaric menace of Dionysos'; with the rise of tragedy it enters into a benign interaction with its opposite.[7] Making the appropriate adjustments, we might translate this into Bakhtinian terms by saying that both monologism and dialogism have a utopian dimension. Imagining a condition in which one person was everybody, the pseudo-Adamite language towards which poetry aspires asks of us a certain binocular vision, a perspective 'beyond good and evil' which is able to hold together at all times both its promise and its mystification.

It is worth following up this issue of 'individuation', for if dialogism is the substratum of all monologism – if from within a sense of the ubiquity of the dialogical we are enabled to 'see' or 'hear' monologism for what it is and does, if (that is to say) we are freed from the mystification of its naturalness – then it is also true that a dialogized heteroglossia as it were *needs* the moment of individuation whose hypostasis generates the monological genres. Bakhtin's revolutionary postulate of the primacy of dialogue (in his strong sense) must be sustained, but it must also be qualified by a consideration we could call its obverse: without individuation, that primal state of all discourse would not only not be known; it would be inert, and animate nothing and nobody. Everybody speaking at once is unimaginable except as noise: not polyphony, but cacophony, aesthetically unpleasing and ethico-politically null.

Perhaps it is now time to give this other side of Bakhtin's case a hearing, and to say that while all 'voices' in the novel are 'world views' and potential 'social languages', those languages and ideologies can only make themselves heard as *voices*. Poetry and drama, along with the 'rhetorical genres', survive as the bearers of this counter-truth to that of the novel. Dialogism is a reality of discourse precariously suspended between twin impossibilities: an experience of one as two which, if realized, would bring us back to one again by reducing two to a mechanical sum of two units. It is what would be lost (though not quite without trace) if the 'as yet unfolded' (*sic*) dialogue 'embedded' in one utterance were actually to be 'unfolded' into 'individual argument and conversation between two persons' (*DN*, 324–25) – as happens, for example, in dramatic dialogue. Drama in the typology of chapter 5 had been described somewhat formalistically as objectivized speech (speech of the second type) organized in relations that are themselves objectivized (*PDP*, 188). In the essay of 1934–35, drama is far more dialogically and hence productively redefined as the suicidal realization of the inner dialogism of all discourse, as the manifestation of that towards which dialogism tends but which it can only reach at the cost of its own dissolution. The individuation which makes it possible to speak of two 'voices' within a single linguistic construction is taken a step further. Laid out sequentially as the lines of speaking subjects empirically present to each other, these voices are articulated as different semantic positions within what then becomes – with the displacement of all difference onto the signified – the same 'unitary' language. We might say that this externalizing move which founds drama as we know it is fatal for dialogism, if it were not also the case that drama is the mirror in which novelistic and other dialogisms recognize their own composed and finished image. Without that dramatic model of individuation constantly before them, the voices of novelistic prose would be scarcely formed. The same goes for resolution: without the provisional closure of plot, dialogism as the irresolvable infinity of dialogue would be mere endlessness.

Bakhtin might, then, insist that the novelistic voices which retain their full power to mean in the face of this abstract dialectic of drama are always more than 'individual dissonances'; that, knowing themselves as 'only surface upheavals of the untamed elements in social heteroglossia', they are at their most characteristic when they more or less explicitly open out all personal disagreement into that heteroglot matrix of sociolinguistic stratification and social contradiction from which they spring in the first place; and that any novel which approaches the condition of drama ends up as 'bad drama', with the narrative in the awkward and absurd position of stage directions in plays (*DN*, 326–27). We can concede all this and yet still argue that the interacting voices of the novel cannot put on the ineluctably social and historical clothing of languages if they do not first of all experience as a moment of their constitution the individuating and finalizing imperative of the dramatic. The novel may weave at will in and out of that 'finite dialogue' of which the drama in its verbal aspect is wholly composed, but without this clarified micro-dialogue as its other the novel's inexhaustible macro-dialogue would not be 'itself'. The potential at least of inscription in manifested (if not necessarily attributed) 'voices' is perhaps the condition of dialogism's elementary audibility or legibility.

These reflections could be summed up by saying that the individuation of drama is not merely the result of an Apollonian reduction of the 'untamed' Dionysian infinity of heteroglossia to persons, but always already within heteroglossia as the precondition of our even beginning to enter and conceive the latter. What post-structuralist discourses speak of as a 'play of signifiers' is just that: a *play*, a drama of signification at the heart of all meaning. This metaphor of 'play', of a 'playing out' or staging, is never far off in Bakhtin's accounts of the varieties of meaning-making. We have seen the trope at work in what I have called the 'difficult drama' which takes place when the word strives to reach its object, that battle with other words in a 'tension-filled environment' (*DN*, 276) which the novel is unique in putting on display, thematizing rather than suppressing. Now, with the poetic genres it is not the case that there is no drama; it is simply that this drama of semiosis takes place in a different theatre. The product of this relocated 'play' is the *symbol*, characteristic sign of poetic discourse and (for Bakhtin) just as 'central' to the theorization of poetry as the 'double-voiced, internally dialogized word' is to the theory of prose (*DN*, 330). The little drama which gives us the poetic symbol or image is 'played out' not between one fully valued word and another but 'between the word and its object'; all of the symbol's play is 'in that space' (*DN*, 328). The distance between the symbol's 'double meaning' and the prose word's ambiguity can be measured by introducing dramatic dialogue as a middle term: where drama gives us two voices within a single language, symbolism can never be other than two meanings within a single voice. It shares with the novel's incarnate contradiction (dialogism) an intersection of meanings; at the same time, it shares with drama the impulse towards unification. Another voice 'break[ing]' into this play of the symbol' destroys the 'poetic plane' and 'translate[s]' it 'onto the plane of prose' (*DN*, 328). Figured diagrammatically, Bakhtin's conception of the dramatic and poetic words might be seen as occupying the middle of a scale which has at its end the novel's orchestration of many languages into a 'world' and at its other extreme the discourse of philosophy, a language of the 'term' and the 'concept' in which (one presumes: Bakhtin does not spell this out) a single meaning inhabits a single voice. Or: at the broad top of an imagined inverted pyramid is a form of mimesis which is dialogically open to the world, which it also structurally replicates in its own infinite difference from itself; at the apex below is a sort of verbal position without magnitude, a form of conceptuality which has renounced all ambiguity in order to keep at bay the world it makes into the object of its monologue.

We have seen that for Bakhtin symbolism differs from dialogism in the space of its signifying event: the varieties of signification that he brings under the comprehensive rubric of the symbol correspond to different dramatic actions, different relationships between the figure's meanings. The relationship may be logical: of part to whole, for example, or of concrete to abstract.[8] Or it may be ontological: 'as a special kind of representational relationship, or as a relationship between essence and appearance'. Bakhtin might have said that symbolism is that form of verbal signification whose productivity could be exhausted by using the categories of either a structuralist or a metaphysical hermeneutic. The slightest touch of irony – of 'another's accent' intruding 'between the word and its object' – does not so much destroy the symbol as refunction it beyond the reach of both of these kinds of analysis (*DN*, 328). Irony or parody cutting across the poetic symbol behaves rather like an unruly fool erupting onto the space where the latter's decorous dance of meaning is being staged.

Bakhtin cites the similes of Lensky's lyrics in *Eugene Onegin* as an instance of this more or less blatant dialogization of the poetic word. Similar English examples could no doubt be found with a sharp satirical edge in Lord Byron, and in a slightly different vein in the novelized quasi-lyrical and narrative poetry of Robert Browning and Arthur Hugh Clough. The less patent, more complex case of Blake's lyric irony will be elaborated later. A related case, one to which Bakhtin gives little space, is the 'novelistic image'. Its difference from the poetic image is worth briefly pursuing, if only because some dominant twentieth-century critical arguments have effected a certain poeticization of the novel as a condition of its being treated as 'art', and Bakhtin can help us to resist such residual power as they still have. One thinks of F.R. Leavis's characteristically tautological dictum about 'major' fiction 'counting' in the same way as 'major' poetry 'counts'; or of the effort to present Dickens as a spontaneous 'symbolist'.[9] The motif of the prison in Charles Dickens's

Little Dorrit, for example, has been seen as a symbol thanks to whose magic potency social criticism becomes high art, as the text's otherwise monstrously disparate sprawl of character zones and narrative lines is conjured into a unity offering aesthetic satisfactions beyond the mere storytelling ingenuity of the 'mystery' plot. Structuralist analysis might trace its productivity as an image in the abstract to its formal combination of metaphor and metonymy – the prison as part of a social whole which is itself prison-like – without ever taking us back to the discursive and historical roots of the life of that particular motif, which surely lie deep in metropolitan English heteroglossia. Dickens's image has none of the radiant translucence and single tone of the symbol: at once opaque and dissonant, it springs from a popular and radical consciousness of long standing and may be guessed as having its origins in or after 1789. Far from effacing the traces of its endless ironic as well as straightforward recycling through countless fictional and polemical contexts, Dickens's multifaceted 'prison' mobilizes these diverse uses and draws its vitality from them. English Jacobinism is one such context: William Godwin's chauvinistic Englishman who exclaims, 'Thank God, we have no Bastille!' finds an echo in the xenophobic politics of the plebeian occupants of Bleeding Heart Yard.[10] Also resonating here is the nickname 'Poor Law Bastilles', given to the workhouses after 1834; Mary Wollstonecraft's Maria, who declares that marriage 'bastilled her for life';[11] and beyond and behind all of these that old tactic of radical polemic whereby the Whiggish critique of French institutions was turned against England itself (as if to underline this, the novel begins in a French prison).[12] The force of this 'novelistic image' is, then, anything but 'symbolic' – not unifying but displacing, moving the text beyond its own boundaries as an aesthetically finalized whole. Centrifugal rather than centripetal, it is less the all-resolving focus of the novel's 'great dialogue' than that dialogue's catalyst, the guarantee that it is unfinishable.

II

And so we come to Blake, first of our generalizable exceptions.[13] If Blake is taken to be a 'Romantic' poet – and he was a latecomer to that company, itself only constituted by criticism after all of its members had already died – then his practice of writing hardly corresponds either to Bakhtin's view of Romantic discourse as a single-voiced authorial expressivity hostile to irony and parody or to the more general view that in the poetic signification of

Romanticism the symbol has triumphed over allegory. For Bakhtin, Romanticism breaks with the 'stylization' of the single-voiced classicist word, only to put in its place a yet purer monologism of utterance from which all hint of refraction through another's word has been eliminated. Combining a Chicago-Aristotelian reading of literary history with a Russian Formalist conceptual vocabulary, we might extend this by saying that the lyric in all its forms, even the 'lowest', becomes the poetic norm of a new literary system, and that in the process both itself and the system are radically changed. As the latter sheds its hierarchy, so the lyric sheds its conventionality, offering itself as the quasi-spontaneous speech-act of a person empirically given and without any difference in kind from the reader. Now while Blake undoubtedly participates in this mutation whereby what Marxists call the 'bourgeois revolution' is at last fought to a finish on the field of poetics – the kinship between his *Songs* and the *Lyrical Ballads* of William Wordsworth and Samuel Taylor Coleridge is evidence enough – his writing from first to last is very plainly both open to the dialogized heteroglossia of his time and alert to the revolutionary possibilities of the allegorized literary language then passing into obsolescence. His solution to the crisis of that language was not to forsake it altogether for an empiricism of 'feeling' but to reinvigorate it, thereby uncovering the ethics and the theology and the politics that lie buried in poetics. It is this act of compelling the poetic to yield up its ethical and theologico-political potential that he calls Imagination. Blake in this way forces upon Bakhtinian thinking an exception not only to its conceptualization of poetry in general but to its characterization of Romantic writing in particular, and seems to hold up before us a stark choice between 'correcting' Bakhtin and 'reclassifying' Blake. The Russian perhaps only knew the Romanticisms of his own country and Germany (and perhaps also France); the Englishman is a maverick, member of a class of one.

There is of course a third possibility, and that is to bring Bakhtin and Blake into dialogue with each other. Our deconstruction of Bakhtin's opposition between the novelistic and the poetic will be interestingly elaborated if we follow through to some sort of answer these hitherto unposed questions: Why was Blake not a novelist? If he was neither (quite) a Romantic nor (quite) a 'neoclassical' poet, what deflected him from taking the path to prose that a superficial reading of Bakhtin might see as the logical choice – at least of so sensitive and politically engaged a listener to the voices and languages of the revolutionary years? Or, to rephrase: what truth was it about poetic discourse and human potentiality that took on exceptional clarity under the signature of William Blake? What I said earlier about the coexisting utopian and demystifying dimensions in Bakhtin's discussion of the poetic genres begins to clarify if we understand how Blake's writing is a powerful hybrid of allegory and parody, the sublime and the grotesque, a peculiar productivity and interaction of modes and effects that are traditionally opposed.

Demonstrating all this demands that we take a detour first of all into the fortunes of these modes as they came down to Blake and as they have since been (mis)represented. Allegory has suffered over the past two hundred years from a critical discourse still under the dominance of symbol, whose terms cast it in an inferior signifying role, constructing it as the crude corporealization of elements from an already given conceptuality, its arbitrary signifiers lacking that necessary relation to a signified with which the symbol instantaneously impresses us.[14] It suited the high-Romantic polemic against allegory to take the classicist conception of its conventional working at face value in order to sustain a notion of the symbol as no mere 'figure' but as a minor miracle of writing in which there is at once and inseparably meaning and materiality: always just enough of each but never too much of either. Nothing that Blake wrote can be understood within these terms: he works in a space before this move towards a punctual specularity of poetic signification is made, and what he retains from the allegorical tradition is its inherent narrativity, its intrinsically unstable dependence upon speaking and acting persons. If it is true that his polemical statements about allegory are (with one exception) denunciatory, his practice shows that what he there denounces is the 'fable' conceived as subordinated to the 'moral' – that is, allegory as narrativity in thrall to conceptuality. For the practice itself must be grasped not as leaping at one bound from the artificiality of the allegorical into the authenticity of the symbolic, but rather as exploiting a contradiction that was then opening up in poetics. 'Allegory' on the one hand was a tissue of 'improbabilities' licensed (within limits) by its 'moral', relegated to the half-life of mere exemplification. On the other hand it is the mode that enables the most unrestricted 'invention', the 'boldest' of 'fiction'. The allegory that Blake renews from within is the name that stood in his time for both the bondage and the freedom of the poetic signifier.

The means of this renewal is our other mode: parody. Whereas the Romantic symbol realizes the monological potential in allegory,

Blake's writing is a continuous opening out of the dialogism that lies only just beneath the surface of an idea that has been made to speak. Parody is an unsublatable moment of that process whereby the always animated signifiers of allegory are freed to mean on their own. We might say that allegorical 'fiction' generates a truth strong enough to challenge the meaning which orthodoxy and authority intend it to deliver and whose very embodiment carries the risk of a subversion in the first place. Parody as the agent of a renovating subversion of allegory is everywhere in Blake; it is there in his claim that his narrative works make up an alternative Scripture, a 'Bible of Hell'; it is also there in his profoundly allusive and ironic lyrics. Typically he takes a dominant cultural text and literalizes it at those highly vulnerable points where it makes a tactical use of allegory: the new narrative produced out of these materials is then offered as the text's occluded subtext, the state of affairs it does not wish us to see or hear. In 'A Poison Tree' and 'The Human Abstract' from the *Songs of Experience* Blake lays bare this device of his writing, above all in the relation between the first stanza and the rest of the poem. The first poem dialogizes a voice of 'forbearance', elaborating out of its casual metaphors a little narrative of murderous consequences which that same voice is ironically forced to tell:

> In the morning glad I see
> My foe outstretched beneath the tree.[15]

In the second poem the abstractions of 'Pity' and 'Mercy', clothed in the tones of ruling-class complacency, are (in a first move) contextually re-accentuated as personifications:

> Pity would be no more
> If we did not make somebody Poor;
> And Mercy no more could be
> If all were as happy as we.[16]

Another voice of vatic intonation then invents other actors in a full-blown allegory of social and psychic alienation which makes up the body of the text:

> And mutual fear brings peace,
> Till the selfish loves increase:
> Then Cruelty knits a snare,
> And spreads his baits with care.[17]

These parodied allegories have their place in a set of lyrics produced in a parodic re-accentuation of the *Songs of Innocence*, themselves in turn already parodies of contemporary verse for children. Into the form which was even then becoming the paradigm of high-Romantic expressivity Blake introduces an unheard-of density of verbal refractions and displacements which extend beyond the parodic to take in the whole range of irony, ambiguity and what Bakhtin calls 'hidden polemic' (*PDP*, 196). It seems we have no choice but to speak in Blake's case, and against the grain of Bakhtin's more categorical distinctions, of a specifically poetic dialogism – one which, while it could never match the range of its novelistic near-relation, is, all the same, no mere rhetorical reduction or rarefaction of the latter, but deeply form-determining, and with its own distinctive effects.

What, then, does this strong poetic dialogism offer that novelistic dialogism can't? To answer this we need to be more specific about the type of allegorizing poetic discourse that is dialogically revitalized in Blake. Let us call it, in a quasi-Bakhtinian coinage, the *apostrophic word*. By this I mean that so-called 'personification allegory' which in his time was exemplified in the 'great' or 'sublime' ode, the major lyric genre in which (normally) an abstract attribute like 'Peace' or 'Liberty' is launched into life by being apostrophized and made the hero(ine) of a short narrative of origins. For an idea to speak or act it has first to be spoken to by the poet; it was from this merely conventional odic gesture that Blake developed a whole ontology by the simple move of refusing to exempt anything from a universal addressivity. The programmatically 'third-person' discourse that tried to escape this condition he called Reason, the ultimate monologism. Blake's claim for the performative status of the apostrophic word is to be read not only in his occasional terse maxims on the topic but also in that transition in his writing which took him from the early lyrics, through the carnivalesque clarification of his great Menippaean satire *The Marriage of Heaven and Hell*, to narrative poems where the notion that everything is alive only in so far as it is created and sustained by acts of apostrophe meets head on the criterion of 'probability'. Truth-claims that were suspended in the lyric held good for the epic kinds; hence, to make lyric 'vision' the continuous texture of narrative, as Blake does in the prophetic books, is to flout the dominant rationality and flaunt the referentiality of the apostrophic word. Like Bakhtin, Blake poses discourses of integral personification against those rationalizing discourses that reify everything they touch. The personification need not be explicit, in the sense of being spelled out, realized semantically: any speech of marked intonation (as Voloshinov observes in 'Discourse in Life and Discourse in Art') turns its referent into an addressee, implicitly calls a hero into being, animates the world in a replay of our onto-genetic and phylogenetic childhood. Blake's fondness for such intonational heightening is to be seen in those intensely pointed and emphatically repeated questions, appeals and exclamations that fill whole lyrics and punctuate the 'epic' writing.

Our dialogue between Bakhtinian theory and Blakean practice might perhaps be brought to a provisional focus by what must surely rank as the best-known Blakean text of this kind. In 'The Tyger' the central issue of any thoroughgoing spirituality is brought before us in poetic writing of the most relentlessly reiterative mate-riality: an utterance that undoes the pseudo-objectivity of the declarative sentence by being made of nothing but questions. To talk about God Blake had to write a poem – a poem, moreover, that was poetic (read: apostrophic) to the nth degree; to transvalue the godhead that he rejected he had at the same time to refract his intentions parodically and polemically through the words of others. In this dense fabric of allusion to aesthetic and theological and political discourses, none is either finally detachable from its source in the current heteroglossia or finally reducible to the others' terms. Blake's revolutionary praise of (his) God is nothing if not oblique, having to fight its way through the outright abuse of anti-Jacobin reaction to reach its object: more than one conservative voice had by 1792–93 begun to recast the 'swinish' people as fearful 'tigers'. Blake's sublime is produced by reminding the arch-conservative Edmund Burke of that passage in his aesthetic treatise where he cites the tiger 'in the gloomy forest' as the quintessence of the sublime of 'power' which rises from 'terror, the common stock of everything that is sublime'.[18] The terrified split subject who speaks the poem is made to realize an image of unbridled Energy in an echo of the terms of William Collins's monstrous figure of 'Danger' in the 'Ode to Fear', whose 'Limbs of Giant Mold/What mortal Eye can fix'd behold?'[19] His quest for an answer is both revealing and creatively misdirected: the artisanal maker that he imagines for the tiger tells us which earthly class subject he most fears; while the 'distant deeps or skies' in which he imagines the making as happening show his fixation upon a conception of the divine Subject as both far removed in time and space and inwardly undi-vided. The poem's climax is yet another, and still more agonized, question: 'Did he who made the Lamb make thee?' In the absence of an answer, the speaker repeats in intensified form the question that invoked the beast at the beginning.

We then understand: the work of creation that he vividly, though mistakenly, thinks of as taking place in some indefinite past is the work of the heteroglot words that speak through him, coming together in his monologue. But we also know that, though his idea of the nature and locus of God is at fault, though in some sense the tiger is of his own making – is a human possibility – his quest for a unified truth, a transcendence, is not. This need to imagine the unconditioned Author of everything is indeed no less human, inasmuch as it is the constitutive obverse of that knowledge of finitude which defines our humanity and which (as both Bakhtin and Blake understand) does not have to entail a disempowering obedience to any hierarchized authority actually in place in the world. Through and beyond the multiple ironies of its poetic dialogism, and taking its strength from them, 'The Tyger' remains a sublime lyric, a poem whose generic memory, extending back to ancient prayer and cultic ritual, ensures that it cannot do other than praise.

III

In Bakhtin's terms, then, Blake's extraordinary project is one of reinventing within an irreversible European modernity the 'proclamatory genres', restoring to poetry its prophetic and performative dimension in an age when irony or speech 'with reservations' has so wholly entered the national vernaculars as to have become codified in their very syntactic forms (*NM70–71*, 132–33). Blake would have agreed with Bakhtin that the old authorial positions whose styles and settings were not a matter of choice have gone for good. However strongly the image of the author as prophet that he assumes in the narrative works alludes to one such superseded speaking subject, it is precisely *an image*, one among many he might have chosen. If he does not write novels, neither does he in any Bakhtinian sense write epics: in texts that refer so immediately to the present and future there is no correlation whatever between a 'high' style and the absolute past; the genre of prophecy speaks to the present by bringing past and future into familiar contact with one another. In Blake an 'old' genre makes a bid for renewed authority in the modern world, openly reviving a 'proclamatory' mode of speech that other authorial images ironize almost to death (a negation which, needless to say, only binds them the more firmly to what they negate). The hard thing perhaps for us to understand is that while this act of discursive renewal is always and necessarily a matter of 'stylization' rather than 'style', it is by no means less authentic for that reason. We might say that modern authorship strives in its Blakean move to be authoritative without being authoritarian, and that this persistence of the will to truth through a discourse that so insistently frames and contextualizes itself is a paradigm of poetry's accommodation to modernity.

The political character of this accommodation is never constant or assured: in late eighteenth-century England it was undoubtedly revolutionary in its implications, if not always in its effects. Percy Bysshe Shelley's 'Ode to the West Wind' is perhaps the last brave attempt to mobilize a hybrid of prophecy and prayer for emancipatory ends, in the long aftermath of the French Revolution. Whatever the future fortunes and political effects of this kind of 'proclamatory' poetic writing in the modern world's European heartland, it has a long life ahead of it in other places, where modernization is a recent experience or has taken a skewed path: South Africa, for example. A play of the 1980s like *Woza Albert!* suggests that in the township heteroglossia from which it manifestly draws its strength we might anywhere find working together (often coinciding in the same text or practice or individual) the radical parodist and the radical *imbongi* (praise singer), latter-day prophet and holy fool alike speaking of the people's freedom as forms of pleasure and forms of worship unite to shadow forth a state beyond or before the cruel commodification of their bodies in the present. It is, moreover, no coincidence that this place where a prophetic poetic discourse has survived not only print culture and literacy but also the colonizer's cultural exterminism should be a prime site of efforts to transform the God who came in the colonizer's missionary train, across a range which runs from the independent African churches in the early days of conversion to the black theology of more recent date; from the spontaneous and local spiritual revolt of the first elites, all the way to the consciously liberationist and global project espoused by black Christians who have sought roles in one or other of the (socialist, liberal or radical-democratic) emancipatory narratives of modernity. Whether oriented to the past or to the future, whether in identifying saints or prophets as ancestors or in identifying the regulative ideas of modern sociopolitical narratives with the Kingdom of God – in short, whether traditionalist or revolutionary – the effect of these phenomena is to show that the authoritative word can be wrested from 'authority' and re-inflected from below as a discourse now of frontal challenge, now of everyday survival, sometimes (again) ambivalently poised between these postures.

We might usefully take some of these reflections into the polemical field opened up in South Africa in the 1990s over the cultural forms appropriate to the post-apartheid condition. The culture of slogans and of the 'spectacle', we are told in the most compelling of the arguments now making itself heard, will (or should) then give way to a new culture of 'irony' and of the quotidian, models for which already exist in some of the writing produced under the old regime of apartheid.[20] Timely as this case is – and I have warmly underwritten it more than once elsewhere – it needs to be hedged about with the kind of caveat that perhaps only the Bakhtinian perspective developed in this essay could make enterable.[21] Anyone brought to acknowledge that the 'proclamatory' genres do not necessarily oppress must also entertain the notion that the 'ironic' genres might not necessarily liberate, or at least not on their own. Strong and positive versions of this counterargument have already surfaced in reference to metropolitan Europe: Russell Berman has, for example, recently argued that the 'charismatic modernism' of the *avant-garde* in our century is complicit with the very bureaucratic rationalization that it is conventionally seen as opposing.[22] At the very least, we might speculate that perhaps the idiom which links the double-voiced genres with civil society and the single-voiced genres with the state is a dangerous idiom – if only because it is self-fulfilling: monologism will seem the language of centralized authority just insofar as we confine that category's empirical instances to the state's monologues; in our loud denunciation of malign voices of authority such benign 'popular' correlatives of those voices as exist might be lost to hearing.

To pose the slogan against irony as if irony were the sole alternative to the slogan's simplification, the only sure guarantee against its illegitimate trespass upon the field of knowledge, is to miss what is distinctive about the forms of modern authority. The slogan, it is true, does not admit of ambiguity or hesitation: as that micro-genre in which the collective praises its own qualities – wishes itself long life or proclaims its own *amandla* or *maatla* (strength, power) – and/or denounces the evils of its others, it cannot live in the company of sceptical tones, let alone admit semantically explicit qualifiers or modifiers of any kind; as the distant echo within modernity of ancient battle-cries, it bears within it the residual magic of all optatives or performatives. At the same time, it has an instrumental cast which puts it in that distinctively modern category of forms which belong to what Bakhtin calls the 'small time' of short-term ends and immediate resolutions. The slogan celebrates the certainties of the collective in an epoch that began in Europe with a revolutionary gesture of doubting everything, and whose hero is the one (literally 'one', typically 'the individual') who claims the right to demur.[23]

It has then to be said that the slogan carries no fixed valency, independent of context. The state-sponsored slogans of the May Day and October marches in the old Soviet Union had of course nothing whatever to do with democracy or the collective and everything to do with a bureaucratic elite devoid of all popular legitimation. What, then, of the slogans of so-called 'national liberation' movements? Any actual movement of that kind will be a hybrid: at its best, a living utopian image of civil-society-in-the-making, a focus for variously oriented social forces; at its worst, a bureaucracy-in-waiting, becoming more like a mirror-image of the state the longer it has to wait in illegality and exile, while its hierarchies harden into military structures of command. The slogan in the latter context, emanating from that source and feeding its finished identity, differs only in tone and content, but scarcely in effect, from the state decree; it is only on entering civil society that a slogan escapes the monopoly of any one movement and can carry the intentions of those who pragmatically put it to use on the ground. There, too, it finds itself in a spectrum of (oral) discourses that, as it were, qualify it from without, challenging its logic of if-not-for-then-against with a counter-logic which says that not to be unambiguously 'for' is not necessarily to be 'against'. The slogan-chanter also laughs or prays, or is exposed to laughter and prayer, and in so far as this happens the slogan is placed in the context of a macro-dialogue without dates or bounds in space. The slogan that does not live at peace with the profane 'carnivalization' of the one form or the sacred 'consummation' of the other may issue at length (and all too often does) in the blow that maims or kills.

Now of course much South African poetry lives in the atmosphere inhabited by the slogan, an atmosphere in which primary and secondary oralities meet and cross-fertilize, and where the written word might paradoxically seem at once superseded and still to come.[24] A literature – that is to say, a tradition specifically of writing – whose organizing principle is the slogan would indeed be giving up on any active role, would not be doing what it does best. Irony is one of its modes, the dominant mode of novelistic prose in particular; and a South Africa in transformation needs novels with their valuable orchestration of incommensurable stories and privacies if the pretensions of the totalizing narratives that obsessed both oligarchy and opposition under the old order are to be cut down to size. But then a culture breaking out of the grip of such narratives also needs friendly forms of authority. Myths, hymns, anthems, prophecies, proverbs: all of these court the danger that they can become terroristic under modern conditions, bearers of exclusive and monopolistic narratives. Properly contextualized, these forms counter the hubris of the 'nation' with a sense (a knowledge only ever agonistically, rather than cognitively, acquired) of the boundlessness of semantic space–time, in which any given community forms only a local and finite coherence. With their focus on the eternities that surround our finitude, they remind us that no speech would begin if besides our interlocutor we did not posit what Bakhtin calls the 'third': an instance of absolute understanding and truly caring listening, a 'superaddressee' more or less personified. If they are not to be the mere means of groups bonding themselves and banding together against their others, these proclamatory forms of the authoritative word need interpreters, and an appropriate technology for their distribution in a 'developing' society.

Writers are those interpreters; print is their medium. The riches of an oral and vatic past are not the less authentic for being 'quoted', ventriloquized, as they cannot but be now. A literature that is the custodian of all times makes the conditions for their continued meaning within our late modernity.[25] The nation that thinks of itself as a village is the enemy of all other villages; condensing the wisdom of its villages in the second-order (though no less authentic) authority of writing and putting it in everybody's hands, the nation – through its writers – redeems itself. The 'battle hymns' of the time of insurgency (as Nadine Gordimer called them) may not be a foundation for the future, but even at their first moment of declamation they had behind them and around them the tones of Ntsikana's hymn and Sontonga's famous anthem: . lodged in comprehensive anthologies, sung at meetings, globally reproduced in recorded sound, these are songs not *of* but *for* the 'nation'.[26] They belong to nobody in this world; what we say in singing them contradicts and forbids any monopoly of their use. Their matter is not thought or even feeling but rather the invocation of that which in some sense thinks us before we think; and what we who sing them 'believe' matters not in the slightest. Calling on God to bless Africa and on the Holy Spirit to 'descend', we celebrate community by imagining what transcends and holds community itself. Blake would have valued (had he known them) these sublime lyrics in which Africa ceaselessly reimages her own bounding outline in eternity. And so too would Bakhtin: for whom the grotesque body was only half the story of our humanity, the novel no absolute model and the absolute a human reality.

6

ETERNITY AND MODERNITY

> There is neither a first nor a last word and there are no
> limits to the dialogic context (it extends into the
> boundless past and the boundless future). Even *past*
> meanings, that is, those born in the dialogue of past
> centuries, can never be stable (finalized, ended once
> and for all) – they will always change (be renewed) in
> the process of subsequent, future development of the
> dialogue. At any moment in the development of the
> dialogue there are immense, boundless masses of
> forgotten contextual meanings, but at certain moments
> of the dialogue's subsequent development along the
> way they are recalled and invigorated in renewed
> form (in a new context). Nothing is absolutely dead:
> every meaning will have its homecoming festival. The
> problem of *great time*.
>
> (*MHS*, 170)

The last thoughts written down by Mikhail Bakhtin before his death
turn not on the meaning of life but rather on the life of meaning.
The gesture is characteristic: the 'meaning of life' could not be other
than a monological 'transcription' and generalization of that force
field of the singular and situated which (for him) is life as it is lived
and endlessly becomes. The whole internally open-ended work of
his life is brought to an external end with the words 'great time', by
which he signifies the immortality of all meanings, the endless
circulation and return of semantic energies, the interaction of live
contexts in infinite dialogue across hundreds and even thousands
of years. 'Great time' is a concept that should speak quite directly to
us as we begin the second Christian millennium in a world where
supposedly forgotten themes and narratives are being revived or

newly inflected, not just by single writers in theory but by whole collectivities in practice.

I

'Every meaning will have its homecoming festival', Bakhtin writes, using a trope which is deliberately archaic and anthropomorphic, not only propelling the idea of an ancient ceremony of welcome into the (open) future but also flaunting its form as a little personification allegory. To see anthropomorphism as a disease of thought is to close oneself to the challenge of a kind of thinking that 'hear[s] voices' (MHS, 169) everywhere and discerns the lineaments of a potential hero in even the most depersonalized and detemporalized discourse. The story of meaning is, like much of Bakhtin's own story, a tale of exile which is often the richer in outcome for the length of its duration. Time in properly human terms is nothing other than the dimension in which meaning opens out. Just as the word in Bakhtin is defined as that which strives always to be heard, which posits implicitly a forever absent ideal or optimal listener, so meanings tendentially seek out the means of their return. A meaning is at home wherever it comes up against a context that will reopen the context(s) it has preserved through time, in a Gadamerian 'fusion of horizons'.[1] By explicitly casting meaning itself in the role of hero, by bringing to life what is otherwise suspended or suppressed, Bakhtin exemplifies in a sort of instant discursive miniature the very realization of potential that he is describing and celebrating.

There had been other candidates for immortality earlier in Bakhtin's work: in the Dostoevsky book it is *personality*; in the Rabelais book it is *the people*: immortalities, respectively, of the spirit and the flesh. The immortality contemplated by the dying Bakhtin is more encompassing, more of the ground of our humanity, than either of these. It is not incompatible with a strong emphasis upon historicity, though it is at odds with any tendency towards a radical relativism. As an eternity of potential, it has nothing in common with that eternity of closure by means of which Bakhtin apophatically thinks the sense of 'historical time' that is for him the great defining discovery of modernity. In this 'naive' eternity of epic the first words and deeds are also the last words and deeds, and the past is the highest value. This 'absolute past' is precisely extra-temporal in so far as those in it cannot imagine that their epoch was ever someone else's future or that it will ever be someone else's past (*EN*, 16–17). In their primal temporal introversion they show no foresight that the likes of us will ever follow them further down the line of time. Bakhtin imagines the eternity of mediaeval Christianity as similarly closed, as a vertical axis of everlasting synchrony from which the horizontal of history at length detaches itself. The exemplary site of this move (for him as for Erich Auerbach)[2] is the *Divine Comedy*, while the eighteenth-century move that decisively launches history as a category of thought bears the proper name of Goethe.

Now these classical and feudal orders of extra-temporality serve Bakhtin mainly in the middle of his career as antitheses of the novel's self-conscious chron(otop)icity. Great time must not, I think, be seen as flatly contradicting his valorization of the novel's orientation towards the 'inconclusive present' (*EN*, 26) or 'unresolved contemporaneity'(*DN*, 349) – its sensitivity to languages of 'the day' (*DN*, 291) – or as marking a turn to 'poetry' with its stately, epochal temporality. This eternity of semantic potential should instead be seen as fashioning for the novel a friendly dialogizing other rather than a purely heuristic opposite, thereby averting the dangers of a fall into 'small time' that might ensue for any hermeneutic that makes a dogma out of the socio-historical relativity and novelty of cultural meanings. It is one thing to use the novel as a battering ram to bring down the bastions of poetics, or indeed to use the still more extreme idiom of carnival against all law or authority whatever; it is quite another thing to build a new hermeneutic on that highly polemical base. With great time Bakhtin seeks to reduce the threat of a radical forgetting posed by both of these powerfully deconstructive categories. His early concept of 'outsideness' in 'aesthetic activity' is now refunctioned in the direction of diachrony and of the reception (rather than production) of cultural texts.

The problem with carnival is that it is one of those hyperbolic concepts that can always go over into their opposites. Starting as a will to freedom, this paradoxical rule of non-identity contains the threat of becoming a finalized unfinalizability, a category without an outside, enshrining 'jolly relativity' as a metaphysical absolute. As an eternal corrective to this possibility, Bakhtin revives and rethinks for other purposes what I will call his *positional* absolute. This category is the wild card among categories in that it requires that we think of uniqueness as multiple, of a non-commutable situatedness as infinitely repeated across the whole of (human: the qualifier is redundant) reality. No one situatedness can be known except from the standpoint of another such situatedness. Applied to history, it means that we neither reduce a work of the past to its conditions nor read it as if it were a product of our time, but always read its uniqueness from our own; that we avoid the abstract objectivity achieved by forever putting ourselves out of the picture and instead think of the work as precisely needing us for the realization of its semantic potential. Besides the (mutually dialogizing) chronotopes within the work, and as the condition of their having their effect, there is this chronotope of the reader 'outside' the work. Reading is the meeting of these chronotopes, by means of which the work is freed from the 'captivity' of time (*IENM*, 5–6).

This redemptive hermeneutic of utopian surplus offered by Bakhtin in his last writings is no different in kind from the aesthetic activity conceptualized in his earliest writings. Works and/or their (internal) authors are now themselves the heroes; readers are the authors that these text-characters everywhere posit and search out. Thanks to this readerly authoring the 'text' becomes the 'work', internalizing – activating within itself – the unforeseen and unforeseeable context(s) in which it finds itself. Or, rather: the 'text' is an analytic abstraction from the work, which is always the text-and/in-a-context, the context-and/in-a-text. The hermeneutic of the late Bakhtin is this 'consummating' activity made reflexive, taken, as it were, to the second power. Qualifying the strong mid-career emphasis upon histor(icit)y is the perspective of a newly reaffirmed philosophical anthropology, a deeply committed phenomenology of the ways we live our human-ness at once in and beyond history. Before we live in those purely conceptual objectivities called 'society' or 'history' we live absolutely in meaning; the infinity and eternity of meaning are both the outcome and the making-good of our own finitude. Meaning is always everywhere because we as individuals can never be, although/because we end both spatially and temporally where and when our bodies end.

II

It should be clear by now that the turn taken by the late Bakhtin is from the grotesque-in-history to the sublime-in-theory, and from an *avant-gardist* agency rooted in the people to one that now devolves upon the practitioner of hermeneutics within the 'human sciences'. In his last essays and notebooks Bakhtin revives the Diltheyan distinction between *Verstehen* and *Erklären* in the new situation presented by the mid-twentieth century, when the 'sciences of the spirit' were adopting (or had widely adopted) the paradigm of language and were no longer in the thrall of the methodology of the natural sciences. The peril faced by these disciplines making up the dominant or emergent field of structuralism in the period after the Second World War was not the lapse into causal explanation: they were founded precisely upon a programmatic rejection of any concern with genesis, any genetic approach to cultural texts. The systemic options of which a text was made up were internal determinants; its realized virtualities were so to speak its composite 'inner' or immanent cause. Bakhtin must at this moment have felt alienated by both official and academic discourses on culture in the Soviet Union: on the one hand, there was 'Marxist' ideology-critique, enshrining a species of vulgar causal explanation rooted in 'class' – in the empirical author's given or chosen place in the social division of labour – and backed always by the violence of repression; on the other, there was the structuralism of the Tartu school, which, like its Western counterpart (though less polemically), abolished any causality other than structural causality. Both putatively 'scientific' discourses about culture would have seemed to Bakhtin little more than rival scientistic ideologies, theoretical monologisms of the same order. The 'linguistic turn' of twentieth-century thought might have promised the institution of a more appropriate paradigm for the human sciences, if the conception of language invoked by these disciplines had been different. Dilthey's work had been done before that turn took place – before language became the model of all social 'objectivation' and interaction.[3] Bakhtin is writing at a time when that paradigm shift had been only too successful, in the age of the growing hegemony of what he calls 'the potential single language of languages' (*PT*, 107). The successful 'revolt against positivism'[4] in the name of those strong claims made for the language paradigm by so many disparate currents of contemporary thought had resulted in the triumph of yet another objectivism.

That paradigm stood, in short, in need of correction. The onto-logical-hermeneutic turn of the late Bakhtin is also in some sense a turn towards the dimension (and problem) of *time*. Why did this happen? Well, the metaphors of both structuralism and of his own popular-carnivalesque deconstruction are predominantly spatial metaphors; space, it would seem, is the privileged dimension of any body of thinking which (like structuralism, notoriously) foregrounds synchrony at the cost of diachrony. In the last writings it is omni-temporality and 'depth of meaning' – he is very careful to say 'not height or breadth' (*PT*, 127) – that preoccupies Bakhtin before all else. And so the Bakhtinian *Dasein* enters the last of its incarnations as 'great time', the plane in which all meaning lives and grows. To be is to understand: understanding is the activity called forth both by texts proper and by those potential texts-to-be called human acts. Texts are events and not those quasi-spatial entities: systems or structures. The text is at once that which is nothing if not understood and yet also that which can never be 'completely translated', in the sense of being subordinated to a 'common logic' (*PT*, 106). Complete translation would effect a logical reduction of the text, its de-realization as a text-event, the resolution of all of its elements into a potential metalanguage and their re-realization in another text. Structuralism is the paranoic ideal of 'complete' translation, inasmuch as it takes the text as far as possible towards the extreme pole of language-as-sign-system – the highest hierarchical level of removal from its radical 'eventness' or historicity. Both 'poles', according to Bakhtin, are 'unconditional': there is the logical absolute of the ultimate metalanguage, and there is the ontological absolute of the 'unique and unrepeatable text' (*PT*, 107). All knowledge begins with such singularities; what is distinctive about hermeneutic understanding is simply that it strives to theorize such singularity and thus to remain within and faithful to that realm of the unique for which 'the text' is so potent a figure. All understanding – even *Erklären* if only it knew itself – is dialogical 'to some degree' (*PT*, 111). Even the comprehension of a foreign language that proceeds by rote learning of its rules partakes of the dialogical: between it and the comprehension of a text in a known language there is no absolute boundary. Bakhtin is always at pains to stress the epistemological and methodological 'impurity' of both the human and the natural sciences: the former mix hermeneutics with a certain (of course subordinate) use of causal explanation, while the latter deceive themselves twice over – first, if they believe they do not begin with singular phenomena and, secondly, if they fail to see that their own moves are as much rhetorical as logical. Causal explanation is after all itself a genre of utterance; rhetorically and dialogically speaking it is equivalent to a 'refutation' (*PT*, 123); internally and in terms of content monological, it is none the less externally and formally caught up in the dialogue that constitutes its disciplinary field.

One way of summing all this up is to say that it is 'the text' rather than 'language' which is truly Bakhtin's paradigm; that we cannot understand deeds except as (possible) texts; that the deed and the text are figures for each other – the potential verbal elabora-

tion of the first being only the other side of the potentially performative, active character of the second. Bakhtin associates this latter
characteristic with premodern speech and writing, above all with
'ancient inscriptions' (*PT*, 115). Modern hermeneutic understanding
is for him not so much a response to the misunderstanding which
comes about as the print culture of modernity dissolves the face-
to-face speaking and teaching of the past, and which was its
justification as a discipline at the beginning; it is rather a late-
modern means of bringing to consciousness the effects of that
'entire about-face in the history of the word when it becomes
expression and pure (actionless) information' (*PT*, 115). The
hermeneutics of our time conducts a rearguard action against the
modern reification of meaning in the methodological discourses of
the humanities. It is this collusion of causal-explanatory methodolo-
gies with the neutralized word that is the antagonist in these last
essays – not the traditional genres or 'feudal ideology', as had been
the case in his earlier work. The antagonism is in any case deeply
modified by an insistence on the necessary hybridity of *all* method-
ologies; so perhaps we should rather say that the work of this phase
abolishes the role of the polemical adversary to which so much of
the force of the early and middle writing is to be attributed.

We are not surprised, then, to find that dialogism is now carefully
dissociated from those antagonistic modes – such as parody and
polemic – with which it had before been all but identified. In place
of the almost routine emphasis upon contradiction we have the notion
of a deep consensus no less dialogical than its opposite; indeed the
infinite shadings of 'agreement' are lauded as the least 'crude' and
'externally ... obvious' (*PT*, 121) of dialogical phenomena.
Submission to authority conceived as dialogical concurrence with
the 'authoritative word' takes the place of – without of course
contradicting or invalidating – those earlier denunciations of an
authoritarian monologism. Bakhtin at his most Gadamerian speaks
of 'the mandatory nature of deep meaning' (*PT*, 121). Like Paul
Ricoeur, he seems to be suggesting that a conflictual intersubjectivity exploitable for its possibilities of freedom or critique emerges
only against the ground of a profoundly consensual intersubjectivity experienced as fate. With the categories of the novel and
carnival what was foregrounded was wilful non-communication,
the deliberate misunderstanding of orthodoxy, authority, spirituality, tradition. Dialogism now becomes the key category of a
communicative rationality that does not so much oppose the instrumental reason of our time as benevolently assert its own more

fundamental and prior (in the Kantian sense, transcendental) status. Not only the carnivalesque force of undermining and forgetting, not only laughter and parody, but also the positive work of under-standing, finds its place in what Hans-Georg Gadamer would call the dialogue (*Gespräch*) 'we are'.[5] Where before the almost exclusive emphasis in Bakhtin was on the present of 'unresolved contempo-raneity' militantly pitted against an oppressive past, we now find him invoking the nexus of past and future as the real ground of a present threatened with the reification that ensues when heuristic methodological moves are allowed to develop ontological preten-sions – in short, when 'method' comes to believe that it is 'truth'. When Bakhtin writes of the 'layering of meaning upon meaning, voice upon voice' or of 'departure beyond the limits of the under-stood' (*PT*, 121), he seems in these sublime evocations of the bottomless depth of the word to be seeking – not (to be sure) some metaphysical ground – (but nonetheless) some profound and underlying dialogical rationality in which both the living and the long-dead and the yet-to-be-born all take part. Beyond the excep-tional moment of carnival or the programmatic novelty of the novel there is this substratum of our *Dasein* as beings whose being it is to understand. The Bakhtin who had sought to intervene in the crisis of late European modernity by projecting the *avant-garde* back into the past – reminding the modern project of its repressed insur-gency – now intervenes precisely by refusing to isolate exemplary moments or instances from the historical record. Without quite deserting that project, he no longer sees it as centrally involving the critical overcoming of tradition; instead we are offered a distinc-tively postmodern perspective in which tradition conceived as the infinite chain of voices past and to come (that long temporal distance which Bakhtin regularly correlates with depth of meaning) is the only basis not simply of our freedom but of all value as such, and without which even critique itself would be meaningless. Our freedom lies in grasping our conditions of possibility rather than in any story of perfection or revolution in this world. Bakhtin deci-sively joins those other philosophers of our century who have broken with the nineteenth-century post-Kantian philosophy of history by reinstating a philosophical anthropology.

'The Problem of the Text' ends (more or less) with Bakhtin's new concept of the 'third', or 'superaddressee'. Just as 'those whose voices are heard in the word before the author comes upon it . . . have their rights' (*PT*, 121), so we always posit in our speaking and writing this 'third' by whom we will be heard and absolutely understood. This Habermasian 'ideal speech situation' is not conceived in Bakhtin as realized or realizable some time or somewhere but rather as always implied in every speech situation whatever and wherever: an 'as if' of every interaction, every bit as ineluctable as it is indispensable. Bakhtin is now more concerned to stress this transcendental instance of 'absolutely just and responsive understanding' than to stress the empirical failures of communication. Our being consists not in our presence on hand but in our ability to recollect and anticipate acts of understanding – to hear and be heard in our turn. The working of the superaddressee can perhaps best be illustrated by Bakhtin's remarks on two very special speech situations: the 'dialogue of the dead' and the 'dialogue of the deaf'. These are (respectively) the dialogue of those who are not present to each other in life but none the less come to hear each other in the afterlife; and the dialogue of those who cannot hear each other at all though they are present to each other and both alive. The first of these – 'the imagined situation of a meeting in the hereafter' (*PT*, 124–25) – almost or actually dispenses with the 'third'; in the second the 'third' is the condition of even the most elementary understanding taking place. All non-pathological exchanges in this world lie somewhere between these two extremes, hypothetically presupposing as they do a third party 'in some metaphysical distance or distant historical time' (*PT*, 126) who will absolutely understand the 'whole self' of the author. 'The author', Bakhtin holds, can never turn over his whole self and his speech work to the complete and *final* will of those who are on hand or nearby. If Bakhtin does not wholly play down the near and the contemporary in these essays, he none the less redresses an inadequate emphasis upon distance and depth, and upon the hearing no less than the speaking subject – more especially the subject who hears the echoes of voices coming, temporally and culturally speaking, from afar. Speakers, it is now acknowledged, are also listeners (always already listeners); and we are reminded of Jean-François Lyotard on the theme of justice when Bakhtin writes of the 'rights' of all voices to be heard and identified as equal to the 'rights' of the speaker.[6] Before we speak, we listen, and after speaking we listen again, and so on endlessly.

III

Those who might think that the postmodern Bakhtin offered here forsakes the modern project altogether need look no further than the opening pages of the 'Notes Made in 1970–71' to be disabused; for there we find a ringing celebration of irony as a feature of all European languages since the onset of modernity. Nevertheless there are two points on which this Bakhtin differs from the outright modernist of the middle period. In the Rabelais book irony is a form of sadly 'reduced' or 'muted' laughter; here we notice that what had been a phenomenon of the decline of the carnivalesque in European history now becomes a great historical gain in itself, and more than that: an aspect not only of certain genres and styles but of whole languages and the cultures they carry in suspension. This quintessentially modern discourse of irony – the 'equivocal language of modern times' – is everywhere we read or listen; our modern speech without fixed occasions is also a speech that is always 'with reservations' (*NM70–71*, 132). Even liberated carnival speech had its specific occasions; the modern language of irony is not denounced for its faint echo of the belly laugh but rather celebrated for its ubiquity, its everydayness, its universal opening up of our freedom. We breathe a linguistic atmosphere that has already been freed for us; we are at home in a language of emancipation. Bakhtin clearly subscribes to a view of language which sees it as subject not just to neutral or arbitrary change but as being in some sense tendentially 'progressive', fraught with implicit value and pre-understanding. Neutral only in so far as they are systems of signs, the European languages have 'precipitated' within their very 'syntactic and lexico-semantic structure[s]' (*NM70–71*, 133) a story of freedom from authority. Irony has historically helped to rid us of the authoritarian word – not to be confused with the authoritative word, which carries authority only insofar as it is 'internally persuasive' (to use a phrase from 'Discourse in the Novel'). Bakhtin effectively deconstructs the modern opposition between reason and authority, at once internalizing and moving beyond the Romantic critique of the enlightenment, along with Gadamer and other twentieth-century hermeneutic thinkers. The second point to be made about this case for the emancipatory force of ironic discourse is that to have broken with this modernist narrative of linguistic freedom – to have 'overcome' it critically or dialectically – would only be to rehearse a typically modernist reflex. The argument for a late postmodern Bakhtin is precisely strengthened by the evidence he here gives of the will to *include* the phases both of his own earlier thought and of earlier European history. Juxtaposing them in this way gives a certain dialogical character to the very form of his meditations – refuses the language of sublation, transformation, supersession. Irony and the authoritative word coexist as peacefully in the postmodern condition as they do in Bakhtin's reflections upon them.

It is, then, not surprising that these reflections are followed straightaway by a brief consideration of *silence*. Raising language to ontological status, as Bakhtin here does, seems almost inescapably to entail imaging its absence. As creatures whose being is language, it behoves us to think through the meaning of the empirical absence of speech. If my transcendental and situational at-homeness in language is not incompatible with the contingent stopping of speech, that is because silence is not simply the lack or failure of speech but is rather what can positively begin when speaking stops. Silence is not the negation of language but its greatest and most wholly human potential: my being (in a Heideggerian phrase) is a being-towards-silence. Silence makes us aware that what founds our humanity is not a ground: it is the ever-shifting boundary between speech and its cessation. Our at-homeness in language is therefore not to be conceived empirically. In contrasting (what the translator renders as) 'quietude' and silence, Bakhtin invokes and adapts the Diltheyan opposition between *Erklären* and *Verstehen*. Quietude can be (causally) explained; silence, being not a condition but an experience, can only be (hermeneutically) understood. In the case of quietude there is nothing that can be heard by anybody who might be listening; we have a mere physical absence of sound in which no listener need be presupposed. The case of silence, however, may be rendered thus: *I do not hear the voice of another*. That is to say: the listening subject must needs be reckoned into the equation. The elaborating subtext of quietude is a sentence in the passive voice (*Nothing was heard*); the subtext of silence is a sentence in the active voice. In these thoughts on silence Bakhtin re-inflects Diltheyan terms in the context not of consciousness (which is where Dilthey himself was) but of the paradigm of language. The inter-subjectivity in which our being consists is language conceived as a chain of speech whose constitutive outside is silence. Language and silence are not so much opposites as forms of – potentials within – each other. Or again: language when it passes into silence is only turned inside out, and as such retains its human shape and consti-tution. The 'logosphere' which is our home is the endless and forever open-ended alternation and interpenetration of silence and 'intelligible sound' (*NM70–71*, 134).

What, then, does Bakhtin mean by going on to describe irony as a 'form of silence' (*NM70–71*, 134)? I can only think he means that a culture of the serious and single tone fixes subjects in positions, cannot imagine an other than itself, must always be verbally proclaiming itself. Irony is a mode of speaking-by-implication whose extreme instance and perhaps most powerful manifestation is saying everything by saying nothing in the empirical sense of speaking audibly for another to hear: in short, speech with such radical 'reservations' that it reserves its right not to manifest itself at all (exemplarily, Jesus before Pontius Pilate). Silence is then the ultimate 'loophole'; speech with reservations so absolute that it reserves itself altogether; the ultimate measure of one who wants to ensure that the last word is never spoken. Bakhtin is suggesting that there may be situations in which to refuse a culture of the last word I must refrain from speaking at all and all articulation must be renounced. Silence is, after all, *all* implication: it is nothing more or less than the absolute rule of implication, and therefore demands that acutest variety of hearing (listening for intelligibility) called *understanding*. Just because it does not activate physiological hearing it brings the deep-semantic or spiritual hearing of understanding into full working and self-awareness. Irony is a form of silence because silence is the transcendental irony of language itself, the world of pure implication that is in constant constitutive tension with its own dense intersubjectivity.

Nowhere is Bakhtin's refusal of the metanarratives of any (Hegelian or Marxist) philosophy of history clearer – nowhere is his alternative of a philosophical anthropology better spelled out – than in his story of 'the witness and the judge' (*NM70–71*, 137). This character (they are not two but one) is not in any sense modern like 'the writer' but hails from the very dawn of consciousness itself. With the appearance anywhere upon the global scene of the witness and the judge, the whole event of Being changes utterly. This is emphatically not the story of being as a higher subject coming to consciousness in Man: like Jürgen Habermas, Bakhtin rejects that solution to modernity's problem of self-grounding which gives primacy to the 'higher' subjectivity of Absolute Spirit, the solitary subject–object of both Nature and History.[7] The whole of Being alters with its very first and most narrowly local acknowledgement, inasmuch as everything else then becomes the unacknowledged. Being is not presence or presence-to-itself; it is that which is forever passing over the border from the uncognized to the cognized. The 'supra-existence' or being-to-the-second-power that is consciousness makes an absolutely new event of being. The tacit polemic with Marxism comes out most evidently in Bakhtin's claim that the 'absolute freedom' of the 'supra-I' is its 'creativity' and that this contrasts with our merely 'relative freedom' to change existence materially (*NM70–71*, 137). Its creative knowing is not and can never be a 'material force' – and not because it is weak but because it has the real (the truly human) power of changing the whole sense of things. Which is to say: the most radical revolution of all is semantic, and it has always already happened. The other side of the misunderstanding of the work of meaning in our constitution is the modern fetishization of material force, the false worship of our very much less than absolute freedom to change existence in itself. For Bakhtin, as for Habermas, both classical 'historical materialism' and Hegelian idealism solve modernity's problem of self-grounding only too well.

Bakhtin returns in the notes of 1970–71 to the issue of epistemological 'impurity', and – in a move that is of a piece with the general leavening of antagonism by consensus in these late writings – insists that reified 'relations among objects' and personified 'relations among subjects' form a continuum of mutual transformation rather than a sharp polarity. We are better able to understand and exercise our 'real freedom' if we realize the 'transitions and combinations' of these relations and actually practise or encounter 'death-dealing analysis' (*NM70–71*, 138–39). In other words, the methodological hybridity of our thinking has a positive and even emancipatory ethico-political charge within the conditions of our late modernity. The *Geisteswissenschaften* constitute an area in which it is 'hardly possible to think about necessity'; but the self-consciousness of this realm of freedom – of '*possibilities* and the *realization* of one of them' (*NM70–71*, 139) – only comes about thanks to a constant thinking and making of the difference between this realm and that other (nomothetic) world of causal determination and necessity. The late-modern sciences of the spirit can only become the active custodians of our freedom if they free themselves from the Eurocentric 'miniature world' of the nineteenth century and boldly claim for themselves that whole world of texts (and potential texts, or acts) which is 'as boundless as the universe' and 'as bottomless as the depths of matter' (*NM70–71*, 140). The epistemological sublime that has been usurped by the sciences of matter and nature must be (re)claimed by the knowledge that takes as its field the infinite depths of meaning.

Bakhtin would seem to be calling for the *Geisteswissenschaften* to modernize themselves, though not in the direction of letting the natural sciences impose their model of objectivity. They must, as it were, catch up with the latter – not by resorting to their methods, but by keeping their difference from each other forever in view, and by claiming for their own special (semantic) dimension the depth and scope of the physical world opened up by the natural sciences. Now this is a paradoxical modernization inasmuch as it commits Bakhtin to a deeper and deeper archaization of thought, a further and further reaching-back to the premodern, a listening to and for the oldest voices, and a reconstruction of the universal conditions of the possibility of our understanding and being-in-the-world. Modernity having brought in its train the mixed legacy of irony and reification, it is no answer simply to revalorize myth over reason: cultures of myth are legitimately and happily closed, deaf to what is outside their bounds; for modern cultures to try to reinvent myth is (as Lyotard has argued) to produce the monster of a monopolistic narrative with global pretensions, a particularism that becomes terroristic because it thinks universally.[8] Fascism is of course the major empirical instance of this sociopolitical teratology. The problem for radical critics of modernity like Bakhtin is, then, that of so redescribing the personalistic universe of myth that it poses no such threat, and that its naivety does not become the basis for an oppressive totalization. In a move that recalls Theodor Adorno and Max Horkheimer in *Dialectic of Enlightenment*, the myth of reason is to be dissolved by unfolding the reason of myth. The interest of emancipation is to be served by bringing communicative and instrumental orders of rationality into dialogue with each other. For this to happen the human sciences must somewhat distance themselves from the *avant-gardist* ethos that proclaims the shock of the new; instead it is their task to confront a self-satisfied modernity with the revelation of the old and the not-yet-born, the past in the yet-to-be and the yet-to-be in the past. The hermeneutics that Bakhtin proposes as the appropriate methodology of the human sciences is assured of being a critical hermeneutics insofar as its deep-semantic knowledge of time is in constant dialogue with the other knowledges of our epoch: that is to say, in so far as it is the complex and inwardly distantiated self-consciousness of a heterogeneous spectrum of (non-violently) coexisting rationalities.

'To understand a given text as the author himself understood it. But our understanding can and should be better' (*NM70–71*, 141). Bakhtin in these words appears to be half-quoting the best-known dictum of Friedrich Schleiermacher, the founder of modern hermeneutics. But then we find him immediately rethinking this maxim in a way that signals his break with this Romantic paradigm and with the whole method that sought to understand under-standing as the marriage of empathy and paraphrase, 'divination' and 'translation'. Reactivating his early work on other–self rela-tions, he reconceives understanding (along lines uncannily close to those of Gadamer and Ricoeur) not as the 'loss' of one's unique position in absolute identification with the other but precisely as the full use of one's 'outsideness', one's spatial and/or temporal and/or cultural exotopy with regard to the other (text). Distance is not to be overcome, but rather to be maximally put to use, as the very condition of 'creative understanding'. Understanding is 'co-creation', the multiplication of meaning thanks to outsideness, which – and again we are reminded particularly of Ricoeur – trans-forms the one who understands. Understanding is quite literally a 'meeting' that places an obligation upon the understanding subject, and the 'highest moment' of such deeply committing under-standing is the meeting with 'a great human being' (*NM70–71*, 142). In understanding, recognition and discovery, apprehension of the known and apprehension of the new are inseparably united. The human sciences will work our salvation by bringing to conscious-ness the 'primary fact[s]' of consciousness itself in a study of the everyday miracle of understanding.

Among such primary realities are the 'complex interrelations' between the small world of my own words and the 'immense, boundless world of others' words' (*NM70–71*, 143) into which I come and which will be there after I am gone: a reality which is not only not conceived but positively obscured by the study of culture, which rarefies and effaces the struggle that takes place between these two verbal worlds of the 'mine' and the 'yours' in the construction of 'objectivity'. 'Objectivity' arises on the ruins of the *I* and the *thou*. Abstraction is not the value-free, ethically neutral act of resolving already lifeless particulars into still more ethereal generalities; it is quite specifically 'abstraction from the *I* and the *thou*'; it is 'life as the object of thought' (*NM70–71*, 143–44). Life cannot become the object of thought without the prior move of turning the intersubjective nexus of first and second persons into the 'position of the third party' (*NM70–71*, 143). Bakhtin's point is that abstract thought by definition unfits itself for conceiving that on the destruction or rarefaction of which it has itself been consti-tuted; that it cannot make a theme of that which it implicitly posits itself against in its very form and constitution. Hermeneutic under-standing by contrast is the self-consciousness of 'the most vital, experienced life': the unmerged *I* and *thou* and *he* will be brought to light only by sciences of the spirit which conceive their own method as the unmerged and unmerging interaction of an *I* and a *thou*, of two 'spirits', the person who understands on the one hand and the understood on the other.

What is understood is, of course, *meaning*; and Bakhtin at this point proffers a definition of (*a*) meaning in negative terms when he writes: 'anything that does not answer a question is devoid of sense for us' (*NM70–71*, 145). We might develop this by saying that the meaning of a text is then to be found on the boundary between the question it answers in its context and the question it in turn asks of me in mine. (*A*) meaning is the living precipitate of an act of understanding – living in so far as it always demands of me another act of intersubjective understanding. The answer to a question which always asks or provokes another one: *that* is a meaning. In reconstructing the question to which a text is *an* (not *the*) answer I cannot but at the same time frame the question it asks of me and prepare an answer accordingly. This answer may not be articulated – may not be a text, but instead those potential texts which are my later deeds. This is what Bakhtin calls 'contextual meaning': meaning that is responsive, universal, omni-temporal. Contextual meaning is 'truly' universal; formal definition, the product of 'abstract thought', is universal only, as it were, in theory, only 'potential meaning' (*NM70–71*, 145). In abstract thought, context carries a connotation of the particular, the less than universal. The universality of contextual meaning is therefore a case of paradoxical hyperbole from the standpoint of such thinking; even a *contradictio in adjecto*. From Bakhtin's point of view it is the claim of abstract thought to be universal that is paradoxical, inasmuch as that order of thought is the product of a particular history and of a determinate mental operation. It is itself the result of an act in a certain historical European context which hubristically elevates its own claim to universality over that of the world of contextual meaning, a world which it at once historically springs from and thematically represses. All of our time and all of our space is filled with contextual meaning. Hermeneutic understanding has privileged access to life as it is intersubjectively lived; it does not seek to supplant abstract thought; by rendering reflexive that meeting of contextual meanings by which we all truly understand, it can tell the story of abstract thought that that thought itself is constitutively unable to tell. Pragmatically, it can help us to put abstract thought in its place: determine where such thinking is appropriate and where not. Before we even begin to think of our world as 'objective' we must remember that we already live in, and are occupied by, an ever-lasting agonistics of contextual meaning that is everywhere in our reality.

We have seen how the notes of 1970–71 began by giving a new face to irony, positively revaluing it as the ubiquitous modern language of freedom rather than as a sort of etiolated remnant of carnival. Near the end of the same text we find Bakhtin giving a new face to the novel, in a structurally similar move. Thirty years earlier he had presented the novel as the genre of contemporaneity *par excellence, the* modern narrative, defined by its difference from the ancient narrative form of epic, which is wedded to the 'absolute past'. Now the operative opposition is between the polyphonic novel (not mentioned since 1929) and what we might call the genre of absolute contemporaneity: journalism. This modern counterpart of ancient rhetoric is the genre of now-as-the-time-of-resolution. Like the law – and is Bakhtin also perhaps thinking of politics here? – journalism assigns guilt and innocence absolutely, and its subjects are 'third part[ies]' (*NM70–71*, 150). It is dominated by a logic of winning and losing and by a kind of dialogue that can be resolved and ended. Bakhtin seems to imply that, unlike true contextual meaning – that greatest of all powers in the world which nevertheless cannot change 'existence itself' – the discourse of jour-nalism is a case of language seeking to approach the condition of an 'empirical force', an instrumentalized language that can be 'trans-lated into action' (*NM70–71*, 152) almost immediately. Journalism is the sort of (relatively) impoverished meaning that can become a material force; the corollary of its relative weakness as meaning is its relative strength as the discursive accompaniment or impulse to material intervention in reality. This discourse of either/or, of winners and losers, of subjects that are categories of persons rather than 'personalities', 'acting agents' (*NM70–71*, 152) rather than hero-ideologues, is also (surely) in some sense the discourse of parties – of *the* Party. However that may be, what is certain is that the polyphonic novel is the form that is at the furthest remove from the discourse of 'small time', with its 'issues that have been resolved within the epoch' (*NM70–71*, 151). Where before Bakhtin had encoded a modernist stance in offering the novel as the genre of modernity, he now openly proclaims the Dostoevskian prototype of modernist fiction as the genre of omni-temporality. Polyphony opens us to a semantic eternity in so far as it resolves the immediate struggles of all epochs into the forever irresolvable 'dialogue on ultimate questions (in the framework of great time)' (*NM70–71*,

151). Like the church in Orthodox theology, its heroes speak and act and think 'before heaven and earth' (*NM70–71*, 152), compelling the intimate and immediate into the ultimate. We can now see the truth of Tzvetan Todorov's observation that in Bakhtin 'Dostoevsky has ceased standing as the object of study' and has 'pass[ed] to the side of the subject'.[9] That is to say, there is an analogy between hermeneutic philosophy and polyphonic poetics: Bakhtin finds in Dostoevsky's fiction a model of the infinite reach of understanding outside fiction, in life. As Dostoevsky does with his heroes, so must we go to work with cultural texts and their meanings; we must become readers (in the widest sense) after the fashion in which he was a writer. Dostoevsky's poetics of fiction is trans-rhetorical in exactly the way that the hermeneutics here espoused by Bakhtin is translinguistic: in both cases the discourse is 'beyond' in the sense of 'outside', a metalanguage but without the (mono)logical implications usually carried by that term. Dostoevsky's (proto-)modernist aesthetic is given a postmodern re-inflection as the model for a critical knowledge of and in late modernity. His nexus of ultimacy and intimacy offers us a paradigm of a sort of politics of the spirit that Bakhtin wishes to launch into the world as the 'consummating' outside of a politics that resolves issues summarily and in the short term – rather in the way that Justice should ideally both embrace and inform the practice of Law. Ethics for Bakhtin is just such a spiritual politics, a realm of deeply obligating imperatives that can never be assimilated to the realm of state decrees and formal legality that it always and everywhere lovingly-critically shadows.

IV

Bakhtin's last reflections in 'Towards a Methodology for the Human Sciences' begin with the word *understanding*, capitalized, and like a single note or chord struck at the start of a piece of music. Understanding is a complex, composite act whose phases – component acts, as it were – have their 'semantic independence', even as they merge in the whole 'empirical act' itself (*MHS*, 159). These phases are: perception; recognition; understanding 'significance' in the 'given context'; and, finally, 'inclusion in the dialogical context' (*MHS*, 159). Only the last of these is in a proper sense actively evaluative, extending beyond the immediate context to deep-universal meanings in the dimension of great time. Now it is here that we find yet another of those striking revaluations of earlier categories that I have twice remarked upon, and this time the category to be re-inflected or rehabilitated (this was after all a moment of many 'rehabilitations' in the then Soviet Union) is the *symbol*. In 'Discourse in the Novel' the symbol had been assimilated to the poetic trope, and it had been construed as the monological correlative of the (dialogized) 'prosaic' symbol (*DN*, 327–29). The symbol was then single-voiced in so far as it rested upon a logical relation of contiguity or similarity, was self-identical and was always adequate to its referential object. Here, by contrast, the symbol becomes the valorized term of a new pair, and its other is now the 'image'. As the word which connotes the world, the symbol is now counterposed to the verbal trope with a limited reference. Indeed 'the image' now seems to be much the same entity as was earlier meant by the (undialogized, unprosaicized) symbol. An image can be made into or understood as a symbol by activating in it the potential infinity of contextual meaning. Correlated with 'world-wide wholeness', and resolving the particular into the primordial, the symbol produces in me 'an awareness that [I] do not coincide with [my] own individual meaning' (*MHS*, 159). In other words, it is the aesthetic resolution of the ethical 'I-for-myself' into 'I-for-another/another-for-me'. The understanding of the symbol is itself symbolic, an instance of 'somewhat rationalized' symbolicity tending towards – without ever reaching – conceptuality: 'there can be *relative* rationalization of the contextual meaning (ordinary scientific analysis) or a deepening with the help of other meanings … through expansion of the remote context' (*MHS*, 160). The symbol is understood only by opening an 'infinity of symbolic contextual meanings'; the image, whilst it *can* be submitted to this kind of understanding, does not demand more than the unfolding of 'significance in the given context' (*MHS*, 160). In the symbol we have that which imperatively calls upon us to effect an unfolding of the remotest contexts; the discursive phenomenon which, more than any other, brings all conceptual analysis up against its limits. With the symbol the hermeneutic circle is stretched to its widest reach before the return to the text is made: it is the textual part which invokes the most extensive contextual whole, the most extensive semantic opening out through time–space.

It does not of course follow that a word with the temporal reach of the symbolic is an ancient phenomenon, a survival: it is as modern as the polyphonic novel. Bakhtin's periodization of the history of meaning moves from an epoch of 'naive mythical personification' through the 'epoch of reification of nature and man' – presumably the mid-life of modernity in the eighteenth and nineteenth centuries – and on to our own time, which he characterizes as that of 'personification of nature and man, but without loss of reification' (*MHS*, 169). The symbol is a feature of this last phase of late modernity, which has seen the rise of philosophies which repersonify 'nature and man' not naively but self-consciously, reflexively, in conscious resistance to high-modern reification, taking this stance in some cases all the way to a total critique of reason of the kind that has prompted Habermas (for example) to relaunch the project of reason under late-modern conditions.[10] This reflexively personifying thought which takes as its field the radically interpersonal nature of our being-in-the-world is Bakhtin's alternative within modernity to the purposive rationality that holds sway over modern life. Its equivalent to the orthodox conceptuality of modern reason is, one presumes, the 'relatively rationalized' (meta)language of symbol: in short, something like the discourse of Bakhtin himself in these late fragments. The universalism of this language is achieved without reification or abstraction, and it is also more encompassing than the universalism of laughter which Bakhtin had championed in his middle period. It is 'not hostile to the mythic, and frequently utilizes its language (transformation into the language of symbols)' (*MHS*, 169). That is to say, it does not share the prejudice of enlightenment reason against myth; on the contrary, it puts myth to use in a way which is appropriate to a late-modern critique of reason that wishes to avoid the 'self-destruction' of reason described by Adorno and Horkheimer. The symbol, along with its quasi-symbolic interpretants (to use a Peircean term), is the most potent signifier of a late-modern discourse which is critical of the concept and yet knows it cannot return to the spontaneous personification and ritual performativity of the premodern.

In all these reflections there is a strong undercurrent of self-reflection; indeed it would seem that the subtextual act of understanding going on in these thoughts on understanding is the effort of the old and dying Bakhtin to understand his own ideas, to make deep sense of his whole career as a thinker and thereby to fashion a philosophy for our postmodernity. For Bakhtin, as for Habermas, the 'place of philosophy' (*MHS*, 161) is on the boundary between exact science and hermeneutic understanding, as the metalanguage of all knowledges. If, then, Bakhtin is plainly no 'postmodernist' in the Lyotardian mould – that view of philosophy hardly characterizes a thinker who doubts the commensurability of language games and is suspicious of all 'meta-'claims – he is certainly in a broad sense postmodern first and last. We might even see his modernist middle period as a digression, an interlude between two phases which reconnect beyond its end, without the last being either a simple or 'dialectical' return to the first. The populist aesthetico-political modernism of the 1930s and early 1940s takes its place within the longer temporality of his whole thinking life. Bakhtin now seeks to situate the phases of his thinking in relation to each other and to situate that thinking as a whole in relation to the context(s) of its inception and reception. The remarks he makes on Dilthey and Hegel as *both* of them monological thinkers signal this reflexive self-consciousness that now comes to characterize his thought. Dilthey's post-Hegelian move fails to establish a properly dialogical order of thinking: narrowly psychological and epistemological, Dilthey's hermeneutic is predicated upon a philosophy of consciousness which eschews Absolute Spirit only to install an equally single-voiced *Einfühlung*. The turn from objective Spirit to psychology as the ground both of understanding and action merely supplants one philosophical monologism with another. The diachronically inflected metaphysics called dialectics, in which philosophy is the sublation of all earlier expressions of Spirit, was not challenged by a revival of empathetic Romantic hermeneutics which extends the definition of 'text' to the events of history. *Einfühlung*, in short, is no challenge to *Aufhebung*. Thought is nothing if not worldly for Bakhtin, in the sense that at its highest and deepest it is both *in* and *about* the world. Thought is a special kind of event in the world because at its fullest stretch it embraces that greatest of all events which *is* the world. In the hermeneutically inspired fundamental ontology Bakhtin is here exploring (for the last time), thought is nothing less than the self-awareness of the multifarious 'eventness' of everything. Or again: there is a great intersubjective project that we call 'the world', and thought is the reflection of this project upon itself which deeply respects and faithfully preserves the open-ended heterogeneity of being.

Occupying his boundary position as a philosopher between the precise and the human sciences, Bakhtin accordingly rethinks the objects of these knowledges – the 'thing' and the 'personality', respectively – not as substances but rather as extremes of a continuum between which all thought oscillates asymptotically. That contact between texts in which alone texts live and are understood is at bottom a 'contact of personalities and not of things (at the extreme)' (*MHS*, 162). Yet Bakhtin also insists – and that last parenthesis begins the suggestion – that thing and personality are hypothetical limiting cases which are never actually encountered in their pure state: there is simply thinking that is tendentially reificatory and thinking that is tendentially personificatory. Reification and personification are not absolute conditions after all, but tendencies subject to mutual modification: in short, relative states. The language of causality and 'material conditions' realizes and absolutizes things: unmodified by the language of interacting texts (personalities), it monopolizes understanding. Bakhtin is seeking a philosophical narrative which neither heroizes the personality nor demonizes the thing, but rather sees both as effects of the way I speak about what is not myself, effects which realize extreme possibilities of speech but which are never fully 'effective'. Bakhtin's old friends *tone* and *intonation* put in a last appearance in this context. The tone of performative utterances can find its way into speech or writing that is not technically performative; the intonation of words that take speech as close as it ever gets to action (words that, in Austin's phrase, 'do things') can take leave of its typical content and inform any aspect of speech. All our understanding is informed by an underlying 'tonality' of consciousness, a quasi-semantic context of inexplicit evaluation on the ground of which 'complete, semantic understanding' arises (*MHS*, 164). Within this accompanying music of cognition are tones that reify, tones that personify. To affect a personality a thing must already have become a (potential) word, a contextual meaning. Aesthetic activity at its strongest is exemplary, inasmuch as it is the one human function that makes it its business to assimilate the world of things to the world of personalities.

And so we come at last to Bakhtin's closing meditation upon great time. An important stage in the train of thought is the reflection on 'form' and 'content' in his last notes – and in particular on the more or less smooth and automatic issue of form into content in premodern times. Form is conceived as generic pre-understanding or 'congealed' content which always precedes the initiative of those who put it to use; it is also seen as an 'implicit context' that does not need to be spelled out because it is assumed in the very implementation of the form. Bakhtin associates form in this sense of tradition with 'general collective creativity' and 'mythological systems' (*MHS*, 166). The cultural texts of post-traditional societies effectively turn this situation inside out, in that the work now thinks of itself as new and does not so much presuppose tradition as challenge me to create the tradition from which its novelty might be supposed to have sprung. Hermeneutic interpretation only becomes at once necessary and possible when innovation has to be deconstructed in what is simultaneously a *re*construction of tradition: the 'before' or 'already' that the work might have acknowledged is brought to light in order that its 'after' or 'not yet' – its reception by a collectivity in principle without bounds – might be realized. Symbols are an instance for Bakhtin of this modern 'form': at one and the same time the 'most stable' and the 'most emotional elements' of discourse (*MHS*, 166), they proclaim within the condition of modernity a universality which is non-conceptual. In order for this non-conceptual universalism to be apprehended, I must move beyond the mere 'recognition' of meaning at the level of the text's iterable technicalities (and their corollary: the anonymous and uncontextualized 'individual consciousness') to attain to – or rather activate – that deep-semantic understanding which is essentially 'evaluative'. The symbol calls forth this understanding beyond 'definition', and is nothing without it. When Bakhtin writes that the work's 'evaluative-semantic aspect' is 'meaningful only to individuals who are related by some common conditions of life . . . by the bonds of brotherhood on a high level' (*MHS*, 166), we are strongly reminded both of the Kantian notion of the aesthetic as founded upon community and of the Wittgensteinian notion of the relation between meaning and 'forms of life'.

Perhaps, then, the difference between 'myth' and 'symbol' in Bakhtin's (late) sense of those terms is that the 'common conditions' that are taken for granted in the texts of the first have to be explicitly posited in the texts of the second. 'Assimilation' to a 'higher . . . at the extreme absolute value' (*MHS*, 166) is the modern surrogate for the implicit pre-understanding and pre-evaluation of premodernity. 'Deep' understanding in our epoch presupposes the transformation of what had been given into a project, the formation of a past which is paradoxically also a future. The category of the aesthetic is the offshoot of an eighteenth-century move in which posited community filled the space vacated by the departure of given community, while at the same time containing any emancipatory ethico-political implications by conceiving the aesthetic as a separate faculty of the same subject that carried the dominant (paradigmatically logical or mathematical) rationality. The Romantic moment saw the partial liberation of the aesthetic as it was freed into an autonomy over against the rational – an autonomy which in the end only reproduced the enlightenment structure of oppositions it had sought to invest with opposite values. Turning the binaries of reason on their heads left them much as they had always been, resulting not in a critique of the modern project but in its gaining a new lease of life, and thereby opening the space for those revivals of its promises that bear the names of Hegel and Marx. Bakhtin represents a twentieth-century hermeneutic or philosophical-anthropological move which revives in a radical way the move that inaugurated the aesthetic as a category, without either keeping it from challenging the dominant conceptuality; or posing it as an anti-conceptuality; or (finally) sweeping it up as a moment in the totalizing conceptuality of the dialectic. With his help we are able to think an agonistics of deep meaning which challenges the dominant conceptuality on ground which is other than of the latter's choosing, and which is not to be superseded by 'philosophy' in the grand march of the Concept in history. The deep 'form' character-istic of modernity is the 'tradition' of post-traditional societies, and it is what we must (re)turn to if we wish to argue that the loss of 'given' community does not have to be made good by the abstract universality of the unsituated thinking subject. Community comes to take up its residence in language conceived neither as a tool nor as a system, but as our only home.

Great time cannot be properly elucidated without, finally, probing further Bakhtin's crucial distinction between 'the work' and 'the text'. The work is the text as performed (read) or poten-tially performed (read); it is what we have when the text is enabled at least partially to realize the far larger and potentially infinite context in which it resonates. Commenting on the notion of 'kin' in one of his earliest essays, Bakhtin writes that we ought to say not 'They are mine' but rather 'I am theirs' (*AH*, 178): his translinguistic project is analogously a hermeneutic which concerns itself not so much with this text's context as with this context's text(s). Most profoundly, this 'extratextual' context is not only not one of inert things – that much we have already seen – it is also not one of words in any lexico-semantic or purely linguistic sense: it is a context of *tones*. It is the never-fully-realized 'intonational-evalua-tive context' against which the text is perceived, in which alone it lives as a *work*. The text is an analytic abstraction from the work conceived as the object of that deep understanding for which the text cannot ever be other than the work, and can only ever be heard over the 'background' from which it emerges. 'The work', Bakhtin writes, 'is enveloped in the music of the intonational-evaluative context in which it is understood and evaluated' (*MHS*, 166). Understanding is, then, listening for context: context conceived as the music of the spheres of meaning, the resonance within which the work is individuated and resonates in its turn. Great time is not an objective state of things; it is a level of understanding in which the remotest of contexts meet and make mutual sense. It is nothing less than outsideness launched into history. It is the temporal dimension of 'I-for-another' and 'the-other-for-me', while 'small time' is the equivalent of 'I-for-myself', the easily memorable past and the merely 'imaginable' future of fear and hope. The cultural text read in the dimension of great time is understood prophetically: that is, as a moment in a process which I use my outsideness to apprehend, but which at the same time I can only apprehend if I also enter imaginatively the realm of its outsideness in respect of me. At the last boundary of his life, going out of the phenomenal world, Bakhtin contemplates 'the future without me' (*MHS*, 167). Understanding in the aspect of great time, I learn to turn my temporal and cultural outsideness inside-out; I learn to transcend in terms of time the category of 'I-for-myself'; I enter the sphere of 'evaluative non-predetermination, unexpectedness ... absolute innovation, miracle' (*MHS*, 167). The new in this deep-semantic sense is of the order of grace: the future neither hoped for nor feared but in which our completion as finite beings lies. We must live in the present recalling at every moment that we are positioned where the anticipation of the past and the memory of the future intersect. Modernist notions of amnesiac novelty have no appeal for the dying Bakhtin; not because he takes an anti-modernist stance but because late modernity both needs and makes available a new sense of the miraculous. The event that nobody living in the category of 'I-for-myself' and 'small time' could have expected is the event that only the community of others-for-others could most deeply understand. We are 'in' great time in so far as texts are for us not mere iterable entities but provisional climaxes in the unceasing music of contexts speaking to each other against all the material odds and across the deepest of empirical divides.

7

PHILOSOPHY AND
THEOLOGY

> Philosophy wanted to be connected with 'contempo-
> rary life', but strictly speaking it should precisely *not*
> be closely linked to "contemporary life', for only then
> can it give 'life' perspective ... Philosophy begins
> where contemporary life ends.[1]
> The novel comes into contact with the spontaneity
> of the inconclusive present; this is what keeps the
> genre from congealing. The novelist is drawn toward
> everything which is not yet completed.
>
> *(EN, 27)*

The first of these two epigraphs is an amalgam of statements made
by Bakhtin in interviews in the last years of his life; the second
comes from 'Epic and Novel', written some thirty years earlier.
Since Bakhtin saw himself as a philosopher, and since he is a known
champion of the novel genre, both propositions carry an implication and intonation which are positive. The first suggests that
philosophy is a discourse which only gives 'life' perspective in so
far as it is distanced from contemporaneity; the novel's thriving
precisely and especially in an element of contemporaneity is the
clear import of the second. Do they therefore contradict each other?
Did Bakhtin change his mind? The short answer to both of these
questions is 'No'; the long answer would be an unfolding of the
dialogical relations these utterances set up simply by being laid
alongside each other. This chapter is a version of that longer answer.

To resolve the issue of how these two categories that are so
strongly affirmed for opposite reasons relate to each other – to reach
the space where their incompatibility emerges as merely apparent –
we could do worse than look at the negotiations of two other categories in one of Bakhtin's earliest writings. Aesthetics is the sector

of philosophy to which Bakhtin was increasingly drawn, and which he went on so thoroughly to historicize that he almost drove it out of philosophy altogether, turning it instead into a sociology of modern culture fronted methodologically by a 'translinguistics' whose privileged object is novelistic prose. Theology is the premodern forerunner of philosophy from which Bakhtin's early aesthetics derives many of its terms. It seems that at this phase a theologically inflected aesthetics – or an aesthetically inflected theology – was for him the only sure means of access and fidelity to that fundamental ethical reality of answerability which is the ground and condition of our whole being-in-the-world. The book-length study entitled 'Author and Hero in Aesthetic Activity' is the place where, uniquely, as never before or later, we see vividly at work this co-inflection of dimensions.

I

I take this work of the early 1920s to be one among many such interventions in that period to make a virtue out of the lateness of Russia's social transformation. If the atheistic and socialist intelligentsia who came to dominate politically after the revolution followed a strategy of aggressive modernization, breaking with the past, catching up with or overtaking the West, there were other intellectuals – among them Bakhtin – for whom the realization elsewhere of possible futures for their country's developmentally belated polity and economy gave its culture a compensatory perspectival advantage over cultures whose polities and economies had modernized 'on time'. Bakhtin's work shows that the desire to fashion an appropriate modernity for Russia by critically activating its 'outsideness' to the West was not simply the knee-jerk reflex of chauvinistic anti-secularists, but rather represented (at least in his case) a real wish to avoid the social and spiritual pathologies of rationalization and instrumentalization that the modern project had spawned in other places.[2]

In 'Author and Hero', then, Bakhtin seeks to free aesthetics from its subordination to epistemology in Western philosophy, drawing to its pole all those impulses of community and intersubjectivity which modern thought had effectively driven into the exile of theology and a specialized spiritual experience. In the aesthetic he finds a modern category which none the less welcomes the lost or sidelined modes and knowledges of other times. The reminder that the other is my lovingly consummating author and I in turn his or hers – that I can never be 'the hero of my own life' (*AH*, 112) – is a reproach to modernity's hubristic claim to self-grounding, its exciting though perverse fiction of the hero as self-authoring. When direct philosophizing became dangerous, Bakhtin turned from a modern category of thought to *the* literary genre of modernity: that is to say, the novel, and first of all the proto-modernist 'polyphonic' novel of Dostoevsky. On the face of it this seems a turnabout: the quasi-authorial autonomy he claims for Dostoevsky's characters is surely just that fiction of self-authoring he had earlier implicitly denounced? But this is not the case: secularity denies or brackets out the Author, reserving Him for last instances and first beginnings, and finally doing away with Him altogether. Bakhtin's conception of novelistic discourse working at full stretch strongly posits the author and thinks of human freedom as nothing if not grounded in a potentially infinite dialogue with the latter. Pushing the freedom of the hero to its limit, we find ourselves back at the authority of the author; life is the difficult and endless passage of one into the other; any other (supposedly unauthored, uncreated) freedom is illusory.[3]

And so it is that we find Bakhtin later in the decade entering with gusto into the spirit of modern writing and finding there not faith cancelled in doubt or spiralling relativism but faith eternally problematized. The obverse of the better-known Bakhtin who celebrates the novelization of the high genres and the carnivalization of the sacred is the Bakhtin who in effect sacralizes the novel, who makes of it a talisman we may wear against the idolatrous temptations of our late-modern world. The objects of modern irony and parody are not the holy or otherworldly as such, but their worldly simulacra. Bakhtin wishes us to see that challenges to representation within representation do not threaten what is beyond representation. On the contrary: they reinforce its claim upon our attention; the grotesque in art does not work against the sublime any more than incarnation works against transcendence. It is in this sense that the novel is our gospel, and (like the Gospels themselves) it offers at every turn a direct route from the everyday into the most elevated. Every character, thanks to the orchestration of dialogism, can be a 'personality', every voice (as he was to put it later) a 'social language'; every element is potentially more than itself, everything exceeds its own bounds, speaks to a context that has no earthly limits. The novel is a holy writ of endlessly permutable content: modern writing as epitomized by the novel is perennially postmodern in so far as it turns any story into the means of breaking open the linear continuum of history and admitting the blazing light of the other.

This view of Bakhtin and the novel is not as bizarre as it may at first sound; it is there already in a bold claim that seems to underlie the careful phenomenological description of 'Author and Hero'. For if the Bakhtin of the middle years dates modernity's onset from the Renaissance, the early Bakhtin is not alone in implicitly mapping the story of modernity upon the much longer narrative of Christianity itself. As a classically trained philologist, Bakhtin would have been familiar with the etymology of 'modern' as a derivative of *modernus*, the term by which fifth-century Christians in the Roman Empire distinguished themselves from older (pagan) believers.[4] The Christians were, then, the first conscious moderns – the first community to make a defining characteristic out of the newness of their binding faith, their historically unprecedented otherness: long before the novel, in short, there was the ancient novelty of the Gospel. Bakhtin's contemporary Erich Auerbach wrote a whole book in 1945 on the premiss that the modernity of modern prose was inspired by the precedent of the Christian story, that behind its junking of the classical 'separation of styles' (*Stiltrennung*) and its discovery of the serious and the tragic in the everyday was a run-of-the-mill police action in Roman Judaea which had shaken the world.[5] If we take in also Auerbach's later work on the semantic revolution whereby Christianity transvalued key words from the classical languages (notably the Latin *humilis*),[6] and on the new faith's deep implication in the polyglossia of the Mediterranean basin (as witness the Hebraized Greek of the New Testament), then it becomes possible to see that many of the motifs that Bakhtin was later to identify with modernity at its most positive and emancipatory find their prototype in an analogous cultural upheaval some fifteen hundred years earlier. Moreover, Auerbach's own studies of that old 'figural' or typological mode whereby persons and events from the Old Testament foreshadowed those of the New might be drafted in to suggest a like relation between early Christianity and those aspects of modernity that Bakhtin and others of like mind would wish to affirm.

In the author of 'Author and Hero', then, we have a crossing of two traditions: on the one hand, an Eastern Christian spirituality boasting a continuous history and only recently released from its long association with a premodern polity; on the other, a Western secular conceptuality which has a similar environing sociopolitical context, but which would have little to say if it were not at once critical of that context and a critical meditation upon a modern history happening elsewhere. What these two traditions of such disparate temporality have in common is a clear 'outsideness' over against modernity as an ongoing historical project, different orders of exotopic witness to its fate whose unique placing within the event of modern historical being might yet help a modernizing Russia to modernize appropriately. They would do this of course without dissolving their own mutual exotopy, without merging. Thus it is that in reading 'Author and Hero' we should not fall into the trap of supposing that either the theology or the aesthetics is the 'truth of' the other. We could indeed say, in a provisional formulation – and paraphrasing Samuel Taylor Coleridge – that the author–hero couple is the repetition in the finite sphere of the infinite 'I–thou' of God; but *only* provisionally, as a working hypothesis with strong support throughout the text: not as a conclusion.

Whatever their relationship in that essay, it is certain that theology and aesthetics have much in common. Both are cognitive discourses which thematize that which is other than, or at least not wholly, cognitive; both are relatively logically ordered metalanguages whose object is either language incommensurably differently oriented and organized or beyond language altogether. It has then to be said that Russian Orthodox theology and the kind of neo-Kantian aesthetics practised by Bakhtin have yet more in common, inasmuch as each allows that the value categories of its object discourse bear a greater existential authenticity than its own. Both, that is to say, strategically rationalize that which exceeds rationality. Russian Orthodox spirituality claims to know no absolute boundary between mysticism and theology, between what Vladimir Lossky calls 'the realm of the common faith and that of personal experience'. Theology is 'an expression, for the profit of all, of that which can be experienced by everyone'.[7] Such a distillation of situational uniqueness into the supra-personal is exactly Bakhtin's notion of cognitive discourse. Aesthetics for Bakhtin should then stand to aesthetic activity as (Orthodox) 'mystical theology' stands to religious experience. Of all the cognitive discourses it is the one that carries the least threat of 'theoreticism', and it is therefore the best placed to challenge epistemology on its own conceptual ground. Thus it is that two streams of thought flow together and mingle in 'Author and Hero': moves within early-twentieth-century German thought to free the aesthetic from its Hegelian sublation in a foundational philosophy meet on the ground of a humbled knowledge the possibilities opened by a traditional Russian spirituality newly freed from its links with the autocracy.

II

Bakhtin begins from the simple truth that you cannot ever be where I am, or see yourself as I see you. I occupy a unique place in being, in so far as I am always (and wherever I might be) outside everyone else. It is on the ground of this ineluctable absolute of the non-commutability of my position with any other – of my outsideness to your experience of yourself and the world, and yours to mine – that Bakhtin builds the whole house of value. He begins with an absolute distinction between two value categories: that of the *I* and that of the *other*. Cognition is indifferent to both; ethics is interested only in the *I*. Aesthetic activity differs from these other sectors of philosophy in that it alone embraces both the I and the other. Indeed it is nothing less than that interaction of both which is instanced in all the manifold phenomenal forms of loving 'consummation' offered as a gift by the other (or author) to the I (or hero). This dyad of author and hero operates in the two dimensions of space and time, the first addressing itself to the hero's body (where the consummation is 'plastic-pictorial': mainly though not exclusively in the visual arts) and the second to the hero's soul (where the consummation is achieved by 'rhythm': more or less confined to 'verbal art'). To space and time Bakhtin adds a third dimension: of 'meaning'. Aesthetic activity constitutes the hero not only as a whole in time and space, but also as a 'whole of meaning'. Aesthetic value is conferred upon 'the hero's meaning-governed attitude in being – that interior place he occupies in the unitary and unique event of being' (*AH*, 138). 'Author and Hero' takes its structure from these three dimensions, examining the hero under the aspect of each in turn, and concentrating under this last (and more inward) dimension upon those genres of speech and writing determined by differing postures of 'meaning', differing modes of 'directedness' towards ends.

The first thing to be said about this early delineation of the 'aesthetic event' and its dependence upon a radical 'outsideness' is that it deals in ideal types, that it is uncompromisingly wedded to pure taxonomic exemplifications. For, given that the planes of author and hero are absolutely distinct and yet equally absolutely in need of each other, it is clear that we have to do here not with a contingent but with a necessary relationship of persons – persons that are (in turn) not empirically on hand but posited transcenden-tally in all such interactions. 'The author' is therefore the 'author-as-author', the one by whom the 'open ethical event' of the hero's life-lived-from-within is totalized and justified from outside. The 'author-as-person' is not only not strictly an author at all, but also not even a hero except in so far as she exists in the context of other lives authorially shaping her own – using their 'excess of . . . seeing and knowing' to do for her what she could never do for herself (AH, 12). Besides being distinct from the plane of the hero, this authorial outsideness is a posture of being neither 'inside' nor 'beside' nor 'against' the hero but purely 'over against' the latter: that is, neither coinciding experientially nor agreeing or disagreeing axiologically with the hero, but simply (where the latter's consciousness is concerned) 'incarnat[ing] meaning in existence' (AH, 12). Where the author loses this stable position – where the aesthetic 'ideal type' fails of realization – various dilutions result, as (allegedly) in Dostoevsky and Kierkegaard, who let the hero 'take possession of the author' (AH, 17). Bakhtin would of course later radically revise this view of Dostoevsky, though whether he would have thought his early author–hero model to be falsified or in need of qualifying by a Dostoevsky now positively valorized is another matter altogether. What is certain is that the aesthetic event always 'presupposes two non-coinciding consciousnesses' (AH, 22); anything in writing or reading which conflates or effaces these tends to syncretize the aesthetic, threatening to transform the event (in the case of their conflation) into an ethical event and (in that of their effacement) into an event of cognition. It is for this reason that the 'religious event' is paradigmatic for aesthetic activity: structurally similar in the strict non-coincidence of constituent consciousnesses, prayer, worship and ritual differ from the aesthetic event only in that the author is not any other (human) other but the (divine) Other of all of us. If the gulf between aesthetic activity and spirituality seems sometimes to narrow almost to vanishing point, if each seems on occasion to be a mere figure for or subset of the other, it is perhaps truer to say that they stand in a relation of infi-nite asymptotic approximation which always stops short of coincidence. Bakhtin clearly sees that we are all heirs to a modern split in knowledge which has the character of a fatality, but which it would be far worse to deny or submit to a too-perfect (Hegelian) reconciliation. An aesthetics distinct from yet friendly towards theology would avert this threat, ensuring for Christian spirituality an appropriately modernized presence within the terrain of profane knowledge, while at the same time challenging the hegemony of those epistemological (subject–object) models on which almost all modern thinking is founded.

At its strongest, then, the argument of 'Author and Hero' becomes a polemic against the shortcomings of 'thought' itself. As we read, it becomes ever clearer that the author's surplus of 'inner and outer seeing' is being offered as an alternative to that universal *aporia* of a typically disembodied and desituated modern subjectivity. The modern subject makes up for its inability vividly and roundedly to image its body in the world by recourse to a 'thought' which relativizes the I and the other – renders them mutually convertible, at the cost of their de-realization. The thought which 'has no difficulty at all in placing *me* on one and the same plane with all *other* human beings' (*AH*, 31) may be the thought which in going abroad from itself conquers nature and the object, proud of its strength. Its weakness lies in its failure to acknowledge in existential terms the real price to be paid for that fiction of thought's power and facility. My consciousness may and can encompass the world, but it can never image my outward appearance and my body's boundaries as encompassed *by* the world. Technological crutches such as the mirror and the photograph are dismissed by Bakhtin as either offering a ghostly vision of myself from the standpoint of a 'possible other' or as 'raw material' for a mechanical 'collation' of myself, while leaving me stranded in mere contingency (*AH*, 32, 34–35). Bakhtin may be on shaky ground in the case of photography: few today would see it as 'authorless'; we would be inclined, rather, to equate it with the painted portrait as alone enabling that subsumption under the category of the other by which I see the whole of myself *in* the world along with everybody else. Bakhtin shows himself to be reviving the older sense of 'aesthetic' as having to do not just with 'art' in a narrow definition but with bodily and sensory experience across the board: it is thus that we find him moving easily from this case of a portrait of myself to my 'absolute need' in life for the other if I am to be born anew as an '*outward* human being on a new plane of being' (*AH*, 35–36). I am not given as an outward body in myself but created as such by the other; I owe my freedom from the solipsism of an 'absolute consciousness' (*AH*, 22) to my bringing-to-birth in the horizon of the other.

Aesthetics for Bakhtin is, then, a pragmatically oriented ontology of the kind that would later show itself in phenomenology of the Merleau-Pontian kind. His aesthetics is a means of escape from the hegemony of epistemology in so far as it begins from that absolute incommensurability of the I and the other which it shares with Christian ethics, and which cognition programmatically denies. Begins from, but at once exceeds: Bakhtin's aesthetics would thrust almost any ethics back into the company of abstract thought, inasmuch as neither cognition nor ethics is anything but 'indifferent to the concrete uniqueness of the image' (*AH*, 41). It is an aesthetics which might be said simultaneously to do two seemingly contrary things: transcendentalizing Christian ethics, reading its injunctions of other-valuing and self-negation back into our very conditions of possibility as beings in the world; while also forestalling any tendency towards a Kantian formal ethics by a strong stress upon 'outward expressedness', upon the body presented along all of its outwardly adverted boundaries to and for the other's loving 'over-shadowing' (*episkiasis*) (*AH*, 41). Bakhtin seeks to preserve the body as a value by positing on the analogy of the outer body an 'inner body' as much in need of consummation from spatial outsideness as the former. Formal ethics attempts the impossible in extrapolating from my self-relation in the inner body to my relation-to-others in the outer body. Bakhtin splits the body in this way as a tactic for giving back to it its full value: only thus can he show for all to see the work of disincarnation secretly performed by a law-like 'morality'.

We could sum all of this up by saying that aesthetics has for Bakhtin the task of tempting ethics away from 'morality' and towards an ontology of the uniquely situated body. In pursuit of this aim, Bakhtin takes his argument into a sharp diachronic tangent, and first of all back to our earliest childhood and the creativity of love in that phase of one's life. Our inchoate inner feeling of ourselves is translated into a clarified 'personality' thanks to words and kisses from the lips of another (typically, initially, a mother); our body as a 'potential value' is likewise further fashioned and sustained by the gaze and speech and embrace of friends throughout our lives (*AH*, 51). Complementing this is a more properly historical excursus into the currents that have shaped the body as a value in European modernity. The logic of Bakhtin's case here seems to be as follows: if the Law disincarnates the subject, then conversely an incarnating ethics will destabilize the Law. To use such an idiom is of course then to recall a much better-known Incarnation, and to commit oneself to a rehearsal of the Christian transvaluation of the valued body. And this is precisely what Bakhtin does, suggesting thereby a fascinating analogy between his project of renewing an ethics of love under the complicated conditions of late modernity and the first launching of that absolute ethical novelty upon the world. Christianity breaks with both the classical emphasis upon the body (when 'everything corporeal was consecrated by the other') and its neo-Platonic denial (when 'the aesthetic value of the body becomes almost extinct'), and does so by means of a complexly hybridized blend of positions – a heteroglot discourse on the body in which the leading and most deeply transformative voice is that of Jesus Himself (*AH*, 53–54). The relevant passage is worth quoting at length:

> In Christ we find a synthesis of unique depth, the synthesis of *ethical solipsism* (man's infinite severity towards himself, i.e., an immaculately pure relationship towards oneself) with *ethical-aesthetic kindness* towards the other. For the first time, there appeared an infinitely deepened *I-for-myself* – not a cold *I-for-myself*, but one of boundless kindness towards the other; an *I-for-myself* that renders full justice to the other as such, disclosing and affirming the other's axiological distinctiveness in all its fullness. All human beings divide for him into himself as the unique one – and all other human beings, into himself as the one bestowing loving mercy – and all others as receiving mercy, into himself as the saviour – and all others as the saved, into himself as the one receiving the burden of sin and expiation – and all others as relieved of this burden and redeemed.
>
> Hence, in all of Christ's norms the *I* and the *other* are contraposed: for myself – absolute sacrifice, for the other, loving mercy. But *I-for-myself* is the other for God. God is no longer defined essentially as the voice of my conscience, as purity of relationship to myself . . . . God is now the heavenly father who is *over me* and can be merciful to me and justify me where I, from within myself, cannot be merciful to myself and cannot justify myself in principle, as long as I remain pure within myself. What I must be for the other, God is for me.
>
> (*AH*, 56)

It is hard to say who is here ventriloquizing whom – Jesus Bakhtin or Bakhtin Jesus? – so completely has this Russian Christian of late modernity identified himself with the founder of Christianity. The terms in which Bakhtin has argued the essential relationship of author and hero are here traced to their spring in the words of the

Gospels. It is as if all the intricate and nuanced phenomenological description of that relationship both before and after this passage had been distilled into a few maxims and had taken on the downright tone of Christian ethical affirmation.

Opening a window as Bakhtin here does onto the spiritual tradition to which his aesthetics is affiliated by no means closes his argument; rather, it adds its own (German-philosophical) idiom to the intellectual heteroglossia of Christianity. That particular mingling of idioms would not anyway have been odd in Russia, where German idealist philosophy arrived in the company of German mysticism and was read together with the latter as its modern continuation. Not unreasonably: had not Hegel's first work been on early Christian communities? And had he not come under the influence of Proclus and Jakob Boehme? We are not surprised, then, to find that in telling the story of the later fortunes of the Gospel ethic Bakhtin distances himself from neo-Platonic elaborations and invokes against these the names of St Bernard of Clairvaux and St Francis of Assisi, those powerful figures of Western mediaeval spirituality to whom the Rhineland mystics owed so much, who feature in prominent episodes of Dante's *Paradiso* and who (as it happens) forge a further link between Bakhtin himself and Auerbach.[8] In so far as these otherwise so different representatives of the *imitatio Christi* stand not for the body's denial but rather for its justification here and now and its transfiguration in eternity, they might be seen as the saints who preside over Bakhtin's 'strictly secular' (*AH*, 149) project in this essay. Creaturely images abound in the style of both mystics, functioning as figural enactments of an Incarnation which means what it says and is no mere disposable historicity, no mere metaphorical shell of physicality. Bakhtin's own style here uses something like the 'low' sublime of both saints to earth and round out a neo-Kantian idiom which might otherwise etherealize the bodiliness of which it speaks. St Bernard's talk of monks as 'acrobats and jugglers'[9] to the world and the popular-grotesque motifs of St Francis's *vita* not only connect with the 'holy fool' of Orthodox tradition, but also place Bakhtin's later preoccupation with carnival in a new light. Bakhtin in any case leaves us in no doubt that by the time of the enlightenment (understood as the birth of secular modernity, in the story the latter tells itself) the ethical-aesthetic valuation of the body in the great mystics of the Middle Ages has long gone and that the body has 'degenerate[d] into an organism as the sum total of the needs of "natural man"' (*AH*, 58). His alternative narrative of modernity will later turn on the figure of Rabelais, who articulates in writing an anonymous culture of the mediaeval folk. Though we might say his bearings in this earlier phase are taken from Dante, the situation is actually more complex than that. Dante is only the near (late-mediaeval, proto-modern) end of a potentially infinite regress and return of mediations, one which takes us through those two exemplary lives so lovingly contextualized in the *Paradiso* to the prototype of that self-negating and other-valued Body of Christ on which all of them model their lives.

If this brief sketch of a history of the body offers one (diachronic) context for Bakhtin's discussion of the hero as a spatial whole, a (much longer) synchronic cross-section of contemporaneous aesthetics offers another. Russian Formalism would preoccupy him in a later critique, dating from 1924; here he examines the opposite tendency of 'expressive aesthetics' which 'defines the essence of aesthetic activity as a co-experiencing of the inner state of an object or of the inner activity of contemplating an object' (*AH*, 62). Bakhtin's objection is that the moment of empathy isolated by this theory remains within the category of the *I* and is thus, 'in essence, *extra-aesthetic*' or at least has nothing specifically aesthetic about it (*AH*, 64). Besides, it enforces an absurd parcelling out of the work into its supposedly co-experienceable elements and cannot account for the whole except by the move of implicitly positing an author – a move which lands it straightaway in the category of the *other*, yet without any sense whatever of the deconstructive deathblow it deals itself in doing so. Co-experiencing cannot for Bakhtin have aesthetic effects except as a moment of in-feeling with the hero which is then fulfilled in an active and co-*creative* consummation of the whole event.

Bakhtin's choice of drama as a case study in his refutation of the aesthetic of empathy is astute, and in several ways. Drama as a hybrid of the verbal and 'plastic-pictorial' enables him to negotiate the borders between two at least of the arts, and thereby more solidly found his claim to a general aesthetics. It is also an acid test of that aesthetic inasmuch as the drama's seemingly authorless delivery of form out of the object itself 'as its own expression' seems superficially to underwrite a theory of the reader-spectator's immediate co-experiencing of that object. Bakhtin draws a detailed distinction between drama-in-performance and the play of children – routinely conflated in other arguments – which requires that in the former the author's 'principled and non-contingent position' outside the life of the hero devolves upon the spectator, and that the actor herself is just such an author-*cum*-onlooker: that is, until the moment of performance (*AH*, 73). In other words, the aesthetic activity of drama contains an empathetic and extra-aesthetic moment, but that moment is punctual and is confined to the actress's relinquishing of her outsideness over against the hero, which then passes exclusively to the audience. In so far as children's play is *all* identification, it is always authorless (until or unless observed); drama, by contrast, is an alternating current of activity–passivity passing constantly between actor and spectator. The miracle of the passive consubstantiality of actor and hero casts the audience in the role of those who actively work the latter's 'aesthetic salvation' (*AH*, 71). If tragedy for Bakhtin is an 'artistic (and religious) performance', then it would seem that all drama is in some sense a profane correlative of the sacred ritual of the Mass (*AH*, 71).

However that may be – and the analogy would need far more spelling out than there is space for here – it is certain that this theory of the drama encompasses a wide range of modern dramatic practice, beyond the polemics spawned by the crisis of drama in our time. It straddles the opposed acting methods of a Konstantin Stanislavsky and a Bertolt Brecht, combining as it does on the one hand a purely technical and extra-aesthetic moment of *Einfühlung* and on the other hand a moment of *Verfremdung* that is decisively aesthetic. That is to say: where naturalism would put both spectator and actor in the category of the *I* and epic theatre would put them both in the category of the *other*, Bakhtin sees the latter giving up authoriality to the former at the point of actorly incarnation. Bakhtin also, incidentally, echoes some of the positions being taken by Luigi Pirandello at just this time.

The length and detail of this critique can be explained by Bakhtin's sensitivity to the view that an 'expressive' aesthetic seems 'especially seductive and convincing' where all the arts of the word are in question – if only because these arts have less 'spatial distinctness' than sculpture and painting and because the 'space' that is needed for a stable outsideness is figurative rather than literal, being either verbally connoted or (as is possible even in drama) cancellable thanks to the engagingly inward resonance of the word. Bakhtin is on far safer (because more specifically verbal) ground when he turns to the problem of the hero as a temporal whole.

III

We are not surprised to find that when Bakhtin turns to this problem 'Author and Hero' becomes less a general-aesthetic project than an aesthetic treatise focused on the verbal arts, a sort of onto-logically inflected poetics that weaves (if anything) more freely than ever back and forth between art-as-such and everyday life. What holds the whole project together none the less is the analogy which Bakhtin maintains throughout between the spatial and the temporal whole, and which licenses him to speak of outsideness in the dimension of time. The soul is the inner whole that is nothing apart from such (axiological-semantic, not necessarily chronological) 'laterness' in the other. The soul is, then, the spirit as it 'looks *from outside,* in the other' (*AH,* 100). The analogy is not between space as literal extension and time as literal duration, inasmuch as both of its terms have already undergone a certain figurative skewing from a 'pure' conceptuality – a metaphorization by which their cognitive abstraction from value is undone and their unity restored. Just as space in verbal art is connoted rather than plastically or pictorially realized in the material, so time is as often as not a hypothetical rather than the real condition of being 'after' the hero. In the hero as a temporal whole the soul is realized 'on the same plane as the other's outer body': that is, in an aesthetic foreshadowing of the 'moment of death' or (ultimately) of 'resurrection in the flesh' (*AH,* 101). The soul can never be mine or spring from my effort within life-as-it-is-lived; it 'descends upon me – like grace upon the sinner, like a gift that is unmerited and unexpected' (*AH,* 101). Pushing his analogical idiom to the limit, Bakhtin declares that the soul is that subtle body or 'inner flesh' that is turned towards me by the other for the contemplation of my 'inner eyes' (*AH,* 102).

The adventure of meaning to which Bakhtin here invites us is like nothing so much as a ladder by which we climb from the headier reaches of conceptuality up into the boldest metaphoricity, then up again into a space where even these distinctions cease to hold and allegory gives way to what the old hermeneutic of the four levels of meaning would have called *anagogy.* The formal homology that he elaborates between spatial and temporal wholes yields oxymoronic metaphors like 'temporal seeing' (*AH,* 103) and 'inward outsideness' (*AH,* 101). Beyond these semantic liberties there beckon those epiphanic states in which such figures reach back towards referential truth, and are no longer metaphoric: the coincidence of body and soul at the moment of death; waking to bodily life forever at the end of all things. One strong implication of this most powerfully charged chapter of Bakhtin's essay says to us that aesthetic activity is an everyday ritual in which these sublime moments of individual and universal ending are proleptically played out. Another – a loophole for the determinedly secular perhaps – allows us to return from heaven to earth, reversing the semantic traffic of that last formulation, and reading those moments of death or apocalypse as figures for ethical-aesthetic activity at work in *this* world.

From this it follows that for Bakhtin the problem of temporal consummation is the problem of life's boundaries in time – of birth and death, but especially of death. Quite simply, neither birth nor death can be an event in my own life: I can no more experience the temporal beginning or end of my life than I can see my body's outline all round and in the world. The world without me and the world without a loved and irreplaceable other are absolutely incommensurable, and the tones proper to them cannot sound together without discord. My death cannot have the narrative weight and urgency in my life that the lives and deaths of those dear to me can and do have. Aesthetic activity anticipates the heroine's death even in the midst of her life; its standpoint is always that of memory or 'the perception of the other under the token of death' (*AH*, 107). Conversely, when she does die – and here Bakhtin, as so often, weaves out of art into life, or rather holds both at once in his conceptual grasp – aesthetic constituents begin to predominate over 'ethical and practical ones' (*AH*, 106). The work of art effects deliberately that valuing of an 'already finished life' in absolute indifference to its meaning, which happens spontaneously in the consciousness of the bereaved (*AH*, 107). I use my unique and extra-temporal position within the beginningless and endless unity of meaning to confer upon the other a unity in space and time. Death by itself (as an empirical fact) is at best neutral and at worst simply absurd where this consummation of the other is concerned; what it ends has no value or meaning; it can consummate nothing, and cannot make up a part of any story we might wish to tell or hear. Not death itself but the difference made to the world by the other's death – and to the other by the world's memory of her – has a reference to value, and hence an aesthetic significance. No longer living from within herself as spirit in the everlasting yet-to-be of meaning, she is now, as it were, *all soul* in so far as she exists only as 'reflected in the loving consciousness of another (another human being, God)' (*AH*, 111). History is the history exclusively of the other: the whole of history is populated by such *whole souls*; that is, by those whose inner exterior is turned towards me and all of those who (like me) have not yet joined the hosts of the dead.

We might sum all this up by saying that whatever transforms the lived experiences of others into moments of their whole inner lives and the latter into that outer form of an inner life called a soul – whatever effects *that*, and wherever – is aesthetic activity. This conception of the aesthetic allows Bakhtin not only to take it beyond 'art' as narrowly defined but also to predicate it across history, back into a past which did not know the modern category of the aesthetic as such. It may well have fallen to enlightened modernity to 'discover' this category for its own purposes; but these need not and will not be ours; and so long as we do not read a consciousness of the category back into the creation of premodern works (and so long as we fully respect the categories *they* recognize), we are not guilty of anachronism. Bakhtin is one of those late-modern thinkers whose critique of modern thought is constructed by exploiting the possibilities of universalization that the category of the aesthetic offers.

Chief among the terms that Bakhtin uses for the 'general conditions' of this aesthetic consummation of an inner life in time is *rhythm*. Rhythm is both detached from the technicalities of the particular arts of music and poetry and generalized away from the confines of 'art', in order that it might be transcendentalized as the rubric under which there takes place all that 'purely temporal ordering' by which the status of a 'positive individual given' is conferred upon lived experience in the other (*AH*, 112, 114). Such rhythmic incarnation is unknown to other forms of reflection, and more: it is a hindrance to their specific ends. Moral reflection upon my own life would be deflected by any such 'inward given' from its legitimate directedness towards the absolute future of meaning, and could only clothe such a self-image in the (essentially non-aesthetic) tones of prayerful and penitential supplication (*AH*, 114). Epistemological reflection transcendentalizes the forms under which the object is apperceived by the unsituated abstract *ego*; not the 'individual form of experiencing an object' (*AH*, 114). Psychology likewise is the value-free 'investigation' of the inward given in abstraction from the *I* and the *other*, not its 'contemplation'. Only in the rhythm of aesthetic activity is any lived experience in the other freed from the future of meaning into the 'absolute past, the past of meaning' (*AH*, 116). Rhythm installs meaning immanently within the lived experience: no longer drawn forward by the *ought* forever posited ahead of it as the possibility of another life, such a life is stilled from within, taking on inner flesh as 'something contentedly present-on-hand' (*AH*, 115).

Adopting yet another idiom: rhythm is that surmounting of the split between the ought and the is which can only enter my self-consciousness at second hand (so to speak), and then only as a source of shame; my lived life is only justified from within by the ought forever posited ahead of it as the possibility of another life. Resonating on the inside of the other's triumphant *Consummatum est* is my hopeless 'Is that all?' The *what-is* is the lack of being which we flee in the perpetual abolition of our past and our present: from within, we are right to fly from that which can none the less only be lifted from us by grace or forgiveness from without. Or, as Bakhtin himself puts it: 'For me myself, only a history of my fall is possible' (*AH*, 123). Sin in Bakhtin's ethical-aesthetic sense is the shameful inner self-contradiction into which I fall when I pretend to a 'self-contented abiding' in the given; a 'falsehood of being' negating the meaning which brought it to birth in the first place; the absurd presumption that I can confer 'rhythm' upon my own life (*AH*, 124). Faith is the rightfully insane belief against all odds that I do not coincide with myself ('But this is not all!'), the desperate refusal of the last word which spurs on my life-as-it-is-lived. All I can do in pronouncing my last word is to turn out from myself and 'surrender myself to the mercy *of the other* (the ultimate sense of deathbed confession)' (*AH*, 128). Your non-coincidence-with-your-self, conversely, is stilled and takes on an inner flesh in my re-membering gaze. In my contemplation your lack of meaning is bodied forth, fills inner space as an aspect of your being. The hero is born in the other's memory of her 'formal' death, a rhythmic re-membering in which death itself is overcome.[10] Bakhtin brilliantly dramatizes the unearthly strangeness of aesthetic consummation by saying that rhythm is what we have when the 'requiem tones at the end [are] already heard in the cradle-song at the beginning' (*AH*, 131). To use the postmodern philosophical terms of Jean-François Lyotard: the author and the hero belong to incommensurable phrasal universes; sin is the trespass of one upon the other; faith is the posture of the hero in hers; love that of the author in his. There is a benign rupture at the heart of being: my *Consummatum* and your 'I can change my life yet!' are neither translatable into each other's terms nor resolvable into a higher instance.

Extrapolating from these observations, we might say that Bakhtin's model of aesthetic activity acknowledges secular moder-nity's projection of regulative ideas into the future but warns it against the assumption that its favoured phrasal universe of the hero is everything there is, or (worse still) that it can smuggle into that universe an idiom of self-consummation. This sinful hubris of modern reason produces in the twentieth century the terroristic heresies of its characteristic politics. Walter Benjamin was writing in the same vein at precisely the time of 'Author and Hero':

> Only the Messiah himself consummates all history, in the sense that he alone redeems, completes, creates its relation to the Messianic. For this reason nothing historical can relate itself on its own account to anything Messianic. Therefore the Kingdom of God is not the *telos* of the historical dynamic; it cannot be set as a goal. From the standpoint of history it is not the goal, but the end. Therefore the order of the profane cannot be built up on the idea of the Divine Kingdom, and therefore theocracy has no political, but only a religious meaning. To have repudiated with utmost vehemence the political significance of theocracy is the cardinal merit of Bloch's *Spirit of Utopia*.
>
> The order of the profane should be erected on the idea of happiness. The relation of this order to the Messianic is one of the essential teachings of the philosophy of history. It is a precondition of a mystical conception of history, containing a problem that can be represented figuratively. If one arrow points to the goal towards which the profane dynamic acts, and another marks the direction of Messianic intensity, then certainly the quest of free humanity for happiness runs counter to the Messianic direction; but just as a force can, through acting, increase another that is acting in the opposite direction, so the order of the profane assists, through being profane, the coming of the Messianic Kingdom. The profane, therefore, although not itself a category of this Kingdom, is a decisive category of its quietest approach.[11]

The lesson that modernity needs to learn is that 'theocracy has no political, but only a religious meaning'; and that the 'profane dynamic' of history which leads a 'free humanity' to seek happiness will only help to bring about the Kingdom of God on condition that it keeps to a course exactly opposed to that of an incommensurable 'Messianic intensity' of suffering. If we make the necessary allowances for Benjamin's Jewish as opposed to Christian theology, this sounds uncannily like a transposition to the sociopolitical sphere of the ethical-aesthetic argument of 'Author and Hero'. At the very least, the Benjaminian fragment helps us to understand how Bakhtin's (also fragmentary, though much longer) intervention speaks to a historical context in which a peculiarly totalizing and triumphalist version of modernity's profane dynamic acknowledged no legitimating narrative other than its own. The pathos of modernity is a pathos of the hero not in itself reprehensible; its pathology is the hero who forgets that there is no history except in the other and that 'consummation' is not the goal towards which history tends but the grace of an ending which comes down upon it.

There is, it is true, nothing quite as vivid in Bakhtin as Benjamin's well-known Angel of History, who is propelled into the future by the storm of progress and yet stares resolutely backwards, counting the cost of that upheaval in the light of the past.[12] What the two contemporaries none the less share is an ability – summed up in that brilliant image – to make us see modernity from outside, to help us think outside its premises. Perhaps the point of their nearest approach is when Bakhtin complements his account of the soul's formation in the 'sorrowfully joyful lightness' of rhythm with a description of the soul's 'surrounding world' (AH, 132). The world-for-me is the 'horizon' of my 'act-performing (forward-looking) consciousness'; the world-as-a-given which is fused with and consecrated by the soul-as-a-given is that soul's 'environment' (AH, 134). The world that already exists has the hopeless finality of a word already uttered and it remains mired in mere unjustified factuality until I introduce into it the other, who is its hero, who does not exist outside it and around whom it arranges itself as a positively valued ambience regardless of meaning. Premodern mythical thought and late-modern 'aestheticizing intuitive philosophy' concur across the millennia with each other and with art at all times in thus seeing the world as the world of 'man-as-the-other': 'All characterizations of present-on-hand being that set [the world] into dramatic motion blaze with the borrowed axiological light of *otherness*' (AH, 134). Being as the environment of the hero is one universal epiphany, the permanent possibility of apocalypse, irradiated by the concentrated essence of potential or actual stories – of all beginnings and middles and endings. When Bakhtin tells us that being conceived as the world's body lives only as the sensitively resonating environment of the soul of the other, and that it dies insofar as it lies within the horizon of spirit, we are in the presence of an aesthetics whose ontological pretensions are at last fully open to view. And more than that: 'environment' begins to take on here something of its late-twentieth-century meaning; Bakhtin's aesthetic ontology legitimates the programme of ecology in so far as it raises a world alive in intimate correlation with the other over a world that 'disintegrates' before the *I-for-myself*.

Ecology is not the only postmodern (hyper-)political project that Bakhtin's aesthetics adumbrates when it moves into the realm of being: feminism is another, or at least feminist *theology*, that radical problematization of the gendering of God which goes much deeper than any merely internal ecclesiastical fight over the priesthood. Once gender enters the argument it becomes possible to read all of 'Author and Hero' as a corrective not only to the 'epistemologism' of modern European philosophy but also to the masculinism of the latter and (much) of Western Christianity besides. And indeed, if we look back across the essay, it is clear that its tonal and stylistic affinities in the West are with the tradition which Western theology specializes as 'mysticism' and which is thus nervously segregated from theology proper on what seem to be gender grounds: either as the spirituality of women themselves (Hildegard of Bingen, Mechthild of Magdeburg) or as a figuring of the love of God which interiorizes/metaphorizes the sexuality of a woman (for example, St Bernard on the *Song of Songs*). To appreciate this dimension we need to resist the reflexes of a highly sensitized feminist conscious-ness – a too-readiness to seize on an apparent instance of male stereotyping – when we find Bakhtin writing of the need of my authoring *I* to be 'totally active' and to 'stand totally outside being in order that [it] should open up before me in its feminine passivity' (*AH*, 136). Bakhtin is writing in a tradition of Orthodox spirituality which has a pedigree stretching back to Plato and *Proverbs* 8, and which had been revived by some of his compatriots at the end of the nineteenth century. On this view, Western spirituality had banished cosmology and left the world bereft by its elevation and abstraction of God; Western secularity had meanwhile deified man. The world forsaken by a God-centred Christianity had made good its loss by the demonic faith of secular humanism. This tradition of Russian spirituality sees these opposites as bedfellows, offering to define itself against both by positing as the substratum of God's consubstantial hypostases in the Trinity a fourth (and feminine) principle known as Sophia, the wisdom of God: Godhead in its aspect of created (rather than creating) oneness, God's body, media-trix between heaven and earth. Bakhtin echoes in his aesthetics on a microcosmic plane the cosmological theory of Vladimir Soloviev, the chief Russian theorist of 'sophiology', for whom everything issues everlastingly from the union of an active Logos and a passive Sophia.[13]

To the *messianic* cast of Benjamin's thought, then, there corresponds a *sophianic* cast in Bakhtin's; and it is nowhere more explicit
than when he openly introduces into his aesthetics the metaphor-
concepts or transcendental agents of a theology which saw itself as
nothing if not also a cosmology and an anthropology. The transcendental gendering for which such a synthesizing project seems to
call at no point becomes a politics of gender, and neither should we
blame it for not doing so. Instead, I would argue, Bakhtin offers
aesthetics itself as a discourse which is 'feminine' in so far as it not
only deeply valorizes the 'naivety' of being as a loving gift of my
creative activity in the world, but also represents a form of thought
which can reach beyond itself in all directions. The boundary of his
discipline to which Bakhtin now takes us is one that enables us to
contemplate in a new light states in which consummation is
subsumed under a rapt *participation*. The modes of my entry into
'the world of otherness', which he subjects to a brief phenomenological description, are *joy* and *the dance*. Joy can only be passive: I
cannot rejoice in myself, but only in the (universal) other – in the
world, or in God. To do this I must renounce my self-activity and
become elemental being in all its defencelessness. Even the minimal
expression of joy in the smile is not truly an expression in the sense
of coming out from myself but rather a reflection of 'the joy of the
affirmed being of others', just as the smile in the icon gives back the
affirmed being of God (*AH*, 137). In the dance Bakhtin finds the
paradox of 'passive activity', a transcendental androgyny in which
yet other epiphanic wonders are played out:

> In dancing, my exterior, visible only to others and existing
> only for others, coalesces with my inner, self-feeling,
> organic activity. In dancing, everything inward in me
> strives to come to the outside, strives to coincide with my
> exterior. In dancing, I become 'bodied' in being to the
> highest degree; I come to participate in the being of others.
> What dances in me is my *present-on-hand* being (that has
> been affirmed from outside) – my *sophianic* being dances in
> me, the other dances in me . . . . Dancing represents the ulti-
> mate limit of my passive self-activity, but the latter occurs
> everywhere in life. I am passively active whenever my
> action is not conditioned by the purely meaning-directed
> activity of my *I-for-myself*, but rather is justified from
> present-on-hand being itself, from nature; that is, whenever
> this present-on-hand being is elementally active in me

rather than the spirit .... Passive self-activity ... does not enrich being with what is in principle unattainable; it does not alter the meaning-governed countenance of being.

(*AH*, 137)

We might see in this account of dance something of Bakhtin's account of acting, if it were not for the more plainly ontological inflection of these remarks, the sublime (almost biblical) parataxis of their style and the implication that I am inwardly possessed by an other who (or which) is not individuated. The *participation mystique* of dance is unlike acting in that it internalizes the justification of my action rather than switching that role back and forth between myself and a determinate audience. Dance does not reconcile body and soul because, for Bakhtin and the spiritual tradition he represents, body and soul are on the same plane in terms of value and never in conflict anyway. What it undoubtedly does is to figure on earth the union of heaven and earth at the end of history; or alternatively: heaven is that ideal coincidence of inner and outer in me which their optimal coincidence in dance encourages us to imagine. Dance, in short, replays the Incarnation in reverse; it is very properly, then, sophianic in so far as the goddess Sophia in her godly–creaturely ambiguity is the guarantee that this *theosis* of 'man' is anything but a loss of 'body'.

The importance of this discussion of these phenomena of rejoicing and the dance is that they do what the study of laughter was to do later in Bakhtin's career: they confirm the inclusiveness, the pan-cultural and pan-historical (in a sense, anthropological) reach of his case. At the same time, their liminal status where the aesthetic is concerned – their placing at that border where art and the holy and the everyday meet, or at least give promise of each other, their very removal from 'art' in any merely modern sense – ensures that we remain decisively in a space beyond the subject–object model and are therefore never in danger of losing that defamiliarizing gaze upon modernity which (as I have suggested) Bakhtin is akin to Benjamin in so valuably offering us. We also have access to the positive side of that critical optic: namely, a posing of the question of being, so notoriously forgotten in modern philosophy and in those theologies that have yielded crucial territory to the latter. For what Martin Heidegger calls the 'forgetting of being' is what Bakhtin might have called our forgetting of the *other*, that other in whom alone I rejoice and who alone dances in me when I dance. The modernity that we see from outside is reminded of those tendentially androgynous experiential encounters with being (experiences of existential *chiasmus*, of encompassing and being encompassed) that it has for so long exiled beyond its purview in favour of the masculine movement of knowing. The paradox of 'passive activity' in such states directs us to the outsideness of outsideness itself, taking us back into the ungrounded ground which is presupposed both in the world of tasks and risks and in the movement of (aesthetic) love by which the heroes of that world are consummated. Reaching this point in the early Bakhtin's thinking, we understand why modern drama expelled the chorus of ancient tragedy, who danced and sang and spoke as the personified 'environment' of the hero. It is as if Bakhtin is inviting us to stand on the side of those who are always there, who were there (historically) before the actor emerged from among them, and who are still there when the hero has left the stage.

IV

This strategy whereby we are made to occupy a space beyond the modern *doxa* and to value being anew is carried over into Bakhtin's discussion of the 'diversity of forms which the meaning-governed whole of the hero assumes' (*AH*, 138). Coming at last to the hero as a 'whole of meaning', we can return to that seeming contradiction of propositions with which I began. If the focus here on forms of speech and writing is a foretaste of the turn Bakhtin will soon take from the act to the word, it is all the more remarkable that the *lacuna* in this discussion is the form that will be the great preoccupation later: the novel. True, there are allusions to novels, but the genre is not theorized as such; and if we could say that this is because Bakhtin did not yet appreciate its specificity, we could equally say that its appearance here would be premature from the standpoint both of the Bakhtin who was learning in writing and of ourselves who learn in reading him. For Bakhtin is here, quite rightly, concerned more with using the aesthetic as a way to reveal what the modern world has sidelined than with that hybrid through which modernity fashioned for itself a vivid self-image in narrative. Thus it is that we begin with spiritual confession and end with hagiography, while the properly modern forms – that is, forms which in their writing are predicated upon, rather than merely retrospectively inviting, our reception of them as art – have to find a place for themselves within this frame. Thus it is, too, that the premodern forms in their turn are viewed as it were from their limits, and that these limits are in no way seen as negative. On the contrary: they are at once internalized by those forms and the very source of their peculiar powers and effects. Indeed aesthetics (for Bakhtin) is the most welcoming of discourses, treating the non-aesthetic as it does not judgingly – as the untrue or historically superseded – but simply as the differently oriented whose difference from the strictly aesthetic is exactly its value.

The thesis of the impossibility of a 'pure' confession provides an example. Though confession might aim at being 'a self-accounting compris[ing] only that which I myself can say about myself' in 'absolute solitariness', it will always and necessarily fall short of that ideal purity, if only because 'the very language of expression' carries a freight of the other which cannot but introduce into it 'aesthetic moments' which clash with its project of self-expression (*AH*, 143, 142). If we then concede with Bakhtin that even at their strongest these intimations of the aesthetic will never let my word about myself be the last word, and that my confession is in principle as endless as the event of being itself, then a further benign impossibility at once stands before us in the form of a counter-vailing 'ultimate limit' which forever qualifies the limit upon pure self-expression (*AH*, 143). For if I can neither purely express myself nor ever fully justify myself, a perspective none the less opens which says that I could never absolutely not be justified. That perspective is the Christian religion, which says that my justification in any absolute sense is not from this but precisely from the *other* world: the gift, in short, of forgiveness. In so far as a self-accounting is also truly a confession it is a turning outwards from myself towards God; it necessarily crosses petitionary with penitential tones.

An aesthetics of thisworldly (aesthetic) justification enables us then to understand as its otherworldly correlative the religious justification from which it borrowed its metaphors in the first place: thus may we explain its hospitality and explanatory reach in respect of the non-aesthetic. But Bakhtin is not content to leave the case there. Purely introverted self-accounting is impossible for a deeper reason still: that I would not bring up the issue of myself if I were truly alone and there were not someone who wished me to be good. Confession presupposes a 'trust in absolute otherness' without which life itself could not begin (*AH*, 144). (We recognize here the outlines of Bakhtin's later concept of the 'third' or 'super-addressee', without which dialogue could not happen.) At the same time, the faith upon which is predicated that very life which my confession puts into question would not be faith without the ineluctably extraverted posture of penitence in the confession itself. The very form of confession posits the impossibility of living my life 'under a guarantee' or 'in a void', since it would then either not be needed or never be contemplated (*AH*, 144). (Again: Bakhtin would later re-inflect these Scylla-and-Charybdis options as the terrible twins 'dogmatism' and 'relativism', both inimical to dialogue. Clearly the superaddressee is the champion he sends into battle against these anti-dialogical demons of abstract thought.) In so far as tones of hope and faith modify its penitential and petitionary tones, confession begins to thematize its conditions of possibility and duly modulates into the (quasi-aesthetic) 'concord' of prayer, in which I explicitly acknowledge that I am not alone, becoming the 'other-for-God'. Prayer may bring to confession aesthetic moments – moments of 'rhythm' – but as a 'performed act', without the immanent consummation of a 'produced work', it can only be repeated endlessly (*AH*, 145). While confession can also – in a modern context perhaps cannot but – undergo aestheticization in my reading, its implied reader is one who (as a fellow sinner afloat in the stream of being alongside the confessing subject rather than standing over against him) answers his act with an act of her own.

Examining from the standpoint of aesthetics forms that date from before the enlightened modernity which invented the category of the aesthetic, Bakhtin reconceives the forms of modernity as belonging not to any linear progression from the premodern but rather in a continuum of mutual illumination and animation, a dimension he will later call 'great time'. By showing, as he does, that the secular forms are transformations of the founding forms of Christian belief, he effects at a stroke the archaization of secularity and the modernization of spirituality. For example, he suggests very strongly the transhistorical power of confessional self-accounting when he claims that the characteristic forms of modern writing are merely confession diverted or perverted: irony and cynicism can be traced to confession which has a theomachic or anthropomachic cast, fighting against the judgement of God or man or both. Confession's worst perversion is invective, which utters in tones of malice all that the other might utter penitentially about herself, marking her as the one who *has no other*. Like his later negative remarks on the 'typological generalization' (*AH*, 183) whereby the hero approaches the condition of an object whose acts are causally (socially, economically) determined, Bakhtin's careful 'placing' of invective founds its critique of a no doubt typical phenomenon of Soviet life in an aesthetic understanding of it: that is, an understanding which does not so much imitate such activities themselves in expelling them beyond the pale of the human as hold open the possibility of their reconversion to the forms they turn inside out. Just as the aesthetic whole of a Dostoevsky novel embraces the rhythmless confessions of its heroes, so the ethical-aesthetic perspective opened by Bakhtin redeems even the perversions of grace. Loving outsideness understands the very forms that abuse or deny their otherness to the other; under the aspect of the aesthetic, despair itself appears a roundabout vindication of faith. Bakhtin's aesthetics might then be read as the theoretical expression of a practical stance towards contemporaneous political developments. Like some other Orthodox intellectuals of his time, Bakhtin adopts towards the atheistic intelligentsia (one branch of which had by then come to dominate the state) an attitude defined not by the polemical negation with which they themselves would greet believers but by the will to transcend all polemic in hermeneutic understanding.

The modern form to which Bakhtin gives most space is autobiography – and for a clear, if unstated, reason. For if any form could be said to incarnate the self-grounding impulse which characterizes modernity, it is this form which accomplishes the self's most immediate self-objectification by internalizing a 'possible other' (*AH*, 152) within lived life, in which I anticipate others' memories of myself and partially assimilate myself to the world of heroes. Measured by ideal-typical criteria of the aesthetic which absolutely distinguish author from hero, and which for Bakhtin are classically epitomized in the lyric, autobiography is a hybrid form: its author is no more the pure artist 'consummating' from without an episode of life-as-it-is-lived than its hero is the purely ethical agent immersed in that life. In other words, the epoch which gives birth to the category of the aesthetic also typically produces a form of self-narrativization which always and necessarily falls short of aesthetic consummation – is always more an act than a *work*. While (auto)biography introduces narrative values missing in confessional self-accounting, its resolute secularism deprives it of that perfect rhythmicizing of prayer into which confession can modulate. Using Bakhtin's later terms, we might say that the author in this form forever strives and equally forever fails to place himself in the shoes of that characteristically modern superaddressee called posterity. The aesthetic is first conceptualized, then, in a context which finds the otherworldly consummation of religious experience, not superseded by a purely aesthetic consummation in all 'art', but rather joined or rivalled by a mode of consummation which is at once quintessentially modern and constitutively imperfect. Adapting Lucien Goldmann's Lukácsian terms, we might say that autobiography is the form of the 'problematic' author. The secular modernity which invents the category of the aesthetic also invents as its characteristic form a genre which 'points beyond its own bounds' and is 'highly insecure and precarious' by comparison with that ideal type of aesthetic consummation, that ancient poetic form which persists down to our time: the lyric (*AH*, 165). In the lyric the author's outsideness is maximally put to use – so much so, indeed, that the author wins the sort of complete victory over the hero which makes the work approach the condition of music. Lyric has as little to do with the merging of author and hero as it has to do with the solipsism of an atomistic *I*. Lyric is essentially choric and therefore communal: it is the state of being possessed by 'a chorus of possible others'. In his quasi-Nietzschean account of the lyric as possession by the spirit of music, Bakhtin seems to be offering not only an ideal-typical instance of aesthetic activity but also a form which (in celebrating love within the human order) connotes an archaic profanity, a germ within the premodern not of individualism exactly but of myself as the one who postulates a world of others, who freely and promiscuously *chooses* community outside all given communities.

However that may be, it is exactly the ethical-aesthetic hybridity of autobiography which will later for Bakhtin give the whole field of novelistic discourse – of modern narrative – its power to intervene in our late modernity. Miming the project of self-grounding which is modernity's great conceptual and experiential innovation, the syncretic and problematic aesthetic activity of modern storytelling none the less so reimagines that project as to neutralize the pathologies to which it has led historically. Dostoevsky matters so much for Bakhtin because his writing keeps faith with modernity's promise of freedom whilst resisting its will to totality. The polyphonic novel is a space in which cynical and ironic voices are given full weight and free play, where heroes sound like (but are not) authors and the author sounds like (but is not) just one hero among others, and where relativism and dogmatism are no longer locked in binary opposition. Modern writing takes on the aspect of a *felix culpa*, a fortunate fall: grace – the reality of absolute understanding, truth-telling and forgiveness – is expelled beyond the space of the text not in order for cynicism to triumph but to preserve both (human) cynicism and (divine) grace in their creative separateness.

Or, to vary the metaphor: in modern writing we have the principle of the minimum dose, a homoeopathic cure for the ills of modernity.[14]

V

Bakhtin's historico-philosophical dialectic of the modern and the premodern in this matter of forms is a complex affair, and only the outlines can be given here. In classical forms like the lyric he posits the principle of an archaic source for modern secularity; in the Christian forms he encodes, conversely, an archaic source for a spirituality no less perennially modern; modernity's true *novel*ties meanwhile are those problematic forms like the autobiography already discussed, forms which invent what he calls 'biographical value', and which subsist on the boundary between the 'produced work' and the 'performed act' (*AH*, 165). It is, however, not this hint of the discursive future but, rather (of all things), the saint's life that comes last in Bakhtin's review, throwing the rest into relief and helping us to finish with a provisional answer to that question of how the theological and the aesthetic relate in his early work which, as I suggested at the beginning of this chapter, would help us to resolve the paradox whereby philosophy and the novel are affirmed by Bakhtin for reasons so diametrically opposed.

Like the icon, the *vita* opens a door directly upon and into eternity. Because the life displayed is a 'significant life in God' – a life always already in the universal other, and therefore beyond the opposition of individual to typical – what is demanded of the author is a renunciation of all initiative, a humbling of himself before tradition on the part of the one representing in order that the represented might have authority (*AH*, 185). Where I am becomes inessential so that all that is essential may pass to the side of the holy person represented; my positional absolute, we might say, is emptied of positionality so that the absolute may shine forth without earthly obstruction. The project of Bakhtin's aesthetics gains a peculiar clarity at this point in 'Author and Hero', emerging as that order of modern knowledge which uses its modernity to understand and embrace premodern forms rather than counterpose itself to them. Hagiography and biography, icon and portrait, are freed from a relationship of merely linear supersession of the former by the latter, and move into a space where they can illuminate and renew each other. In this project, Bakhtin perhaps figures on the geopolitical plane a wished-for relationship of Orthodox

Russia and Western Europe which was doomed not to be realized in his time. If we read 'Author and Hero' in the appropriate spirit we will not be tempted to consign it to the status of the early work of someone who later knew better than to dwell on theology and the experience it seeks to understand. Instead we will find in it not only the intercultural resonance I have just mentioned, but much else besides. Among this residue of implication is that which comes from meditating upon the great significant absence at its heart – an absence as conspicuous as that of the epic in the chronotope essay: the novel. We reflect that it is in the borderland of biographical value – the space of the aesthetic hybrid – that he will soon place this genre, leaving behind him for good the ideal-typical analysis of 'Author and Hero' and staking all upon this irreverent newcomer and its fortunes in history. Philosophy expands to take into its long view this quintessential form of contemporaneity. The novel, for its part, in all its aesthetic hybridity, has the role of keeping philosophy this side of an abstract theoreticism by focusing always upon that aesthetic-ethical boundary where culture engages most directly with the world of answerable deeds: that world which Bakhtin had already sought to describe in *Toward a Philosophy of the Act* (the subject of Chapter 8), and in which all of us, without exception or exemption, *live*.

8

'FIRST PHILOSOPHY' AND THE 'FIRST' BAKHTIN

> An act of our activity, of our actual experiencing, is like a two-faced Janus. It looks in two opposite directions: it looks at the objective unity of a domain of culture and at the never-repeated uniqueness of an actually lived and experienced life.
>
> (*TPA*, 2)

Mikhail Bakhtin's last work is marked off from his earliest by a small but absolutely critical shift of emphasis: if in the early 1920s he puts his faith in a 'first philosophy' (*prima philosophia*), by the end of his life he has moved onto the terrain of the human sciences, and philosophy's task is now not the business of resolving the modern crisis by itself – in an introspection and self-correction offered to other disciplines as exemplary – but to hold the ring between the different sectors of modern knowledge as (in Jürgen Habermas' expression) their 'stand-in and interpreter'.[1] Or, as he puts it in *Toward a Philosophy of the Act*, its task is to bring the 'special' orders of answerability proper to each of these sectors 'into communion with' that fundamental 'moral' or 'personal' answerability by which alone they break free from their suspended animation in mere possibility and have any real effect in the world (*TPA*, 3). Philosophy is to make them aware of the ethical charge which necessarily informs them, but for which they themselves do not (and cannot) have any terms. In this very early work – its title is, incidentally, an editorial coinage – there is no hint that these new fields of the social even exist. As Bakhtin comes to acknowledge their existence, as indeed he enters into spirited dialogue with them (to begin with obliquely, through the polemics of his friends Pavel Medvedev and Valentin Voloshinov), so he diverts his project; but without ever wholly forsaking it. 'Dialogism', 'chronotope', 'great time', the defining motifs of his mature work: all of these are here *in potentia*.

I

Each of these later categories is an instance of that philosophy 'by other means' which was later to characterize Bakhtin's thinking. However, rather than draw attention to those points in the text at which these categories are foreshadowed – or, perhaps we should say, those passages which he appears to be recalling when in later years he comes to elaborate them – I would like to point, by way of introduction, to two other features of this early work. The first of these is a reference almost in passing to language as having arisen historically in the distant epoch of 'participative thinking' (*TPA*, 8), and as therefore having an act-oriented or performative character at odds with the abstract or theoretical thinking which it has been made to subserve in the modern world. The other noteworthy feature is the ambivalence in this text surrounding 'aesthetic activity'. Sometimes firmly assigned along with 'theory' to the realm of objectified 'culture', it is then held out at other times as that branch of culture which is closest in its 'architectonic structure' to the ethical reality of the world-as-event – as the moment of practical reason which, in more nearly approximating that world's actuality, brings us closer to the answerable deed than any 'pure', theoretical reason ever could. If there is a winning emphasis, it is the second of these; not indeed explicitly spelled out, but if anything the more eloquently witnessed for being tacit: namely, in the long analysis of a poem by Alexander Pushkin with which this early fragment ends.

Why, it may be asked, is there this ambivalence – this oscillating emphasis between the enthusiastic privileging of art, on the one hand, and its dismissive relegation, on the other? It would seem that Bakhtin is at pains to heed the claims of the life-world; but that he is equally under an imperative to neutralize the seductions of the aesthetic, in particular as it is exemplified in the contemporary vitalist philosophy (notably that of Henri Bergson), which he sees as disablingly 'aestheticized' (*TPA*, 13). Aestheticized philosophy can conjure only an illusion of resonance with the 'life' of 'once-occurrent being'. Whilst aesthetic activity may not give us any more direct access to the world of deeds and their performers than 'theory' can, it is – however 'objectified' – at least a *form* of participation. Having then put an unequivocal distance between himself and 'aestheticized' philosophy in *Toward a Philosophy of the Act*, Bakhtin spends the rest of his career thinking through and by means of works of (verbal) art and their writers. Indeed it would appear that the whole of his later focus on literature – and of course above all on the novel as the type *par excellence* of modern writing – can be traced back to this early work. This whole move can be seen to rest on an implicit logic which is at least quasi-syllogistic: the major premiss concerns the (participative) character of natural language, and the minor premiss the character of literature as a particular (aesthetic) use of language. To spell the matter out somewhat more bluntly: if you put the hint about the close relation between articulated language and participative thinking alongside the observations about aesthetic activity as a form of objectified participation in being-as-event, what you then logically get is a championing of literature as a discourse which has its headquarters not far from the centre of ethical operations in the world of answerable deeds. That is to say: an aesthetic activity whose medium or material is language can offer, if not an entry into that world, at least an adumbration of it. In language we find not some Dionysian other of reason but the sedimented residue of an archaic practical reason with which modern writing is, alone among the discourses of cultural modernity, still in touch. This is surely the logic of analysing the Pushkin poem and then choosing only to write the section of his projected study that concerned aesthetics. It is also the logic that lies behind the decision never to write again except in a certain connection with aesthetics or poetics. What Bakhtin would later call translinguistics is nothing other than a poetics of language in all of its varieties. In his view, such a poetics transcends mere methodology and technicality (such as he saw exemplified in the Russian Formalists) in being articulated upon a general aesthetics which in turn acknowledges its place within a universe of moral answerability.

That will have to do for now as a preliminary resolution of the question of the ambiguity surrounding 'aesthetic activity' in *Toward a Philosophy of the Act*; refinements will follow in my later argument. As the prolegomenon to a systematic treatise in the neo-Kantian mould, however, it is haunted by a far more pervasive ambiguity at the level of its style. Consider: there must always be a certain tension hedging about the project of bringing under a phenomenological description – or, as Bakhtin sometimes puts it, 'disclosing' – the structure of the ought and of the moral and historically actual subject that is its bearer, inasmuch as a cognitive discourse is being called upon to expose the limits of cognition, to do what cognition cannot do from its own ground: that is, to investigate, to reveal in its elements, the structure of the deed, including even that performed act of abstraction or de-situation in which cognition itself is founded. Like Martin Heidegger, Bakhtin sees an analogy between cognition and technology: what the abstracting act institutes is an 'immanent law' which does what it wills and is frightening, 'irresponsibly destructive' (*TPA*, 7). The purely theoretical world of cognition is one in which I cannot *live*; if it were the only world, I would, quite simply, not be here. Its only legitimation is that it 'enriches' being as one of being's moments; it is only illegitimate in so far as it lightens the heaviness of being, claiming to include that in which it is itself included and without which it could neither begin nor be sustained. As a cognitive discourse which is paradoxically critical of this hubristic overreaching of cognition, *Toward a Philosophy of the Act* must constantly not only remind us of that in which cognition is included, but also so name that more inclusive context as not to bring it under the sign of an abstract universal. Hence it is that we have the mantric repetition of the hyphenated adjectival construction 'once-occurrent' variously qualifying 'event' and 'deed' and 'being': to have put this attribute in the category of the already understood would have been to have damagingly conceded the commutability or substitutability of the irreducibly singular, thus perilously diluting in the signifier the uniqueness that is thereby signified. Patterning after what they most crucially and centrally represent – the act as a document with a signature appended to its 'text' – these repetitions have the effect always of nudging the common noun or noun-phrase towards the condition of the proper noun. As in the earliest Greek drama, being is a play in which I am the only actor. As with God in a prayer, being is not so much referred to as invoked, called upon. Cognitive discourse, we might say, is here made to feel the pressure of other uses of language. Or, again, we could say that the tone of this discourse is one from which a prayerful intonation has been removed but which retains nonetheless the repetitions of supplication; and that what we then hear inwardly as we read is nothing other than the sound made by the concept as it goes about the business of its self-transcendence.

II

Our exposition of *Toward a Philosophy of the Act* might begin with the observation that these features I have just isolated of the tone and form of Bakhtin's writing have their reflex at the semantic level. We seldom, if ever, for example, hear here of 'the self': instead we have 'I', the philosophical 'I' which performatively institutes uniqueness every time it is used, inviting the reader to think not of some third-person universal subject but of himself or herself as that which resists all extrapolation – as that around which being uniquely (unprecedentedly, unrepeatably) arranges itself, in a way that it has never done before or elsewhere and will never do again. Also characteristic of this paradoxical discourse is the use (as in 'Author and Hero in Aesthetic Activity') of oxymoronic metaphors. 'Value', for example, is variously correlated with light and with flesh and blood, in a tropology which – at least for the kind of theoreticist thinking that sets up or perpetuates all of the other oppositions of modern binarism – would seem absurdly to conflate opacity with translucency. From the standpoint of anyone who understands the tradition of icons, however, there is no paradox: these are figures precisely of transfiguration; abstraction is at once dark and disembodied, whilst for participative thinking bodies are always suffused with the light of value. Invoking a perspective in which incarnation completes rather than contradicts transcendence, Bakhtin fuses enlightenment and Revelation in the figures he uses. Or, rather: he connects enlightenment with the Revelation it represses or brackets out from its past. Alexandar Mihailovic speaks of a 'Christological subtext' in all of Bakhtin's writing.[2] Whilst by no means disagreeing, I think it would be truer to say that in his earliest work what we observe very clearly is a redemption of that tragic misreading of the Western enlightenment project by the Russian intelligentsia which was so astutely pointed out in 1909 by the *Landmarks* (*Vekhi*) contributors: those extraordinary *pre*-revolutionary post-Marxists – Semyon Frank, Sergei Bulgakov and Nikolai Berdyaev among them – who typically moved (back) to Orthodox Christianity through a neo-Kantian phase, and of whom Bakhtin might arguably be seen as a younger follower. Far from extracting from that narrative the single motif of atheism, vulgarizing it and elevating to philosophical heights its most extreme and polemical modes, Bakhtin uses his placing within a spiritual tradition that strongly emphasizes incarnation and transfiguration to bring out such a subtext in the philosophical discourse of modernity itself.[3] If Immanuel Kant practised critique in order at once to clean up reason's act and to save traditional faith beyond its borders, Bakhtin makes critical use of his own inherited faith to resituate modern rationality within the wider context of answerability.

We will see later that this work of a critically inflected faith within reason's borders ensures that reason promiscuously crosses *all* cultural borders. Methodologically speaking, such a move can be rendered either as the deconstructive use of the third Kantian critique against the first two – so positioning the *Critique of Judgement* that it challenges the local and temporal insularity of the latter rather than founding their certainty – or it can be rendered as a certain resurrection of the supreme figure of self-sacrifice in Western culture from the (merely superficial) exile to which Western secular thought has consigned Him. The figure of Christ appears as the thematization of Bakhtin's project of teasing out those 'unconscious or masked' (*TPA*, 8) vestiges of participative thinking in philosophy which the anti-cognitive intuitionism of 'aestheticized' philosophy in the contemporary West is, for all its promise, incapable of delivering save as a 'negligible admixture' (*TPA*, 13). From within the content or product of 'aesthetic seeing' there is 'no way out into life'. If, however, we understand aesthetic seeing not as passive empathizing with an object but as an active empathy – as involving a moment of objectifying, of 'return into oneself' – then the fiction of my inessentiality to the world, my ethical nullity, is exploded (*TPA*, 14). The great paradigm of this self-renunciation (which is not removal of myself from the world but rather a confirmation of my necessity to the accomplishment of its very being) is of course Jesus Himself. Self-renunciation produces not a world in which I do not exist or which does not need me, but rather a powerful enactment of being-as-event. Bakhtin implies that this is the highest form of self-activity available to mankind when he writes that by removing Himself from the world, Jesus changes it utterly; the world in which He has been is utterly different from the world before He came. All strongly being-enacting acts are henceforth summed up in that epochal deed of self-abstraction. While theory can grasp the sense of the world which Jesus has filled precisely (if paradoxically) by leaving, it loses the historicity of the event; history conversely grasps the event at the cost of the sense; the intuition of art gives us both together but at the risk of losing 'our own position in relation to [the event]' (*TPA*, 16). I lose my unique place in being when I use 'aesthetic seeing' as a way in to 'aesthetic being' – when, that is, I mistake the *product* for the answerable *act* of such seeing. Bakhtin's claim that 'aesthetic being' is closer to the life of being than the 'theoretical world' is made within the context of this clear warning against mistaking one for the other. In Levinasian vein, Bakhtin seems to be saying that it is only from within an ethics of radical alterity that a first philosophy can be launched. Privileging the aesthetic dimension of experience can help us to undo the dominance of theoretical cognition, but it cannot have a direct part in the building of a fundamental ontology to take its place. In this (reconstructive rather than deconstructive) task there is no substitute for that order of participative understanding and phenomenological disclosure of the act in which none of its moments or relations is universalized.

We might note in passing that the spectrum of contemporary thought which Bakhtin finds wanting extends well beyond vitalism to embrace the official philosophy of the (then) new Soviet state. Marxism is acknowledged as giving promise of access to the 'living' world of the act – Bakhtin is no doubt thinking of Marx's eleventh thesis on Feuerbach about changing the world instead of interpreting it – whilst failing to discriminate the is from the ought. Contemporary philosophy in general is symptomatic of a crisis whereby we feel most at home where we are not ourselves and are instead inwardly possessed by the immanent logic of some sector of knowledge. A philosophy which cannot include within itself the 'process of my thinking', which can only echo its internal legitimation, which deals only in the special obligations of particular intellectual functions: such a philosophy cannot offer the basis of a first philosophy (TPA, 21). However that may be, it is certain that no tradition of modern ethics fares any better for Bakhtin: not even the Kantian tradition, in which practical reason is invoked as guaranteeing reason's powers in general by showing it at work in a humanly constituted sphere of 'freedom', among objects of its own making, without empirical constraints – at work, in short, unconditionally. 'Content ethics' risks describing as ethical norms those which are not specifically ethical at all; norms which arise not from some necessity internal to themselves but which are simply theoretical propositions deriving from particular disciplines (or which syncretize several such) and have the ought tacked onto them from the outside. 'Formal ethics' in the Kantian style rescues the ought from this contingency by (correctly) rethinking it as a category neither of the material of enunciated maxims or laws themselves nor – as is the case with law and religion – of the tradition which transmits them, but solely of the consciousness that determines them. Where it too falls down, though, is in 'theoretizing' the ought: the categorical imperative is wrong not because of the obligatoriness that makes it an imperative – 'a performed act must be absolutely non-contingent' – but because 'legality itself

187

is the content of the law' (*TPA*, 25). The actual deed is lost in its purely theoretical justification; universal validity is bought at too high a cost experientially speaking. What is more, the will in formal ethics renders itself passive in prescribing a law to itself, confining its self-activity (suicidally) to that single overriding prescription. Kantian 'practical reason' is, then, for Bakhtin, no less 'theoretical' than the other domains of Kant's philosophy: its principle is that not of the 'actually performed act' but of the 'possible generation of already performed acts in a theoretical transcription of them' (*TPA*, 27).

It is worth stopping to reflect on how Bakhtin proceeds here. His critique of Kantian ethics is the best kind of immanent critique in so far as it turns its object inside out on the new ground valuably established by that very object: in elevating the singularity of the deed over all universals, he is not so much contradicting Kant as using the strength of the Kantian argument – namely, its insistence on non-contingency – against itself. Otherwise put: in a move that has all the extremism and provocation of Adornian negative dialectics or Derridean deconstruction, Bakhtin effectively parodies the categorical imperative. He also, as it happens, anticipates the critique of Saussurean linguistics that he will later ventriloquize through the work of Voloshinov. The answerability of the performed act (knowable only from *within* its performance) ensures that its theoretically valid meaning occupies the same 'unitary' plane as its peculiar tone and historicity; or, better still: answerability in the deed *is nothing other than* that unity. Rationalistic ethics behaves rather like Saussurean linguistics: its supreme law echoes the latter's reduction of *langue* in consigning *parole* (the singular speech-act) to contingency. In then attributing rationality only to what is objective and reducible to logic, it forgets that rationality is 'blind and elemental' without the centre of 'an answerable consciousness' (*TPA*, 29). Only from the standpoint of the dominant rationalism of modern philosophy could the philosophy of the act that Bakhtin is here proposing seem in any way subjectivist or irrational. Far from being less than rational, the thinking which at once informs and understands the answerable act is (as it were) *hyper*-rational. This sublation of the rational encompasses the field of the rational as a lesser light is dimmed by a greater, whilst still partaking of the character of light. Even that 'transcendental unity of objective culture' which rationalism achieves by bracketing out the performed act can only have effect when we 'actually think' it and it 'shines with the borrowed light of our answerability' (*TPA*, 30).

Interestingly it is here – before the explicit linguistic turn he will later take, some would say under Ernst Cassirer's influence – that Bakhtin first makes the claims for that special truth of language to the world of deeds which I noted earlier.[4] Quite simply, rationalism's fallacy is to suppose that only that which is logical is expressible. Using a phraseology that suggests a riposte over the centuries to the father of rationalism (with whom this text is clearly in what Bakhtin would later call 'hidden polemic': transcendental philosophy begins, after all, not with Kant but with René Descartes), Bakhtin says that the clarity and distinctness of the event to its participant is actually guaranteed by language itself. It is the abstract that is (strictly) unutterable; not the act in its concreteness at all, but rather pure conceptuality that must always fall short of full understanding. For Bakhtin in this phase understanding in the proper sense is a quasi-spatial affair: it is a matter of orienting oneself answerably to the world as ostensively defined – as given and set-as-a-task in all its unrepeatable concreteness around and under and over me in the event of being. Understanding only takes place, after all, thanks to the participative thinking facilitated by language itself, its privileged medium. The corollary of this is that what is purely given cannot be experienced; and, conversely, what is truly experienced cannot be merely given. Like the world after Christ's coming, the object grows in my experience of it: it is not the same as it was before it swam into my ken, appearing as it does simultaneously and inseparably under the aspect of the is as well as the ought. Understanding is the work of my 'living word', which does not know an object 'totally given' (*TPA*, 32). My word spoken about the object mobilizes it towards what is yet-to-be-determined about it, making it into a moment of the event. (The definite article in that last clause is mandatory: *an* event would be a mere instance; *the* event is an actuality. Grammatically speaking, the world of the act is a world not only of proper names, but also of definite articles.) What indissolubly links the event to the word is the intonation which belongs to both – or, at least, to their interface within my deed. It is not the context of culture that actualizes my deed; on the contrary, it is my deed of 'active thinking' that actualizes (potentially, the whole of) culture itself. The monadic seclusion of the thought's 'possible content' is opened up and broken through by the tone of its performance in the boundless theatre of an answerable consciousness (*TPA*, 34, 36). The living word and the living deed are at once the closest of ontological bedfellows in reality and figures for each other in this phenomenological description of them.

That reference to Descartes in the last paragraph portends more than at first sight appears. For it soon becomes clear as one reads *Toward a Philosophy of the Act* that Bakhtin's retrospective itinerary through Western thinking does not stop at Kant but pushes back to the *cogito: ergo* sum.[5] Like the categorical imperative, the *cogito* is here subject to a certain parodic reworking, a re-accentuation in the most literal sense. If Descartes's stress in his elementary resolution of ontological doubt is upon the verb of his premiss 'I think', Bakhtin's emphasis is upon the personal pronoun in that clause. Of far more weight than my experience of *thinking* – an experience which is immediately made existentially null by that brutal *ergo*, vaporized in the thin air of a logical deduction – is the fact that the experience is *mine*. It is the inescapably tonal 'experiencing of an experience' as *my* experience and not anybody else's (the fact that '*I* think – perform a deed by thinking') that bonds into a unity all of its constituent moments and is 'answerably rational' (*TPA*, 36–37). From an abstractly rational – that is to say, rational*ist* – standpoint this richly meaningful tone which radically 'owns' an experience is so much dross, the stuff of art rather than positive knowledge. 'Truth' being (on this view) composed solely of moments which are universal, in the sense of being serially commutable across persons or self-identically iterable by me or anyone else – truth being thus conceived, this affirmative tonality of actively owning a thought or feeling is relegated to the outer darkness of the merely impression-istic and individual. It cannot be the basis of the unity of an act of thinking or feeling. For Bakhtin, though, the very term 'unity' is compromised by its association with this rationalist notion of truth, and – rather like Emmanuel Levinas in his claim that any drawing of the other into a 'we' is the work of a power-laden, totalizing conceptuality – he proposes that 'uniqueness' should be put in its place. Such a unique correlation of moments has nothing in common with 'the contentual constancy of a principle, of a right, of a law, and even less so of being' (*TPA*, 38). Bakhtin suggests that we might rethink this correlation in the 'act-performing consciousness' as a species of loving, being-true-to: in short, faith. Faith here is not dogmatic adherence: the analogue implicitly invoked in this refer-ence to one of the Christian virtues is that of being true to one's word, as in a relationship of deep love or solemn trust. An episte-mology based on possible contents can be no basis for an ethics: what obliges me in an obligation is not its content but my signature under it, the answerable world of the act being one not of 'rough drafts' without signature but of fair copies duly signed and binding the doer (*TPA*, 44). Cognitive certainty founded in the unity of a deed's universal relations can only be a 'technical' moment in the deed's more encompassing performative reality.

Ontological certainty cannot, in short, be reduced to such cognitive certainty. Bakhtin returns Descartes' *cogito* to the performative acknowledgement which it denies. The *cogito* subordinates that acknowledgement to the task of achieving a mode of certainty, when of course in Bakhtin's view the reverse should obtain: that task itself should be subordinate to such prior and active acknowledgement. In the performed act I affirm my participation in the whole of being; but then this affirmation that I have an ineluctable part in being withers into a cognitive certainty at the moment that it is made of (or on behalf of) anyone or everyone else. The being in which I acknowledge my active part is whole and indivisible; no part of it, that is, can be assigned to anyone else as a place which is other than the locus of *my* unrepeatable deed; my deed's uniqueness and my coextension in it with all being are simply two sides of the same ethical and ontological coin. Because 'there is no alibi in being' – because there is no place where I can claim to be other than where I answerably now am – where I am is everywhere: in the deed, immediacy and ultimacy coincide. The 'non-alibi in being' (*TPA*, 40) has not only forensic but also Christological connotations: those who do not believe Jesus to be the Christ, or who deny Him as Peter does, essentially claim to live from some other place than where they are (for example in the Law). My existence is not a predicate of an arbitrary individual from which I then logically extrapolate the existence of possible others; it is *an* event *in* being which is also and inseparably *the* event *of* being. Bakhtin's 'I think' and his 'I, too, *exist*' (*TPA*, 40) resist any logical correlation in the sense that they cannot be used to reconstruct the *cogito*, in which the transcendental subject of modern philosophy is founded. These locutions encompass cognitive certainty, which must not be allowed to encompass – still less replace – *them*. It is tempting to use this formulation: they are propositions of equal weight. Better, however, to say that they are (truly speaking) not propositions at all but rather irreducible affirmations. Like performatives in the Austinian definition, they cannot be quoted – rendered indirectly – and still retain what J.L. Austin himself would call their 'illocutionary' force. They cannot be made to follow a *that*, as the propositional content of an utterance. Instead we would need to call them (something like) alternative and equally valid verbal performances of my – already performative – participation in the event of being. As propositions, they would have no place in being; they would instead be relegated to the condition of possible being: that purely theoretical world where there is no centre from which I can begin – from which, that is, I can at once enact and come upon being. In this restless realm, where not the is and the ought but only the 'could' and the 'could not' rule, nothing can properly begin. In this sea of mere possibility, the place I occupy is 'insignificantly minute', dwarfed by what surrounds it. The totality of values and knowledge of the whole of 'historical mankind' mean nothing to me unless I have a 'particular emotional-volitional attitude' towards them. Historical mankind must itself be brought into correlation with my unique participation, must indeed glow with value in my intoning invocation of it, before the perennial values held by it can be any concern of mine. There is no such thing, in short, as man-in-general: 'I exist and a particular concrete other exists' (*TPA*, 47). Mortality as a concept levels all actual deaths to a single meaning: my death, your death, his or hers – these do not admit of any such *Gleichschaltung*. Belonging as they do to different 'phrasal universes' (in Jean-François Lyotard's expression), being incommensurable, they cannot come into mutual contradiction. Whereas empathy with being leads to a loss of oneself and a concomitant erasure of these differences, participation neither conflates nor counterposes, its terms always counting as persons and relating each to the other always in what we might call a *co-inherent distinctiveness*.

Having said this, we need then also to say that for Bakhtin participation has nothing in common with the surrogacy of symbolic representation. The small space occupied by my act does not merely symbolically betoken the boundless world of being: counterposition is not, that is, sublated in symbolic portending: there *can* be no such counterposition when, from the unique place of my self-activity, the small expands always – actually, and not just symbolically – to fill the boundless whole. In making participation a moment of representation one becomes an impostor, a 'pretender'. The rituals of religion and politics are legitimate only insofar as the representative roles they demand are self-consciously forms of 'specialized action' encompassed within an ultimate (personal) answerability, from which alone they gain their force (*TPA*, 52). Anything else is pharisaism, the pride that passes itself off as humility. Bakhtin is perhaps thinking here of the Russian intelligentsia, who were viewed by the *Landmarks* contributors as just such humble-prideful individuals in the sense that their humility before 'the people' is a disguised form of pride.[6] Against the example of such latter-day Pharisees, the actively self-sacrificing individual imitates Christ. Viewed from the standpoint of its politics, the pathology of modernity is exactly this heroization of the political. Institutionalism and ritualism, whether in religion or in politics, come to the same thing; both are for Bakhtin symptoms of a deeper crisis of modernity which takes the form of a diversion of all the energy of the act into 'the autonomous domain of culture'. All spirit and ideality having migrated thanks to theory into the realm of 'culture', the deed decomposes into the brute materiality either of economic interest or of instinctual drive. That objective realm, which is the repository of the finished products of the deed, attracts to itself and then monopolizes the dimension of spirit which properly belongs only to the act performed within being-as-event. Art and theory in their historically established autonomy together conspire to empty the deed; feeding off its axiological and ontological riches, they leave it depleted. As the latter-day pagan cult of possession-inspiration, 'art' thus conceived is powerless to restore to the deed the performative energy which theory has drained from it. Aesthetic activity and the act itself can only safely be correlated for the purposes of a first philosophy by an examination of the 'concrete architectonics' that they share. In his very first published work, 'Art and Answerability', Bakhtin had insisted that if life was 'vulgar prose', the unwittingly colluding guilty parties were a theoretical knowledge which reduced the act to biology or the economic and an artistic practice which dissolved active answering in a passive possession (AA, 1–3). By different routes, both lead to solipsism and to the construction of a world without an outside. The Romantic counter-enlightenment has in this sense made things worse, whatever its intentions: art and theory together make up a self-legitimating world of culture which threatens the deed with a greater danger of reduction than did theory on its own.

It is this situation which gives special urgency to Bakhtin's project at the end of this fragment: namely, the task of at once using the internal architectonic of aesthetic seeing as a ready paradigm for the architectonics of the deed itself *and* insisting on their fundamental ontological difference. His aim, he says, is not to create a 'logically unified system of values' but rather to describe the 'concrete architectonic of value-governed experiencing of the world' (TPA, 60–61). To emphasize the architectonics common to both aesthetic seeing and actual doing is to establish a space anterior to logic and system which can include the latter without being conflated with them. 'Art' and 'life' will then at least be so articulated upon one another that 'theory' can no longer appear to be a self-legitimating mode of superior (because putatively universal) understanding. As an 'architectonic interrelation' of two 'valuatively' affirmed *others*, art is a secondary – or, better, second-order – architectonics; an architectonics of architectonics: otherness raised to the second power, in so far as both the *I* and the *other in* the work are *others* for the artist-contemplator *outside* it (*TPA*, 63). Only by correlating 'art' and 'life' in this way can 'theory' find its proper level. Otherwise, theory can get away with substituting an abstract system of hierarchized contents for the concrete architectonic of valuative contexts (with their indivisible form-content). Such a system, like all merely logical constructs, combines a strict internal necessity with utter contingency in relation to everything else. From this it should be plain that Bakhtin conceives of the Kantian triad of cognitive, ethical and aesthetic in Trinitarian terms, as so many interpenetrating hypostases of the human: his escape from the binary oppositions of cognitive discourse is made good thanks to just such hyper-conceptual *ternaries*. *Towards a Philosophy of the Act* elaborates an aesthetics of ethics as a first philosophy; his next work, 'Author and Hero', offers a complementary ethics of aesthetics. The two works together ensure that 'art' and 'life' are articulated architectonically rather than logically (or indeed dialectically). Whilst 'art' as such may not itself offer an exit from conceptuality into the life-world, its reconceptualization in these two early works – as 'aesthetic activity' or as 'aesthetic seeing' – offers a figure for the understanding of the life-world which is firmly removed from the categories for the understanding of experience on offer from cognitive discourse. The traditional self-understanding of art inherited from the nineteenth century is that of the counter-enlightenment, and from Bakhtin's perspective it is both a wrong turning and an opportunity: a wrong turning because it confirms theoretical reason in its place; an opportunity because it gives serious ontological weight to the only modern and secular discourse ('art') which truly figures the Other.

III

How better to show this new conception of the aesthetic as inter-personal action than in a correlative act of (close) reading? Bakhtin's choice of the untitled Pushkin lyric traditionally called 'Parting' is richly suggestive in itself, before his analysis even begins. Besides picking up on the motifs of love and death which he connects on a formal level with aesthetic activity, it cannot surely be a coincidence that he chooses for his illustration a text that thematizes the transcultural by a poet – Russia's great 'national' poet, what is more – whose ethnic background was partly African. (The heroine Amalia Riznich's first and second names signal yet another ethnic hybrid of Austrian and Italian.) It is also a poem from exactly the period which saw the elaboration of that late-modern conception of art which essentially modernism never wholly overcame, but which Bakhtin is here provocatively contesting. The poem, moreover, takes us in imagination to the Mediterranean basin, cradle of those founding Classical and Christian cultures which fused to form the culture of the West. Italy is seen through Russian eyes, Russia through Italian eyes: Bakhtin's later explanation of dialogism in terms of saying *I* in the language of the other and *you* in my own language is already on the horizon here. All of this – and indeed the whole fragment – needs to be read in the context of the Westernizing *versus* Slavophile polemic in early-twentieth-century Russia, that battle of positions which themselves might be mapped upon the broader and longer-term European opposition of enlightenment universalism and counter-enlightenment particularism. Of course the otherness actually contemplated by the speaker of the poem is not so much cultural as ontological or existential: namely, that other of mortal life on earth which is the afterlife of the hero's assured eventual meeting with his beloved, who for the time being – or eternity – has (in words that echo the Orthodox prayer for the dead) 'fallen asleep forever' (*TPA*, 66). Bakhtin chooses this poem, then, because it is a richly ambivalent elegy-eulogy to our human 'intercreaturality'.[7] As creatures of the Creator, we are creatures of earth and death, and all our values are absolutely bound up with these co-ordinates of our mortality. Paradoxically, though, it is only through time that eternity is known. Eternity is a projection (Bakhtin has already argued) not of mathematical time – this would be mere endlessness, the sheer vertiginous terror of a dimension without *me* – but rather of time saturated with the value which it gains from my very finitude; which is to say: the other side of the (chronotopic) incarnation of time in space is its transcendence in eternity. As we have seen in 'Author and Hero', poetry even at its most lyrical is for Bakhtin not the expression of a solitary *I*, but rather the choric staging of our intercreatural being as creatures *among* other creatures and *of* the Creator. This mutual indwelling of what Bakhtin calls 'valuative contexts' (*TPA*, 67) makes time and space take on flesh and blood, and it is the special business of poetry verbally to enact this interpenetration. Poems like this one thematize that function of their writing; and their affirmation of the multiplicity and immortality of consciousness (a theme which Bakhtin will elaborate some forty years later and for which the paradigm is clearly the Trinity) is welcoming – as only it can be – to the hybridity of cultural identities.[8] Here is the text of the poem:

Bound for the shores of your distant homeland
You were leaving this foreign land.
In that unforgettable hour, in that sorrowful hour,
I wept before you for a long time
My hands, growing ever colder,
Strained to hold you back,
My moans implored you not to break off
The terrible anguish of parting.

But you tore away your lips
From our bitter kiss;
From a land of gloomy exile
You called me to another land.
You said: 'On the day of our meeting
Beneath an eternally blue sky
In the shade of olive trees,
We shall once more, beloved, unite our kisses of love.

But there – alas! – where the sky's vault
Shines with blue radiance,
Where the waters slumber beneath the cliffs,
You have fallen asleep forever.
Your beauty and your sufferings
Have vanished in the grave –
And the kiss of our meeting has vanished as well . . .
But I am waiting for that kiss – you owe it to me . . .

This poem brings into the foreground that translation of cultures into each other's terms which Bakhtin's later sociology of discourse was to theorize and which forms so great a part of what pass for theories of hybridity and 'postcoloniality' today. My motherland is another land to you; this world which we share and by which we apophatically know the next is not a world of 'man in general'; rather, it is a rich intercreaturality of persons crossed with a rich transculturality of communal identities. Art as a form of 'objective' love ('lovingly interested attention' as a principle of shaping) offers a way of seeing which brings out this manifold and irreducible inner alterity of the human. From *outside* the contemplated world, the artist lovingly 'affirms and founds' that 'concrete actuality' of a person which is art's 'supreme value-centre' irrespective of the values assigned to the same person *within* that world (*TPA*, 63–64). These values can never become the principle of art's shaping-from-without of what (in the moment of empathy) is seen from within.

Let us turn now to the detail of Bakhtin's analysis. He sees the poem as made up of two interpenetrating value-contexts within a single aesthetic event: the movement from other land to motherland issues from the heroine's context while at the same time being real-ized as an event in the hero's life. The unique places that the two of them fill are brought into interaction without ever quite losing their distinctiveness. This 'intense interpenetration' takes place within the creaturality – the finitude as human beings under God's love – which they share (*TPA*, 69). What takes precedence, however, over this common condition from which both begin, and which qualifies all of their creatural life, is the projected event of their meeting here-after. Because Italy as the place where she might again live and where they might meet has become by the end of the poem the place where she no longer is, it is qualified inescapably by that fact of her having died – of her having, that is, left this world altogether and not just one place in it. The elegiac tone of their parting and their 'unrealized meeting' (*TPA*, 70) in this life gives way – and in so doing lends all of its creatural force – to the tone of assurance accompanying the thought of their future meeting in the next. All the pathos of their twofold parting (hers from him, then hers from the world specified as the space of their anticipated earthly meeting) turns and is made to flow into the muted joy of that closing affirmation of a heavenly reunion. Italy and Russia as self-identical places separated by so many miles cease to be such: instead they live within the ongoing event, occupying a place in its architectonic structure which is in turn constituted by two unique horizons in an intersection no less unique. This intersection (not fusion, not merging) of horizons has something of the character of a complex chiastic embrace: the event-context Italy-as-other/Russia-as-mother enfolds within itself the event-context Russia-as-other/Italy-as-mother. The hero's unique place and part in being is, then, far from being monadically closed off. Moreover, 'the Italy of all mankind' enters into the making of his consciousness (*TPA*, 71). Standing in his turn outside this whole architectonic complex is the artist himself – not in the guise of some disembodied World Spirit but as a bodied other to the poem's world who correlates the hero's context with 'the value of human beings and of the human' only in so far as he is himself thus bodied and participating in being (*TPA*, 72).

Venturing so deeply into the intricacies of a particular instance of aesthetic seeing by no means has the effect of ejecting Bakhtin from the philosophical ground which he wishes to occupy and lumping him along with some kind of anti-theoretical 'practical criticism': the other side of contesting theoreticism is, after all, the reconstitution of theory as a discourse which thematizes its own answerability. That he has no desire of leaving theory to the theorists but seeks rather to make the strongest bid he can for their ground is clear from the very term that he uses for the common structure of aesthetic seeing and ethical doing. No commentator known to me has stopped to reflect on the fruitful paradox of 'architectonic(s)' as a term. The *Shorter Oxford English Dictionary* defines this metaphoric coinage as 'the science . . . of the systematic arrangement of knowledge' and records its first use in English as dating back to 1838.[9] Philosophical systems, especially those of the German idealist tradition just then passing its peak, are even today regularly praised for the 'architectonic' beauty of their construction. The fundamental structure of both ethics and aesthetics – the counterposition of the *I* and the *other* – is, then, perversely named with the name of what one could be forgiven for thinking it is resolutely set against: logic, system. The sense of so doing is, however, quite plain when we recall (once again) that Bakhtin is not opposing reason with the irrational. When we posit something more fundamental than rationality we do not move into a primordial structureless oneness or in-itself. We encounter rather a structure, and of the most concrete kind: the structure of which all other structures are moments, more or less rationalized. Architectonics as the aesthetics of knowledge – the way in which a whole system strikes the inner eye – is therefore very appropriately subjected to a further metaphorization, a sort of parodic transfer of meaning yielding metasystematic commentary. For Bakhtin, what institutes and orders, with all (indeed more than) the authority of system, is the act in its performance. The institutional and the systematic are not so much negated as relocated and redefined. Metaphorizing over again high-modern philosophy's metaphor for the beauty of its own structuring, Bakhtin brings architectonics back from abstraction and thereby builds before us a house of value as many-mansioned as that promised to believers by Jesus in the gospel of John. As the church houses the faithful, as system embraces the abstractly rational or intelligible, so the architectonic of two or more valuative contexts constructs a space for the answerable. Whatever effect the first of these two have in the world they have thanks to the ever-alternating foundation of the third.

IV

In the closing paragraph of this fragmentary manuscript Bakhtin entertains us with a glimpse of how his project in it relates to the discourse of Christianity – how its peculiar modernization of Christian discourse differs signally from all earlier modernizations. Bakhtin's modernization is not a replication of that process whereby Revelation over the centuries has made so many successive concessions to secular reason that the cognitive discourse which defends its claims (theology) opened the way first for deism and at last for atheism. Thinkers like Bakhtin would have seen the Russian intelligentsia as consolidating (and, in so doing, clarifying) this error by abstracting the cultural *product* of Western development from the *acts* – the history – that produced it. Bakhtin seeks to correct both this gross abstraction and the whole Western development itself by getting beyond – perhaps it would be better to say *behind* – modernity's self-understanding as an unequivocally positive and progressive break from the past of myth and superstition. He retraces its itinerary – through Kant, through Descartes, and still further back – and then in thought he takes a new path forward, such that enlightenment appears in its true guise as a moment of Revelation: not, that is, as a negation of Revelation but as a dimension of Revelation's historical unfolding. Enlightenment is a Christian heresy which deifies man: (human) *theosis* without (divine) *kenosis*. From the enlightenment's standpoint Revelation is nothing other than the dogmatic issuing of ideas from authority, the transmission of certain contents from a source not to be questioned. In a lecture of 1925 recorded by Lev Pumpiansky, Bakhtin will argue that Revelation speaks not of certain idea-contents or truths but rather of the obligating force of the personhood of God.[10] It is in this sense that Revelation calls upon me to answer with my life for what it shows me. Enlightenment misunderstands Revelation by imposing upon the latter its own epistemological model of the cognizing subject over against the object, conveniently forgetting that Revelation's model of the self is that of the hero answering to his Author before the whole world. Bakhtin finds this forgotten concrete-architectonic core of Revelation in Dante, in the mediaeval mystery plays and in tragedy, and it is this early-modern cultural phenomenon that he seeks to revive under late-modern conditions. The *logos* (reason, the narrowly rational word) of modernity is in no sense rejected; rather, it is redeemed as a moment in the ongoing unceasing event of the Johannine *Logos* (the Word made flesh). On this view, Revelation is not confined to the closed canon of Holy Writ: the meaning of 'modernity' that Bakhtin wishes to put into circulation is that of an epoch in which Revelation, so far from losing its force, actually expands to fill the whole expressive and intellectual culture of humankind (including the natural sciences). The residue of incarnated narrative truth which survives the heresy of the enlightenment's self-misunderstanding is given the generic name of 'art', which in Bakhtin may be taken as a code for the non-cognitive orders of meaning.

When he speaks, then, of giving 'adequate scientific expression' to the architectonic of the *I* and the *other* – 'think[ing them] through more essentially and fully' – what Bakhtin intends is not yet another modernizing of Christian spirituality on modernity's terms, as if Christian discourse were something of the past, belonging to the prehistory of modern humanity (*TPA*, 75). On the contrary: he is calling for a late-modern philosophy which will at bottom be a hermeneutic committed to a reading-forward from critical points in the past – a past which is thought of as being as open as the future. Prophecy has not come to an end: it has simply multiplied its forms; and the discourses we call 'literature' and 'philosophy' are the names of two of these forms (it is, after all, only their modern separation from each other that disguises their status as components of an ongoing prophetic discourse). Revelation and the Incarnation represent, in short, not punctual moments in the past but a continuing and omni-temporal agonistics of history. At once and without contradiction religious philosopher and philosopher of religion, Bakhtin takes his distance equally from dogmatic sceptics and dogmatic theists. If late modernity is a time of crisis – of, that is, the modern pathology at its extreme point – it is also a time in which the mutual outsideness of enlightenment and Revelation yields insights that could never have been there for the self-understanding of either on its own. If enlightenment is a fall, it is, like the Fall of Man, *felix culpa*, a happy one in the long term, a dialogical test undergone by Revelation, helping Christianity to break out of the pseudo-eternal vertical of its dogmatic enclosure in the Middle Ages. Modernity at its best is, then, not so much a triumph of enlightenment as an opportunity for Revelation to reinvigorate itself – to re-enter the horizontal of historical experience. The story of the modern world cannot be reduced to the story it has so often told itself: that is, of *logos* winning out over *mythos*; in the Christian Revelation, as Hans Blumenberg has argued, *logos* and *mythos* have been intertwined from the beginning.

V

The mention of Blumenberg's name opens the possibility of some concluding reflections on the lessons Bakhtin has to teach the late twentieth century. Those who have in recent years in different ways and often with divergent agendas dwelt on the Bakhtinian debt to the work of Cassirer – I am thinking in particular of Craig Brandist and Brian Poole – would do well to acknowledge Bakhtin's uncannily close prefiguration of Blumenberg's critique of the philosopher of 'symbolic forms' in his monumental *Work on Myth*.[11] With Blumenberg it is as if a way has been found beyond the *aporia* which threatens when we place Max Horkheimer and Theodor Adorno's (in)famous apophthegm of 1947 – 'Myth is already enlightenment; and enlightenment has reverted to myth' – alongside Cassirer's *The Myth of the State* of the year before.[12] The polemical hyperbole of the first, with its vision of a reason totally and culpably instrumental-ized, its paradoxical critical discrediting of the whole tradition of critique; the latter's shocked discovery in contemplating the phenomenon of Nazism that myth has not, after all, been rendered obsolete by reason: neither of these is a necessary deduction. Blumenberg's laborious scholarship established some thirty years later what Bakhtin's early fragment seems to have been anticipating some thirty years earlier – namely, that *mythos* and *logos* are not opposites locked in a unilinear teleology (one succeeding the other historically) but, rather, perennial dimensions of the human project, and that myth can therefore never be decisively 'brought to an end'.[13] The enlightenment's demonization of myth itself bears all the marks of myth in the 'bad' sense established by that very demo-nization; and it merely repeats under new conditions the early-Christian polemic against paganism. In truth the seeds of reason are there in myth's inbuilt reflexivity, in its 'work' on itself. Christianity is distinguished by Blumenberg as being the first reli-gion to achieve a 'distance from myth' in that it creates an 'abstract system of dogma' that frees it from particular spaces and 'autochthonous familiarities', thereby ensuring that it is truly a world religion speaking telegraphically across the boundaries of culture and language.[14] In effect, Blumenberg credits Christianity with the founding of the very conceptuality that the enlightenment was to turn against it. Bakhtin undoes in much the same way the whole modern myth of myth's supersession – under which we would need to include the Romantic valorization of its premodern pastness and those philosophical systems like Hegel's which offer philosophy itself as the final myth. The ethnocentricity of all such arguments – up to and including Cassirer's – has no place in Bakhtin, for whom a philosophical reinvention of the intercreatural essence of Christian metaphysics and its elaboration to match the complexities of a post-traditional age is the first task of an ethics that will be truly transcultural.

Two commentators on Bakhtin have latterly seen his work as correcting the ethnocentricity of the whole tradition of critique that stems from Kant. Wlad Godzich goes for the formal ethics of Kant himself; Greg Nielsen for the twentieth-century discourse ethics of Habermas. The inference to be drawn from both is that what enables this correction is the careful discrimination whereby Bakhtin asserts the claims of the aesthetic alongside (indeed, in a complex and nuanced way, *over*) the cognitive and moral spheres of value, and which I have sought to explicate in this chapter. Nielsen's argument seems to be that Habermasian discourse-ethical universals are over-juridified and over-rationalized: life-world solidarities – that is, intra-cultural versions of 'the good' – can only be transcended by normative notions of 'the right'. As the aesthetics of social action, Bakhtinian dialogism provides a model for the expansion of solidarity to take in relations of ethical interaction *between* life-worlds. Even when (as in the 'ideal speech situation') the better argument wins, something is left unaccounted for: 'the creative content of actual dialogue has to do with the extra, unfinished residue that actors produce in their discursive associations, despite the rational motivations that might be deduced from their actions'.[15] Transculturation takes place when hybrids are formed in the contact of disparate life-worlds. Habermas underrates the 'aesthetic dimension' of 'practical discourse';[16] with Bakhtin's help, however, we can see that 'it shoulders an intuitive content of intersubjectivity as well as a rational force of unification or binding effect'.[17] Crossing the boundaries between life-worlds means that 'the expressive must play a larger role than either the objective or authoritative validity claims in communicative actions'.[18] It is, Nielsen concludes, 'not a binding reason but a gesture of care and even affection that lays the basis for intersubjectivity'.[19] In short: Bakhtin's translinguistic conception of style is inherently friendly towards the transcultural; style is the domain of the hybrid and of hybridization. In so far as it is the forerunner of his translinguistics of the work, his early architectonics of the deed shows itself to be motivated by the same transcultural(ist) impulse.

Godzich's case is more historically inflected than Nielsen's. Modernity for Bakhtin and his 'circle' is 'the epoch that resulted from the confrontation with Otherness and then sought to avoid this Otherness at all cost by elaborating a complex strategy for its containment'. In a detour through Kant they 'seek to restore this Otherness to its rightful . . . place'. Kant's 'canonical organization of Western rationality' contained in their view 'a particular flaw'[20]: whilst the imagination in ordinary cases of the failure of determinate judgement provides 'a concept of reason' with which the understanding can work – whilst we all have 'direct experience' of one such idea in the categorical imperative, permitting us 'to recognize the existence of other human beings and to engage in ethical acts'[21] – what Godzich calls 'intercultural interaction' (namely, face-to-face encounter of a European with an exotic creature) thwarts the working of imagination's first aid to the understanding, producing in the European the reflex either of fight or flight in the face of a cognitively unmasterable alterity. The ethical is 'unable to account for an Other that is not a member of the community ruled by the categorical imperative'.[22] Bakhtin accordingly 'correct[s] Kant's architectonics'[23] by insisting that 'the proper meaning of an ethical act is one that is undertaken when the understanding is no longer a guide to our behaviour'. It is this 'practical sphere'[24] (which constructs the human world) that is reconciled with the cognitive (which constructs the world of nature). Now whilst – the argument continues – both cognitive and practical have transcendental status, the aesthetic experiences the world as constructed by those other value spheres and is therefore 'caught in the finite'.[25] Where the first two *Critiques* presuppose the transcendental subject and seek merely to ensure 'cognitive certainty' for it, the third 'turns to the constitution of the subject itself' and 'forces it to recognize itself as an historical being'.[26] The subject which acknowledges its own historicity cannot constitute the Other as an object, sharing as it does that common historicity. In place of the 'theoretical instance' we have the 'anthropological instance' which 'recognizes the limitations of the understanding and the possibility of differing modes of subject constitution in space and time'.[27]

If we take the intercultural in Godzich to be synonymous with the transcultural in Nielsen, then we can recast their insights in terms appropriate to the present argument. The inference to be drawn from both commentators is one that I have already drawn: that it is careful discrimination which enables the 'correction' whereby Bakhtin is seen as refounding the claims of the aesthetic over the cognitive and the ethical. Within the aesthetic it is of course (as we have seen) the *literary* that comes to dominate Bakhtin's thinking from henceforth. The analysis of the Pushkin poem is evidence enough to suggest that the move from philosophy to literature was not simply (or at least not in its initial impulse) Aesopian. With this move to the art form whose material is language, what I have called the intercreatural modulates into the *dialogical*: it is through the parity of two or more voices on the same plane rather than the mortality of two human beings under God that art and the life-world are mutually articulated. Within literature it is then the novel that clarifies for Bakhtin what it is about literary discourse as a whole that can 'save' (late) modernity. So far from being the counterpart of philosophy in Hegel's system (as Brandist argues), the novel keeps alive that renegotiation of the tension between *mythos* and *logos* which – rather than any real or potential triumph of the latter – marks the very beginning of modernity. The novel's weddedness to the plane of the horizontal recaptures the raw energy of the creatural that then entered writing, before rationalism rendered the *logos*'s travesty of myth hegemonic and in the name of the universal fatally narrowed modernity's gaze. Consigning myth to the premodern meant consigning virtually all of humankind to the darkness of a past that the emitter of that hubristic discourse had (by definition) outgrown. The reader hostile to the postcolonial will detect in that last sentence of mine something of its (to him, merely modish) pathos; and it is true both that I have already dropped the dreaded word into the discourse of this essay and that I have on an earlier occasion linked Bakhtin's name with the condition it describes. However, I was not then – and I am not now – in the business of dignifying that agenda with his name. Equally, I do not go along with those Russian and North American writers on Bakhtin for whom he must never be tempted from what they see (respectively) as his ethnic or disciplinary home ground. My project in this chapter has been to open a space beyond those egregious alternatives and to show their proponents that their disagreement is shortsighted – better still: that Bakhtin is already in a place where their opposition has no meaning.

To find a critique of ethnocentricity in Bakhtin which is compatible with that of 'postcolonialism' is not in any way to 'politicize'

his work (I leave that move to Western Marxists, Russian national-
ists and some North American scholars). After all, what else is the
postcolonial but the space where the political simplicities of the
anti-colonial are interrupted, diverting it along a tangent into the
anti-foundational? The history of colonial power and anti-colonial
resistance becomes less a story of winners and losers in Manichaean
opposition and separation than a holistic experience, the study of
which is a privileged source of insights into our whole late-modern
condition. Strongest among these is the acknowledgment that
hybridity in the field of culture is not the exception but the rule;
that there are no 'essences' or pure identities. Nothing would be
gained by saying that Bakhtin anticipates this insight: rather, let us
say that he brings the intercultural and the intertextual and the
intercreatural into one and the same perspective, and that for him
the discourse we call literature is where this coextension can best be
seen (and heard and felt). Arguments about the ubiquity and antiquity of the hybrid are only a late-modern rendering-conscious of an
age-old alternative ontology preserved in the vivid suggestion of
the forms of literature throughout that long exile from Western
knowledge which has given literature itself its separate identity.
Whilst finding persuasive the case made by Godzich and Nielsen
for Bakhtin's detheoreticized neo-Kantianism, I would none the less
wish to enter a special plea of my own. It is this: that in Bakhtin we
cannot ignore the specific aesthetic of the literary; and that we
cannot fully understand him without bringing the Christian dimension of his thinking into the frame. Other heirs to the neo-Kantian
tradition simply do not break, as he does, with the whole epistemology and ontology of the transcendental subject and with the
prejudice against prejudice of the enlightenment. 'Intersubjectivity' –
a term that I have elsewhere used uncritically, but which I now
wish partly to disown – is the conceptual and terminological sign of
this failure. Using this category to question high modernity's
recourse to a higher subject or *Geist* (Habermas) is no better than
acknowledging the variety of 'symbolic forms' (Cassirer). Bakhtin is
of course in no sense setting literature up as a secular surrogate for
the religious discourse of Christianity. Secularity, after all, is only
the name we give to the situation in which stories of different kinds
place themselves peacefully alongside each other, none bidding for
a monopoly upon truth. Literature recommends itself to Bakhtin as
a form of narrative knowledge which actively seeks this non-coer-
cive juxtaposition of narratives. Christianity in the early phase
represented by Johannine proto-theology developed an intercreat-

ural metaphysic in conditions of intercultural meeting and mixing precipitated by the world's first truly extensive empire. Literature mimes the telegraphy – the solidarity across disparate life-worlds – for which Christianity provided a model, without seeking to replace it: it simply does so under conditions of modernity, when the discrediting of master-codes coincided with the coming of print culture and the passage of face-to-face into what Benedict Anderson would call 'imagined' forms of community. Literature's peculiar form of the intercreatural is that reproduction of the intertextual along the whole verbal scale from languages themselves to works right down to the inside of individual words for which Bakhtin finds the name *dialogism*. The thin abstraction and transcendentalism of 'intersubjectivity' can never capture this phenomenon. What, then, is this literature which, sensitively conceived, can heal the splits of modernity? The quasi-auto-ethnography of microcommunities; the cherishing and loving understanding of minorities of one; the figuring of personalities precisely as microcommunities; works as strangers which make ethical demands upon us – which to know and fully familiarize is to condemn to death. Bakhtin's aesthetics of ethics modulates into an ethics of aesthetics; then into a poetics of language; then into a semiotics of the grotesque body; then into a semantics of time–space; finally, into a hermeneutics of being: through all of these shifts of focus, his thinking takes him ineluctably into this territory of the literary and keeps him there. It also makes the late twentieth century's sensitivities about the ethnocentric and its positive valuation of the transcultural less a matter of the political correctness of today than a recurrence to the unfinished business of critical moments in the history of the last two thousand years of that discourse which radiated from Jerusalem and Rome and Constantinople to embrace the world.

Bakhtin would have us see this recurrence (or its potential) as the subtext of all the European literatures; for however much they might have contributed to the making of national vernaculars and therefore to the consolidation of nation-states which at length spawned empires – in other words, whatever their complicity in the building of Western global hegemony and 'Eurocentricity' – the works of those literatures bear in their minute particulars not only an incarnational logic but also a memory at least of the moment when the modern European world first parted company with the mutual deafness of cultures in the Middle Ages (a moment for which Bakhtin's literary trinity of Dante, Rabelais and Shakespeare may be read as a code). Literature does not promise the substantial recovery of this moment; it does something infinitely preferable: it makes its gains and insights mobile, portable in all dimensions. At the time of writing *Toward a Philosophy of the Act*, the polemical distinction between the 'poetic genres' (literature as an agent of centralization) and 'the novel' (its centrifugal aspect) – a source of much unfortunate misunderstanding for Bakhtin's commentators – lay in the future; for the time being a short Russian love lyric – he will use it again in 'Author and Hero' – is the first hint of that 'philosophy by other means' of which I spoke at the beginning of this chapter. Perhaps that should be rephrased as 'philosophy *by means of the Other*'. For Bakhtin did not, after all, so much want philosophy to disappear into the expert cultures and sectoral divisions of the social and human sciences as express the hope that it might reconstitute itself as their interpreter in a permanent detour through the caring and always carnal knowledges of the Other, which plays and poems and novels hold out to us – that is, if only we can learn to see them neither as effusions of subjects nor as products subjectlessly constructed but as complex world-disclosing events. Art for Mikhail Bakhtin, in short, neither stands above life nor portends its own sublation in it. Moving beyond those characteristic aesthetics of the two centuries we have now put behind us – beyond, that is, both Romanticism and the *avant-garde* – he conceives art quite simply (but with infinite implication) as the speech in which widely sundered life-worlds address each other.

APPENDIX

On the naming of 'free indirect discourse'

There are no less than seventeen attributable terms for 'free indirect discourse', on my count. In chronological order of coinage, they run thus: 'peculiar mixture of direct and indirect speech' (Adolf Tobler, *Zeitschrift fur romanische Philologie*, 21, 1897); 'veiled speech' (Kalepky, *Zeitschrift fur romansiche Philologie*, 23, 1899); 'free indirect style' (Charles Bally, *Germanisch-romanische Monatsschrift*, 4, 1912); 'disguised speech' (Kalepky, *Germanisch-romanische Monatsschrift*, 5, 1913); 'speech as fact' (Eugen Lerch, *Germanisch-romanische Monatsschrift*, 6, 1914); 'experienced speech' (Etienne Lorck, *Die erlebte Rede* [Heidelberg: 1921]); 'pseudo-objective speech' (Leo Spitzer, *Germanisch-romanische Monatsschrift*, 9, 1921); 'independent form of indirect discourse' (George Curme, *A Grammar of the German Language* [New York: 1922]); 'quasi-direct speech' (Gertraud Lerch, *Idealistische Neuphilologie* [Heidelberg: 1922]); 'semi-direct discourse' (Legrand, *Stylistique française* [Paris: 1922]) ; 'represented speech' (Otto Jespersen, *The Philosophy of Grammar* [London: 1924]); 'semi-indirect style' (E. Kruisinga, *A Handbook of Present-day English* [Utrecht: 1925]); 'half-direct speech' (Leo Spitzer, *Germanisch-romanische Monatsschrift*, 14, 1928); 'indirect interior monologue' (Edouard Dujardin, *Le Monologue interieur* [Paris: 1931]); 'substitutionary speech' (Bernard Fehr, *English Studies*, 20, 3, 1938); 'narrated monologue' (Kurt Müller-Vollmer, unpublished paper, 1965); 'improper direct discourse' (Kalik-Teljatnikova, *Le Français moderne*, 33:4, 34:2, 1966). Curme's description may well have first appeared in the 1904 edition of his German grammar. The term 'narrated monologue' has gained circulation thanks to Dorrit Cohn: see her 'Narrated Monologue: Definition of a Fictional Style', *Comparative Literature*, 18:2, 1966, pp. 97–112; also her *Transparent Minds* (Princeton: Princeton University Press, 1978) pp. 99–140. The final tally may well be eighteen: I have not been able to establish where 'seemingly indirect discourse' – cited in Uspensky (1973) as an English term – is to be found.

NOTES

INTRODUCTION

1 Katerina Clark and Michael Holquist, *Mikhail Bakhtin* (Cambridge, MA: The Belknap Press of Harvard University Press, 1984), p. 317.
2 See Lucien Goldmann, 'The Sociology of Literature: Status and Problems of Method', *International Social Science Journal*, 19:4, 1967, pp. 493–516. The extract I read was 'Discourse Types in Prose', in Ladislaw Matejka and Kristina Pomorska (eds), *Readings in Russian Poetics: Formalist and Structuralist Views* (Cambridge, MA: MIT Press, 1971), pp. 176–196.
3 See section VI of my 'On the Borders of Bakhtin: Dialogization, Decolonization', in Ken Hirschkop and David Shepherd (eds), *Bakhtin and Cultural Theory* (Manchester: Manchester University Press, 1989), pp. 39–67.
4 Jacques Derrida, 'Deconstruction and the Other', in Richard Kearney (ed.), *Dialogues with Contemporary Continental Thinkers* (Manchester: Manchester University Press, 1984), p. 123.

CHAPTER 1

1 Tzvetan Todorov, *Mikhail Bakhtin: The Dialogical Principle* (Manchester: Manchester University Press, 1984), p. 118.
2 Karl Marx, *Grundrisse: Foundations of the Critique of Political Economy*, trans. Martin Nicolaus (Harmondsworth: Penguin Books, 1973), p. 162.
3 Bloch does this in *Das Prinzip Hoffnung* (1959); see 'Ernst Bloch', in Fredric Jameson, *Marxism and Form: Twentieth-Century Dialectical Theories of Literature* (Princeton: Princeton University Press, 1971), pp. 141–42. Brian Poole has shown how Bakhtin's dialogue with Cassirer extends to his 'mature works', where it becomes (to put the matter politely) less dialogue than ventriloquism and verbatim quotation, so that – at least in his use of *Individuum und Kosmos in der Philosophie der Renaissance* (1927) – he is 'somewhat closer' to the Marburg philsopher 'than has hitherto been suspected'. See Brian Poole, 'Bakhtin and Cassirer: The Philosophical Origins of Bakhtin's Carnival Messianism', in Peter Hitchcock (ed.), *South Atlantic Quarterly*, 97:3–4 (special issue on Bakhtin), pp. 537–78.

4 Voloshinov cites vol. 1 of the *Philosophy of Symbolic Forms* in a footnote to the first chapter of *Marxism and the Philosophy of Language* (*MPL*, 11); Bakhtin cites the same book in the text of 'Forms of Time and of the Chronotope in the Novel' (*FTC*, 251).

5 Georg Lukács, *History and Class Consciousness: Studies in Marxist Dialectics*, trans. Rodney Livingstone (London: Merlin Press, 1971), p. 105.

6 See Michael Ryan, *Marxism and Deconstruction: A Critical Articulation* (Baltimore and London: The Johns Hopkins University Press, 1982).

7 'A state of mind is utopian when it is incongruous with the state of reality within which it occurs': thus Mannheim in *Ideology and Utopia: An Introduction to the Sociology of Knowledge* (London: Routledge and Kegan Paul, 1966), p. 173.

8 Graham Pechey, 'Bakhtin, Marxism and Post-structuralism', in Francis Barker *et al.* (eds), *Literature, Politics and Theory* (London: Methuen, 1986), p. 121.

9 'Homophonic' is not to be confused with the adjective from *homophone*; it is the Bakhtinian term for novels with a monological 'dominant'; 'polyphony' is the converse case of dialogism in dominance.

10 Ken Hirschkop, 'The Social and the Subject in Bakhtin', *Poetics Today*, 6:4, 1985, p. 774. This marks the beginning of a long and friendly dialogue with the work of Hirschkop, whose patient interrogation of Bakhtin has been exemplary. His *Mikhail Bakhtin: An Aesthetic for Democracy* (Oxford: Oxford University Press, 1999) is the (provisional) culmination of that quest. For my response to this book, see 'Towards a Culture of Democracy: Ken Hirschkop on Bakhtin', *Dialogism*, 5–6, 2002.

11 Quintin Hoare and Geoffrey Nowell-Smith (eds), *Selections from the Prison Notebooks of Antonio Gramsci* (London: Lawrence and Wishart, 1971), p. 437.

12 Karl Radek, 'Contemporary World Literature and the Tasks of Proletarian Art', in Maxim Gorky *et al.*, *Soviet Writers' Congress 1934: The Debate on Socialist Realism and Modernism in the Soviet Union* (London: Lawrence and Wishart, 1977 [1934]), p. 152.

13 Gramsci defines 'civil society' in *Prison Notebooks* as 'the ensemble of organisms commonly called "private"' (Hoare and Nowell-Smith, *Selections from the Prison Notebooks of Antonio Gramsci*, p. 12); Marx's 'civil society' is more or less a synonym for (or at least includes) the economy.

14 Anatoly Lunacharsky, *On Literature and Art* (Moscow: Progress Publishers, 1973), p. 88.

15 Lunacharsky, *On Literature and Art*, p. 99.

16 Lunacharsky, *On Literature and Art*, p. 102.

17 Lunacharsky, *On Literature and Art*, p. 105.

18 *Shorter Oxford English Dictionary* entry on 'polyphony'.

19 Jameson, *Marxism and Form*, p. 373; Hoare and Nowell-Smith, *Selections from the Prison Notebooks of Antonio Gramsci*, p. 417.

20 Hoare and Nowell-Smith, *Selections from the Prison Notebooks of Antonio Gramsci*, p. 405.

21 Jameson, *Marxism and Form*, p. 365.

22 Frantz Fanon, *The Wretched of the Earth*, trans. Costance Farrington (Harmondsworth: Penguin Books, 1967), p. 31.

23 See Paulo Freire, *Pedagogy of the Oppressed*, trans. Myra Bergman Ramos (Harmondsworth: Penguin Books, 1972), *passim* but especially chs 3 and 4 (pp. 60–150); and Augusto Boal, *Theatre of the Oppressed*, trans. Charles A. and Maria-Odilia Leal-Mcbride (London: Pluto Press, 1979), pp. 120–56.

24 Fredric Jameson, 'Periodizing the 60s', in *The Ideologies of Theory*, vol. 2 (London: Routledge, 1988), p. 188.

CHAPTER 2

1 Two interventions on this topic are to be found, for example, in a single issue of the *Oxford Literary Review*, 4:2, 1980: John Frow, 'System and History: A Critique of Russian Formalism', pp. 56–71; and my own 'Formalism and Marxism' (a long review of Tony Bennett's *Formalism and Marxism* and Medvedev's *Formal Method in Literary Scholarship*), pp. 72–81. Frow's essay was later reprinted as a chapter entitled 'Russian Formalism and the Concept of Literary System' in his *Marxism and Literary History* (Oxford: Basil Blackwell, 1986), pp. 83–102. I return to the topic in my 'Bakhtin, Marxism and Post-structuralism', in Francis Barker *et al.*, *Literature, Politics and Theory* (London: Methuen, 1986), pp. 104–25. The mistaken premiss of this essay – that Bakhtin was 'a Marxist' – does not, I think, invalidate my more general characterization of Formalism as a theory and method.

2 Mikhail Mikhaylovich (*sic*) Bakhtin, 'Toward the Aesthetics of the Word', *Dispositio*, IV, 11–12, 1979, pp. 299–315.

3 Mark Kaiser, 'P.N. Medvedev's "The Collapse of Formalism"', in B.A. Stolz *et al.* (eds), *Language and Literary Theory* (Ann Arbor, MI: Michigan Slavic Publications, 1984), pp. 405–41. After a brief introduction, Kaiser provides a translation only of new material, along with a guide to material that remains unchanged from the 1928 text.

4 'If the science of literature wishes to become scientific it must recognize the "device" as its sole "hero"': thus Roman Jakobson in his *Noveskaja Russkaja poezija: Nabrosok pervyj* (Prague, 1921). Quoted in Peter Steiner, *Russian Formalism: A Metapoetics* (Ithaca and London: Cornell University Press, 1984), p. 213.

5 For an account of these anti-formalist arguments, see 'Marxism versus Formalism', ch. VI of Victor Erlich, *Russian Formalism: History-Doctrine* (The Hague: Mouton, 1969), pp. 99–117.

6 See Roman Jakobson and Yury Tynyanov, 'Problems of Research in Literature and Language', in *Russian Poetics in Translation*, 1977, pp. 49–51. The first English translation of these theses appeared in *New Left Review*; another version is to be found in Ladislav Matejka and Katerina Pomorska (eds), *Readings in Russian Poetics* (Cambridge MA: MIT Press, 1971).

7 I am thinking of (for example) the positions taken on 'art' and its relation to 'the ideological' in Pierre Macherey, *A Theory of Literary Production*, trans. Geoffrey Wall (London: Routledge and Kegan Paul, 1978 [1966]); and in Louis Althusser, *For Marx*, trans. Ben Brewster (London: Allen Lane, 1969 [1965]).

8 Etienne Balibar and Pierre Macherey, 'On Literature as an Ideological Form: Some Marxist Propositions', *Oxford Literary Review*, 3, 1978, pp. 4–12. The original of this essay was first published in 1974. Its warm reception in anglophone Marxist circles may be judged by its rapid reappearance in no less than three other places: in *Praxis 5*, 1980, pp. 43–58; in Robert Young (ed.), *Untying the Text* (Boston and London: Routledge and Kegan Paul, 1981), pp. 79–99; and in Philip Rice and Patricia Waugh (eds), *Modern Literary Theory: A Reader* (London: Edward Arnold, 1996), pp. 61–68.

9 See Maxim Gorky *et al.*, *Soviet Writers' Congress 1934: The Debate on Socialist Realism and Modernism* (London: Lawrence and Wishart, 1977), *passim*.

10 Kaiser, 'P.N. Medvedev's "Collapse of Formalism"', pp. 411 and 419.

11 Kaiser, 'P.N. Medvedev's "Collapse of Formalism"', p. 411.

12 Kaiser, 'P.N. Medvedev's "Collapse of Formalism"', p. 414.

13 Kaiser, 'P.N. Medvedev's "Collapse of Formalism"', p. 414.

14 Kaiser, 'P.N. Medvedev's "Collapse of Formalism"', p. 439.

15 On this migration of structuralism, see J.G. Merquior, *From Prague to Paris: A Critique of Structuralist and Post-structuralist Thought* (London: Verso, 1986).

16 Russell Berman, 'The Routinization of Charismatic Modernism and the Problem of Postmodernity', *Cultural Critique*, 5, 1987, p. 58.

CHAPTER 3

1 See Brian McHale, 'Free Indirect Discourse: A Survey of Recent Accounts', *PTL: A Journal of Descriptive Poetics and Theory of Literature*, 3, 1978, pp. 249–87. McHale is unusual and innovative in his insistence on the 'literariness' of free indirect discourse; neo-Firthian linguists had hitherto sought to trace it back to everyday orality.

2 Tzvetan Todorov, *Mikhail Bakhtin: The Dialogical Principle* (Manchester: Manchester University Press, 1984), pp. 75–76.

3 Michael Gregory, 'Aspects of Varieties Differentiation', *Journal of Linguistics*, 3, 1967.

4 I have dealt with this incomplete deconstruction of 'form' in Russian-Formalist discourse in my 'Bakhtin, Marxism and Post-structuralism', in Francis Barker *et al.* (eds), *Literature, Politics and Theory* (London: Methuen, 1986), pp. 104–25.

5 Adapted for post-structuralist uses by Roland Barthes, the *histoire-discours* couple originates in a soberly linguistic context: see Emile Benveniste, 'Correlations of Tense in the French Verb', in *Problems in General Linguistics*, trans. Mary Elizabeth Meek (Coral Gables, FL: University of Miami Press), pp. 205–15.

6 L.C. Harmer, *French Language Today: Its Characteristics and Tendencies* (London and New York: Hutchinson's University Library, 1954), pp. 300–01. Quoting from *Iron in the Soul* by Jean-Paul Sartre, Harmer writes: 'the practice of interpolating direct speech into the narrative in the original texts might well be called "style direct libre"'. The term has been widely adopted by anglophone stylisticians and linguists, among them Michael Gregory and Norman Page (see note 17).

7 Erich Auerbach, *Mimesis: The Representation of Reality in Western Literature* (Princeton: Princeton University Press, 1968), pp. 523–24.

8 Quoted in Roy Pascal, *The Dual Voice* (Manchester: Manchester University Press, 1977), pp. 10–11.

9 Gregory, 'Aspects of Varieties Differentiation'.

10 Robert Young, 'Back to Bakhtin', *Cultural Critique*, 2, 1986, p. 87. Young writes: 'the crucial role of Bakhtin in the development of post-structuralist thought is passed over'.

11 Boris Uspensky, *A Poetics of Composition: The Structure of the Artistic Text and Typology of a Compositional Form* (Berkeley: University of California Press, 1973), pp. 34–36.

12 I have lost this reference. As far as I can recall, it comes from an intervention by Kristeva at the Edinburgh Festival or the Institute of Contemporary Arts in the 1970s which appeared as 'Signifying Practice'(?) in a pamphlet publication.

13 See note 12.

14 For an itemization of this 'problematic' naming, see the Appendix to this volume.

15 By 'Jamesian theory' I mean not so much the positions taken by Henry James himself as the dogma of 'impersonality' – of the story 'telling itself' – found in Percy Lubbock's *The Craft of Fiction* (London: Jonathan Cape, 1921) and in Joseph Warren Beach's *The Twentieth-Century Novel: Studies in Technique* (New York and London: The Century Co., 1932). For a critique of these arguments from a Chicago-Aristotelian standpoint, see Wayne Booth, *The Rhetoric of Fiction* (Chicago and London: University of Chicago Press, 1961). The post-structuralist case for the 'death of the author' occupies a space beyond all of these positions, and we should not be misled by its superficial likeness to the first of them.

16 See Marguerite Lips, *Le Style indirect libre* (Paris: Payot, 1926), and Lisa Glauser, *Die erlebte Rede im englischen Roman* (Berlin: A. Francke, 1948).

17 The reference here is of course to Pascal, *The Dual Voice*. Before Pascal's monograph, anglophone monoglots had to make do with the odd article in journals of linguistics or of comparative literature, or with single chapters in longer works such as Stephen Ullmann, *Style in the French Novel* (Cambridge: Cambridge University Press, 1957), and Norman Page, *Speech in the English Novel* (London: Longman, 1973). Since Pascal, there has (besides Cohn: see note 14) been the important work of Ann Banfield: see her *Unspeakable Sentences: Narration and Representation in the Language of Fiction* (London: Routledge and Kegan Paul, 1982). For a highly provocative Bakhtin-oriented essay on the role of FID in the modern 'silencing' of prose, see Charles Lock, 'Double Voicing, Sharing Words: Bakhtin's Dialogism and the History of the Theory of Free Indirect Discourse', in Jorgen Bruhn and Jan Lundquist (eds), *The Novelness of Bakhtin* (Copenhagen: Museum Tusculanum Press, 2001), pp. 71–87.

18 See Jane Spencer, *Rise of the Woman Novelist: Aphra Behn to Jane Austen* (Oxford: Basil Blackwell, 1986).

19 McHale, 'Free Indirect Discourse: A Survey of Recent Accounts', p. 275.

20 Todorov, *Mikhail Bakhtin: The Dialogical Principle*, p. 102.

CHAPTER 4

1 See George Steiner, *Heidegger* (London: Fontana Press, 1978), p. 27.

2 The 'revisionist critique' here referred to was launched by Martin Bernal in the first volume of *Black Athena: The Afroasiatic Roots of Classical Civilization* (London: Free Association Books, 1987).

3 That Bakhtin favoured a realist over a modernist aesthetic is the working premiss of Caryl Emerson and Gary Saul Morson in their co-written *Mikhail Bakhtin: Creation of a Prosaics* (Stanford: Stanford University Press, 1990).

4 For another view of the realism–reflexivity opposition, which also uses Bakhtin as the agent of its undoing, see Ann Jefferson, 'Realism Reconsidered: Bakhtin's Dialogism and the "Will to Reference"', *Australian Journal of French Studies*, 23:2, 1986, pp. 169–84.

5 Bertolt Brecht, 'Against Georg Lukács', in Ernst Bloch *et al.*, *Aesthetics and Politics* (London: Verso, 1977), pp. 68–85. The phrase quoted in this sentence is my translation of the title of another essay, not yet (to my knowledge) translated into English: see Bertolt Brecht, 'Weite und Vielfalt der realistischen Schreibweise', in *Über Realismus* (Frankfurt am Main: Suhrkamp Verlag, 1971), pp. 88–97. To propose an intertextual relationship between Lukács and Bakhtin is not of course to say anything new: at the time of writing this chapter the best account known to me was Michel Aucouturier, 'The History of the Novel in Russia in the 1930s: Lukács and Bakhtin', in John Garrard (ed.), *The Russian Novel from Pushkin to Pasternak* (New Haven and London: Yale University Press, 1983), pp. 229–40. Other essays include: Eva Corredor, 'Lukács and Bakhtin: A Dialogue on Fiction', *University of Ottawa Quarterly*, 53:1, 1983, pp. 97–107; and Prabhakara Jha, 'Lukács, Bakhtin and the Sociology of the Novel', *Diogenes*, 129, 1985, pp. 63–90. We now, however, have the benefit of a whole monograph on this relationship in Galin Tihanov, *The Master and the Slave: Lukács, Bakhtin, and the Ideas of Their Time* (Oxford: Clarendon Press, 2000). Tihanov's contention is that in 'striving to overturn Lukács, [Bakhtin] remained in his force-field' (p. 15). (See also note 17 below.)

6 Fredric Jameson, *Marxism and Form: Twentieth-Century Dialectical Theories of Literature* (Princeton: Princeton University Press, 1971), p. 163.

7 Georg Lukács, 'Essay on the Novel', *International Literature*, 5, 1936, pp. 73–74.

8 Georg Lukács, *The Theory of the Novel* (London: Merlin Press, 1971 [1920]), pp. 72–73.

9 Lukács, *The Theory of the Novel*, p. 74.

10 Jameson, *Marxism and Form*, p. 180.

11 Lukács, *The Theory of the Novel*, p. 29.

12 Lukács, *The Theory of the Novel*, p. 29.

13 Maxim Gorky, 'Soviet Literature', in Maxim Gorky *et al.*, *Soviet Writers' Congress 1934: The Debate on Socialist Realism and Modernism in the Soviet Union* (London: Lawrence and Wishart, 1977 [1934]), pp. 28 and 30.

14 Gorky, 'Soviet Literature', p. 43.

15 Gorky, 'Soviet Literature', p. 36.
16 Gorky, 'Soviet Literature', p. 53.
17 For an argument which brings 'Discourse in the Novel' into the frame of anti-Lukácsian polemic – and into alignment with the case I am making here – see John Neubauer, 'Bakhtin versus Lukács: Inscriptions of Homelessness in Theories of the Novel', *Poetics Today*, 17:4, 1996, pp. 531–46. Neubauer writes: 'Bakhtin developed his theory of the novel by refiguring [Lukácsian] *transcendental* homelessness into *linguistic* homelessness' (p. 532).
18 Gorky, 'Soviet Literature', p. 36.
19 Gorky, 'Soviet Literature', p. 36
20 See Erich Auerbach, *Mimesis: The Representation of Reality in Western Literature* (Princeton: Princeton University Press, 1953 [1949]), pp. 174–202. In particular one should note Auerbach's claim that Dante's 'beyond' is 'changeless and of all time yet full of history' (p. 197). Compare also with the passage here quoted from Bakhtin (*FTC*, 157–58) the following from Auerbach: 'the images and ideas that fill this vertical world are in their turn filled with a powerful desire to escape this world, to set out along the historically productive horizontal, to to be distributed not upward, but forward' (p. 157). The likeness between Bakhtin's reading of Dante and Auerbach's may have to do with their common relationship to the tradition of German philology (their readings of Rabelais are also extraordinarily alike, even in points of phraseology); Bakhtin might also have read Auerbach's *Dante als Dichter der irdischen Welt* (Berlin and Leipzig: Walter de Gruyter, 1929).
21 Gorky, 'Soviet Literature', p. 43.
22 I was thinking here of Colin MacCabe, *James Joyce and the Revolution of the Word* (London: Macmillan, 1978), and Dominic Manganiello, *Joyce's Politics* (London: Routledge and Kegan Paul, 1980).
23 Samuel Beckett *et al.*, *Our Exagmination Round his Factification for Incamination of 'Work in Progress'* (London: Faber and Faber, 1929), p. 16.
24 Emile Benveniste, 'Remarks on the Function of Language in Freudian Theory', in *Problems in General Linguistics* (Coral Gables, FL: University of Miami Press, 1971), p. 74.
25 See Michel Foucault, *The History of Sexuality: An Introduction* (Harmondsworth: Penguin Books, 1981).
26 Erich Auerbach, 'Figura', in *Scenes from The Drama of European Literature* (Manchester: Manchester University Press, 1984). Auerbach writes:

> The figural interpretation changed the Old Testament from a book of laws and a history of the people of Israel into a series of figures of Christ and the Redemption .... In this form and in this context ... the Celtic and Germanic peoples, for example, could accept the Old Testament; it was a part of the universal religion of salvation and a necessary component of the equally magnificent and universal vision of history that was conveyed to them along with this religion .... Figural interpretation establishes a connection between two events and persons, the first of which signifies not only itself but also the second, while the second encompasses or fulfils the first. The two poles of the figures are separate in time,

but both, being real events or figures, are within time, within the stream of historical life.

(pp. 52–53)

27 I had assumed that this quotation from Kristeva comes from her *Revolution in Poetic Language*, but I cannot find it anywhere in that book. It is possible that it comes from the same source as my other fugitive Kristeva reference (see Chapter 3, note 12).

28 See Peter Bürger, *The Theory of the Avant-Garde* (Manchester: Manchester University Press, 1984), p. 49:

> The avantgardistes proposed the sublation of art – sublation in the Hegelian sense of the term: art was not to be simply destroyed, but transferred to the praxis of life where it could be preserved, albeit in a changed form.

CHAPTER 5

1 The bulk of this chapter was written in late 1989; the concluding section on South Africa dates from September 1993. At the time of writing in 1989 there was no English translation of Bakhtin's earliest writings, where the 'theological' dimension of his thinking is quite explicit. Though I have of course since read these essays and indeed written about them, I have chosen not to rewrite this essay in their light. The remarks I make in the course of the chapter on Bakhtin's (seemingly negative) attitude towards 'poetry' should be supplemented by a reading of the important work of Michael Eskin: see his *Ethics and Dialogue in the Works of Levinas, Bakhtin, Mandel'shtam and Celan* (Oxford: Oxford University Press, 2000) and 'Bakhtin and Poetry', *Poetics Today* 21:2 (Summer 2000), pp. 379–91.

2 For further reflections on Christ in Bakhtin/Dostoevsky, see the chapter 'Human and Interhuman: Mikhail Bakhtin' in Tzvetan Todorov, *Literature and Its Theorists* (New York: Cornell University Press, 1987).

3 See Julia Kristeva, *Desire in Language: A Semiotic Approach to Literature and Art*, ed. Leon S. Roudiez, trans. Thomas Gora, Alice Jardine and Leon S. Roudiez (Oxford: Blackwell,1980), pp. 70–72.

4 See Ken Hirschkop, 'Bakhtin, Discourse, and Democracy', *New Left Review*, 160, 1986.

5 See Ken Hirschkop, 'Dialogism as a Challenge to Literary Criticism', in Catriona Kelly *et al.* (eds), *Discontinuous Discourses in Modern Russian Literature* (Basingstoke: Macmillan, 1989), p. 27.

6 See Friedrich Nietzsche, *The Birth of Tragedy*, trans. Francis Golffing (New York: Doubleday, 1956), pp. 42–43; and James Curtis, 'Michael (*sic*) Bakhtin, Nietzsche, and Russian Pre-Revolutionary Thought', in B.G. Rosenthal (ed.), *Nietzsche in Russia* (Princeton: Princeton University Press, 1986).

7 Nietzsche, *The Birth of Tragedy*, p. 35.

8 Though Bakhtin does not use these terms, we can recognize here the classic figures of metonymy and metaphor later to be correlated by Roman Jakobson with 'contiguity' and 'similarity' and elevated to the

status of semiotic universals. See Roman Jakobson and Morris Halle, *Fundamentals of Language* (The Hague: Mouton, 1956).

9 See F.R. Leavis, *The Great Tradition* (London: Chatto and Windus, 1948), p. 2.

10 See William Godwin, *The Adventures of Caleb Williams; Or, Things as They Are*, ed. David McCracken (Oxford: Oxford University Press, 1970), p. 181.

11 Mary Wollstonecraft, *Maria*, ed. Janet Todd (Harmondsworth: Penguin Books, 1992), p. 115.

12 For a discussion of this transvaluation by radical writers of key elements of the Whiggish national self-image (with special reference to Blake's 'London'), see Graham Pechey, 'The London Motif in Some Eighteenth-century Contexts: A Semiotic Study', *Literature and History*, 4, 1976.

13 Much of the rest of this section draws on a paper I presented to the University of Essex Sociology of Literature Conference in 1981: see Graham Pechey, 'Mutations of Romantic Discourse', in Francis Barker *et al.* (eds), *1789: Reading Writing Revolution* (Colchester: University of Essex, 1982).

14 The great and pioneering exception to this unanimity among post-Romantic commentators upon allegory (long before Paul de Man) is if course Walter Benjamin: see *Origins of German Tragic Drama* (London: New Left Books, 1977), p. 159 ff.

15 Geoffrey Keynes (ed.), *Poetry and Prose of William Blake* (London: Nonesuch Library, 1961), p. 77.

16 Keynes, *Poetry and Prose of William Blake*, p. 75.

17 Keynes, *Poetry and Prose of William Blake*, p. 75.

18 Edmund Burke, *A Philosophical Inquiry into the Origin of our Ideas of the Sublime and the Beautiful*, ed. David Womersley (Harmondsworth: Penguin Books, 1998), p. 109.

19 Austin Poole (ed.), *Poems of Gray and Collins* (London: Oxford University Press, 1961), p. 246.

20 See Njabulo S. Ndebele, *South African Literature and Culture: Rediscovery of the Ordinary*, intro. by Graham Pechey (Manchester: Manchester University Press, 1994).

21 Graham Pechey, 'Post-Apartheid Narratives', in Francis Barker *et al.* (eds), *Colonial Discourse/Postcolonial Theory* (Manchester: Manchester University Press, 1994).

22 See Russell Berman, 'The Routinization of Charismatic Modernism and the Problem of Postmodernity', *Cultural Critique*, 5, 1987, pp. 49–68.

23 The best examination of the slogan as a micro-genre in the context of South Africa in the last days of the struggle against the apartheid regime is a novel which has a slogan for its title: Menan du Plessis's *Longlive!* (Cape Town: David Philip, 1989). See my review of this book, 'Voices of Struggle', *Southern African Review of Books*, 3:2, 1989–90, pp. 3–5.

24 Jeremy Cronin, '"Even under the Rine of Terror": Insurgent South African Poetry', in Martin Trump (ed.), *Rendering Things Visible: Essays in South African Literary Culture* (Johannesburg: Ravan Press, 1990), pp. 295–306.

25 These remarks were strongly inspired by my reading – repeatedly over many years – of Njabulo Ndebele's poem 'The Revolution of the Aged':

see Stephen Gray, *The Penguin Book of Southern African Verse* (Harmondsworth: Penguin Books, 1989), pp. 296–98.

26 Non-South African readers will need to be told that the reference here is to the 'Great Hymn' by Ntsikana (one of the first black South African converts to Christianity in the early nineteenth century) and to the South African national anthem 'Nkosi Sikelel' iAfrika'. For texts, see Gray, *The Penguin Book of Southern African Verse*, pp. 47–48 and 149–50.

CHAPTER 6

` 1 *Horizontverschmelzung* in the original German: see Hans-Georg Gadamer, *Truth and Method* (London: Sheed and Ward, 1975), p. 273. According to Robert Holub in his *Jurgen Habermas: Critic in the Public Sphere* (London: Routledge, 1991), this is one of Gadamer's 'most notorious metaphors'.

2 Auerbach's claim that Dante's 'beyond' is 'changeless and of all time and yet full of history' (*Mimesis: The Representation of Reality in Western Literature* (Princeton: Princeton University Press, 1968), p. 197) coincides closely with Bakhtin's notion of a 'tension' between 'living historical time' and the 'extra-temporal otherworldly ideal' that governs the form of the *Divine Comedy*. See also Chapter 4, note 19.

3 See György Markus, 'The Paradigm of Language: Wittgenstein, Lévi-Strauss, Gadamer', in John Fekete (ed.), *The Structural Allegory* (Manchester: Manchester University Press, 1984), pp. 104–29.

4 This expression was coined by H. Stuart Hughes in his *Consciousness and Society* (Brighton: Harvester Press, 1979), pp. 33–66. His aim was to decribe the 'turn towards the subjective' in late-nineteenth-century thought; I have chosen here to extend its use to the later 'turn' in the twentieth century away from the philosophy of consciousness and towards the 'language' paradigm, in the belief that these rather different currents of late modernity converge in their common rejection models of objectivity derived from the natural sciences.

5 Gadamer, *Truth and Method*, p. xxiv.

6 See David Carroll, 'Narrative, Heterogeneity, and the Question of the Political: Bakhtin and Lyotard', in Murray Krieger (ed.), *The Aims of Representation: Subject/Text/History* (New York: Columbia University Press, 1987). For another staging of the dialogue between Bakhtin and Lyotard, see Anton Simons, *Het groteske van de taal: Over het werk van Mikhail Bakhtin* (Amsterdam: Uitgeverij Sua, 1990), pp. 161–67.

7 See Holub, *Jurgen Habermas*, pp. 153–54. Holub's discussion of the Habermas–Gadamer debate (pp. 49–77) is essential reading for anyone concerned to locate the late Bakhtin within the currents of late-twentieth-century thinking, as is Michael Gardiner's chapter on 'Bakhtin's Critical Hermeneutics' in *The Dialogics of Critique: M.M. Bakhtin and the Theory of Ideology* (London: Routledge, 1992), pp. 99–140.

8 'We respect the Amazon peoples to the extent that they are not modern, but when modern men make themselves into Amazons, it is monstrous' (quoted in Carroll, 'Narrative, Heterogeneity, and the

Question of the Political', p. 101). See also Lyotard's 'Notes on Legitimation', *Oxford Literary Review*, 9, 116–17. Lyotard here argues that totalitarianism is thoroughly modern in its combination of 'legitimation by myth' with the 'powers of universalization' that belong to republican discourse.

9 Tzvetan Todorov, *Mikhail Bakhtin: The Dialogical Principle* (Manchester: Manchester University Press, 1984), p. 107.

10 This statement should be qualified by the observation that Habermas's project breaks with the high-modern paradigm by embracing a version of the 'linguistic turn' common to a number of philosophical projects in the twentieth century.

CHAPTER 7

1 Sergei Bocharov, 'Conversations with Bakhtin', *PMLA*, 109:5, 1994, p. 1,019 (from an interview that took place on 29 October 1974).

2 In this paragraph and the two following I have borrowed formulations and lines of argument from my 'The Post-Apartheid Sublime: Rediscovering the Extraordinary', in Derek Attridge and Rosemary Jolly (eds), *Writing South Africa: Literature, Apartheid and Democracy 1970–1995* (Cambridge: Cambridge University Press, 1997), pp. 57–74. See also note 13 below.

3 For Bakhtin's recorded reflections on 'spiritual freedom' as 'true freedom', see Nikolai Rzhevsky, 'Kozhinov on Bakhtin', *New Literary History*, 25, 1994, pp. 429–44. This article, among others, is also the source of the assertion in my first paragraph that Bakhtin thought of himself as a philosopher: see p. 435.

4 This observation is made by Jürgen Habermas: see his 'Modernity – An Incomplete Project', in Hal Foster (ed.), *Postmodern Culture* (London: Pluto Press, 1985), pp. 3–15 (p. 3).

5 See the 'Epilogue' to Erich Auerbach, *Mimesis: The Representation of Reality in Western Literature* (Princeton: Princeton University Press, 1953), p. 555. For an early-twentieth-century Russian view of the relationship of Christianity and Western modernity from an intellectual with whom the early Bakhtin may have identified, see James Pain and Nicolas Zernov (eds) *A Bulgakov Anthology* (London: SPCK, 1976). The following observation might be taken as representative: 'The new Europe has been spiritually nurtured and educated by the Christian Church, and modern European culture with its science and learning is Christian in origin, although it is beginning to forget this' (p. 62).

6 See especially 'Sermo Humilis', in Erich Auerbach, *Literary Language and Its Public in Late Latin Antiquity and in the Middle Ages*, trans. Ralph Manheim (Princeton: Princeton University Press, 1965), pp. 27–66.

7 Vladimir Lossky, *The Mystical Theology of the Eastern Church* (Cambridge and London: James Clarke & Co. Ltd, 1957), pp. 14 and 9.

8 See editorial notes nos. 80 and 81 to 'Author and Hero in Aesthetic Activity' (*AH*, 243) and *Rabelais and His World* (*RW*, 56–57, 78); also Erich Auerbach, 'St Francis of Assisi in Dante's *Commedia*', in *Scenes from the Drama of European Literature*, trans. Catherine Garvin (Manchester: Manchester University Press, 1984), pp. 79–98.

9 Rowan Williams, *The Wound of Knowledge: Christian Spirituality from the New Testament to St John of the Cross* (London: Darton, Longman & Todd, 1979), p. 108.

10 The feminization of the hero in this sentence, whilst not Bakhtin's own explicit formulation, is consonant with the Sophianic cast of his aesthetic ontology; it also has not a little to do with the death of my wife (to whom this book is dedicated) in the year before this chapter was first composed.

11 Walter Benjamin, 'Theologico-Political Fragment', in *One-Way Street, and Other Writings*, trans. Edmund Jephcott and Kingsley Shorter (London and New York: Verso, 1979), pp. 155–56.

12 Walter Benjamin, 'Theses on the Philosophy of History', in *Illuminations: Essays and Reflections*, trans. Harry Zohn (London: Jonathan Cape, 1970), pp. 255–66 (pp. 259–60).

13 In the preparation of this brief excursus on sophiology I have drawn on the following: Caitlin Matthews, *Sophia Goddess of Wisdom: The Divine Feminine from Black Goddess to World-Soul* (London: Mandala, 1991); and S.D. Cioran, *Vladimir Solov'ev and the Knighthood of the Divine Sophia* (Waterloo, Ontario: Wilfrid Laurier University Press, 1977).

14 This paragraph also draws on the terms of my 'Post-Apartheid Sublime' essay.

CHAPTER 8

1 See Jürgen Habermas, 'Philosophy as Stand-in and Interpreter', in Kenneth Baynes *et al.* (eds), *After Philosophy: End or Transformation?* (Cambridge, MA: MIT Press, 1987), pp. 296–315.

2 See Alexandar Mihailovic, *Corporeal Words: Mikhail Bakhtin's Theology of Discourse* (Evanston, IL: Northwestern University Press, 1997), *passim*.

3 Boris Shragin and Albert Todd (eds), *Landmarks: A Collection of Essays on the Russian Intelligentsia*, trans. Marian Schwarz (New York: Karz Howard, 1977 [1909]). See especially Bulgakov's 'Heroism and Asceticism', in which he writes:

> Nowadays it is common for people to to forget that western European culture has religious roots . . . . The cultural history of the western European world constitutes a single coherent whole in which both the Middle Ages and the Reformation still live and occupy their own inevitable place alongside the trends of modern times . . . . Our intelligentsia never went further in its Westernism than the superficial assimilation of the west's latest political and social ideas.
>
> (pp. 31–33)

4 This reading of Cassirer's influence upon Bakhtin is exemplified in Craig Brandist, 'Bakhtin, Cassirer, and Symbolic Forms', *Radical Philosophy*, 89 (September–October) 1997, pp. 20–27.

5 Boris Grozovskii, 'The Idea of the Other in Rene Descartes's *Meditations*: A Hermeneutic Investigation into the History of Philosophy', in Carol

Adlam *et al.* (eds), *Face to Face: Bakhtin in Russia and the West* (Sheffield: Sheffield Academic Press, 1997), pp. 58–80.

6 See Bulgakov's 'Heroism and Asceticism', in Shragin and Todd, *Landmarks*, pp. 54–55.

7 'Intercreaturality' is a neologism of mine which has its source partly in the writing of Vitalii Makhlin on Bakhtin and partly in that of Erich Auerbach on a late-mediaeval variety of realism. Makhlin poses the question 'How might [a meaning] possess a certain corporeal reality?', and continues: 'Bakhtin's answer . . . implies that the incarnate unity of any material signifying activity ("answerability") constitutes not "the subject", but rather a "creature" [*tvar'*] in its relation to other creatures and to the Creator' ('Face to Face: Bakhtin's Programme and the Architectonics of Being-as-Event in the Twentieth Century', in Adlam *et al.* (eds), *Face to Face*, p. 48). The inspiration for adding the 'inter-' prefix comes from the example of Julia Kristeva, whose neologism 'intertextuality' tropes on Edmund Husserl's 'intersubjectivity'. For a fuller discussion of the term, see my 'Intercultural, Intercreatural: Bakhtin and the Uniqueness of "Literary Seeing"', in Boguslaw Zylko (ed.), *Bakhtin and His Intellectual Ambience* (Gdansk: Wydawnictwo Uniwersytetu Gdanskiego, 2002), pp. 276–91.

8 'Consciousness is in essence multiple': see 'Towards a Reworking of the Dostoevsky Book', in M.M. Bakhtin, *Problems of Dostoevsky's Poetics*, ed. and trans. Caryl Emerson (Manchester: Manchester University Press, 1984), p. 288.

9 *Shorter Oxford English Dictionary, On Historical Principles*, ed. C.T. Onions (Oxford: Oxford University Press, 1955), p. 94.

10 See the lecture given by Bakhtin on 1 November 1925, recorded by Pumpiansky. An English translation of these notes of Pumpiansky's is to be found in the appendix to Susan Felch and Paul Contino (eds), *Bakhtin and Religion: A Feeling for Faith* (Evanston, IL: Northwestern University Press, 2001).

11 Hans Blumenberg, *Work on Myth* (Cambridge, MA: MIT Press, 1990); Brandist, 'Bakhtin, Cassirer, and Symbolic Forms'. The essay by Poole is his 'Bakhtin and Cassirer: Philosophical Origins of Bakhtin's Carnival Messianism', *South Atlantic Quarterly*, 97:3–4, pp. 537–78.

12 Theodor Adorno and Max Horkheimer, *Dialectic of Enlightenment* (London and New York: Verso, 1979), p. xvi; Ernst Cassirer, *The Myth of the State* (London: Oxford University Press, 1946).

13 For an explanation of (the impossibility of) 'bringing myth to an end', see chapter 4 of part 2 of Blumenberg, *Work on Myth*.

14 Blumenberg, *Work on Myth*, pp. 96–97.

15 Greg Nielsen, 'Bakhtin and Habermas: Toward a Transcultural Ethics', *Theory and Society*, 24, 1995, p. 813.

16 Nielsen, 'Bakhtin and Habermas', pp. 811–12.

17 Nielsen, 'Bakhtin and Habermas', p. 819.

18 Nielsen, 'Bakhtin and Habermas', p. 819.

19 Nielsen, 'Bakhtin and Habermas', p. 823.

20 Wlad Godzich, 'Correcting Kant: Bakhtin and Intercultural Interactions', *boundary 2*, 18:1, 1991, p. 7.

21 Godzich, 'Correcting Kant', p. 9.

22 Godzich, 'Correcting Kant', p. 12.
23 Godzich, 'Correcting Kant', p. 10.
24 Godzich, 'Correcting Kant', p. 11.
25 Godzich, 'Correcting Kant', p. 12.
26 Godzich, 'Correcting Kant', p. 13.
27 Godzich, 'Correcting Kant', p. 14.

BIBLIOGRAPHY

WORKS OF BAKHTIN AND HIS CIRCLE

Bakhtin, M.M. *Rabelais and His World*, trans. Hélène Iswolsky (Cambridge, MA: MIT Press, 1968).

——. *The Dialogic Imagination*, ed. Michael Holquist, trans. Caryl Emerson and Michael Holquist (Austin and London: University of Texas Press, 1981).

——. *Problems of Dostoevsky's Poetics*, ed. and trans. Caryl Emerson (Manchester: Manchester University Press, 1984).

——. *Speech Genres and Other Late Essays*, ed. Caryl Emerson and Michael Holquist, trans. Vern W. McGee (Austin and London: University of Texas Press, 1986).

——. *Art and Answerability: Early Philosophical Essays*, ed. Michael Holquist and Vadim Liapunov, trans. Vadim Liapunov (Austin and London: University of Texas Press, 1990).

——. *Toward a Philosophy of the Act*, ed. Vadim Liapunov and Michael Holquist, trans. Vadim Liapunov (Austin and London: University of Texas Press, 1993).

Medvedev, P.N. *The Formal Method in Literary Scholarship*, trans. Albert J. Wehrle (Baltimore and London: The Johns Hopkins University Press, 1978).

Voloshinov, V.N. *Marxism and the Philosophy of Language*, trans. Ladislav Matejka and I.R. Titunik (New York and London: Seminar Press, 1973).

——. *Freudianism: A Marxist Critique*, ed. Neal H. Bruss, trans. I.R. Titunik (New York: Academic Press, 1976).

OTHER WORKS

Adorno, Theodor and Max Horkheimer. *Dialectic of Enlightenment* (London and New York: Verso, 1979).

Althusser, Louis. *For Marx*, trans. Ben Brewster (London: Allen Lane, 1969 [1965]).

Aucouturier, Michel. 'The History of the Novel in Russia in the 1930s: Lukács and Bakhtin', in John Garrard (ed.), *The Russian Novel from Pushkin to Pasternak* (New Haven and London: Yale University Press, 1983), pp. 229–40.

Auerbach, Erich. *Dante als Dichter der irdischen Welt* (Berlin and Leipzig: Walter de Gruyter, 1929).

——. *Mimesis: The Representation of Reality in Western Literature* (Princeton: Princeton University Press, 1953 [1949]).

——. *Literary Language and Its Public in Late Latin Antiquity and in the Middle Ages*, trans. Ralph Manheim (Princeton: Princeton University Press, 1965).

——. *Scenes from the Drama of European Literature* (Manchester: Manchester University Press, 1984).

——. 'St Francis of Assisi in Dante's *Commedia*', in *Scenes from the Drama of European Literature*, trans. Catherine Garvin (Manchester: Manchester University Press, 1984), pp. 79–98.

Bakhtin, Mikhail Mikhaylovich (*sic*). 'Toward the Aesthetics of the Word', *Dispositio*, IV, 11–12, 1979, pp. 299–315.

Balibar, Etienne and Pierre Macherey. 'On Literature as an Ideological Form: Some Marxist Propositions', *Oxford Literary Review*, 3, 1978, p. 4.

Banfield, Ann. *Unspeakable Sentences: Narration and Representation in the Language of Fiction* (London: Routledge and Kegan Paul, 1982).

Barker, Francis, Peter Hulme, Margaret Iversen and Diana Loxley. *Literature, Politics and Theory* (London: Methuen, 1986).

Beach, Joseph Warren. *The Twentieth-Century Novel: Studies in Technique* (New York and London: The Century Co., 1932).

Beckett, Samuel *et al. Our Exagmination Round His Factification for Incamination of 'Work in Progress'* (London: Faber and Faber, 1929).

Benjamin, Walter. 'Theses on the Philosophy of History', in *Illuminations: Essays and Reflections*, trans. Harry Zohn (London: Jonathan Cape, 1970), pp. 255–66.

——.*Origins of German Tragic Drama* (London: New Left Books, 1977).

——. 'Theologico-Political Fragment', in *One-Way Street, and Other Writings*, trans. Edmund Jephcott and Kingsley Shorter (London and New York: Verso, 1979).

Benveniste, Emile. *Problems in General Linguistics* (Coral Gables, FL: University of Miami Press, 1971).

Berman, Russell. 'The Routinization of Charismatic Modernism and the Problem of Postmodernity', *Cultural Critique*, 5, 1987.

Bernal, Martin. *Black Athena: The Afroasiatic Roots of Classical Civilization* (London: Free Association Books, 1987).

Blumenberg, Hans. *Work on Myth* (Cambridge, MA: MIT Press, 1990).

Boal, Augusto. *Theatre of the Oppressed*, trans. Charles A. and Maria-Odilia Leal-Mcbride (London: Pluto Press, 1979).

Bocharov, Sergei. 'Conversations with Bakhtin', *PMLA* 109:5, 1994.

Booth, Wayne. *The Rhetoric of Fiction* (Chicago and London: University of Chicago Press, 1961).

Brandist, Craig. 'Bakhtin, Cassirer, and Symbolic Forms', *Radical Philosophy*, 89 (September–October), 1997, pp. 20–27.

Brecht, Bertolt. 'Weite und Vielfalt der realistischen Schreibweise', in *Über Realismus* (Frankfurt am Main: Suhrkamp Verlag, 1971), pp. 88–97.

——. 'Against Georg Lukács', in Ernst Bloch, Georg Lukacs, Bertolt Brecht, Walter Benjamin and Theodor Adorno, *Aesthetics and Politics* (London: Verso, 1977), pp. 68–85.

Bürger, Peter. *The Theory of the Avant-Garde* (Manchester: Manchester University Press, 1984).

Burke, Edmund. *A Philosophical Inquiry into the Origin of Our Ideas of the Sublime and the Beautiful*, ed. David Womersley (Harmondsworth: Penguin Books, 1998).

Carroll, David. 'Narrative, Heterogeneity, and the Question of the Political: Bakhtin and Lyotard', in Murray Krieger (ed.), *The Aims of Representation: Subject/Text/History* (New York: Columbia University Press, 1987).

Cassirer, Ernst. *The Myth of the State* (London: Oxford University Press, 1946).

Cioran, S.D. *Vladimir Solov'ev and the Knighthood of the Divine Sophia* (Waterloo, Ontario: Wilfrid Laurier University Press, 1977).

Clark, Katerina and Michael Holquist. *Mikhail Bakhtin* (Cambridge, MA: The Belknap Press of Harvard University Press, 1984).

Corredor, Eva. 'Lukács and Bakhtin: A Dialogue on Fiction', *University of Ottawa Quarterly*, 53:1, 1983, pp. 97–107.

Cronin, Jeremy. '"Even under the Rine of Terror": Insurgent South African Poetry', in Martin Trump (ed.), *Rendering Things Visible: Essays in South African Literary Culture* (Johannesburg: Ravan Press, 1990), pp. 295–306.

Curtis, James. 'Michael [*sic*] Bakhtin, Nietzsche, and Russian Pre-Revolutionary Thought', in B.G. Rosenthal (ed.), *Nietzsche in Russia* (Princeton: Princeton University Press, 1986).

Derrida, Jacques. 'Deconstruction and the Other', in Richard Kearney (ed.), *Dialogues with Contemporary Continental Thinkers* (Manchester: Manchester University Press, 1984).

du Plessis, Menan. *Longlive!* (Cape Town: David Philip, 1989).

Emerson, Caryl and Gary Saul Morson. *Mikhail Bakhtin: Creation of a Prosaics* (Stanford: Stanford University Press, 1990).

Erlich, Victor. *Russian Formalism: History-Doctrine* (The Hague: Mouton, 1969).

Eskin, Michael. *Ethics and Dialogue in the Works of Levinas, Bakhtin, Mandel'shtam and Celan* (Oxford: Oxford University Press, 2000).

——. 'Bakhtin and Poetry', *Poetics Today*, 21:2 (Summer), 2000, pp. 379–91.

Fanon, Frantz. *The Wretched of the Earth*, trans. Costance Farrington (Harmondsworth: Penguin Books, 1967), p. 31.

Felch, Susan and Paul Contino (eds). *Bakhtin and Religion: A Feeling for Faith* (Evanston, IL: Northwestern University Press, 2001).

Foucault, Michel. *The History of Sexuality: An Introduction* (Harmondsworth: Penguin Books, 1981).

Freire, Paulo. *Pedagogy of the Oppressed*, trans. Myra Bergman Ramos (Harmondsworth: Penguin Books, 1972).

Frow, John. 'System and History: A Critique of Russian Formalism', *Oxford Literary Review*, 4:2, 1980, pp. 56–71.

——. *Marxism and Literary History* (Oxford: Basil Blackwell, 1986).

Gadamer, Hans-Georg. *Truth and Method* (London: Sheed and Ward, 1975).

Gardiner, Michael. *The Dialogics of Critique: M.M. Bakhtin and the Theory of Ideology* (London: Routledge, 1992).

Glauser, Lisa. *Die erlebte Rede im englischen Roman* (Berlin: A. Francke, 1948).

Godwin, William *The Adventures of Caleb Williams; Or, Things as They Are*, ed. David McCracken (Oxford: Oxford University Press, 1970).

Godzich, Wlad. 'Correcting Kant: Bakhtin and Intercultural Interactions', *boundary 2*, 18:1, 1991.

Goldmann, Lucien. 'The Sociology of Literature: Status and Problems of Method', *International Social Science Journal*, 19:4, 1967, pp. 493–516.

Gorky, Maxim. 'Soviet Literature', in Maxim Gorky *et al.*, *Soviet Writers' Congress 1934: The Debate on Socialist Realism and Modernism in the Soviet Union* (London: Lawrence and Wishart, 1977 [1934]).

Gorky, Maxim, Karl Radek, Nikolai Bukharin, Andrey Zhdanov *et al. Soviet Writers' Congress 1934: The Debate on Socialist Realism and Modernism* (London: Lawrence and Wishart, 1977).

Gray, Stephen (ed.). *The Penguin Book of Southern African Verse* (Harmondsworth: Penguin Books, 1989).

Gregory, Michael. 'Aspects of Varieties Differentiation', *Journal of Linguistics*, 3, 1967.

Grozovskii, Boris. 'The Idea of the Other in René Descartes's *Meditations*: A Hermeneutic Investigation into the History of Philosophy', in Carol Adlam, Rachel Falconer, Vitalii Makhlin and Alastair Renfrew (eds), *Face to Face: Bakhtin in Russia and the West* (Sheffield: Sheffield Academic Press, 1997).

Habermas, Jürgen. 'Modernity – An Incomplete Project', in Hal Foster (ed.), *Postmodern Culture* (London: Pluto Press, 1985), pp. 3–15.

——. 'Philosophy as Stand-in and Interpreter', in Kenneth Baynes, James Bohman, and Thomas McCarthy (eds), *After Philosophy: End or Transformation?* (Cambridge, MA: MIT Press, 1987), pp. 296–315.

Harmer, L.C. *French Language Today: Its Characteristics and Tendencies* (London and New York: Hutchinson's University Library, 1954).

Hirschkop, Ken. 'The Social and the Subject in Bakhtin', *Poetics Today*, 6:4, 1985.

——. 'Bakhtin, Discourse, and Democracy', *New Left Review*, 160, 1986.

——. 'Dialogism as a Challenge to Literary Criticism', in Catriona Kelly, Michael Makin and David Shepherd (eds), *Discontinuous Discourses in Modern Russian Literature* (Basingstoke: Macmillan, 1989).

——. *Mikhail Bakhtin: An Aesthetic for Democracy* (Oxford: Oxford University Press, 1999).

Hoare, Quintin and Geoffrey Nowell-Smith (eds). *Selections from the Prison Notebooks of Antonio Gramsci* (London: Lawrence and Wishart, 1971).

Holub, Robert. *Jurgen Habermas: Critic in the Public Sphere* (London: Routledge, 1991).

Hughes, H. Stuart. *Consciousness and Society* (Brighton: Harvester Press, 1979).

Jakobson, Roman. *Noveskaja Russkaja poezija: Nabrosok pervyj* (Prague, 1921).

Jakobson, Roman and Morris Halle. *Fundamentals of Language* (The Hague: Mouton, 1956).

Jakobson, Roman and Yury Tynyanov. 'Problems of Research in Literature and Language', in *Russian Poetics in Translation*, 1977, pp. 49–51.

Jameson, Fredric. *Marxism and Form: Twentieth-Century Dialectical Theories of Literature* (Princeton: Princeton University Press, 1971).

Jameson, Fredric. 'Periodizing the 60s', in *The Ideologies of Theory*, vol. 2 (London: Routledge, 1988).

Jefferson, Ann. 'Realism Reconsidered: Bakhtin's Dialogism and the "Will to Reference"', *Australian Journal of French Studies*, 23:2, 1986, pp. 169–84.

Jha, Prabhakara, 'Lukács, Bakhtin and the Sociology of the Novel', *Diogenes*, 129, 1985, pp. 63–90.

Kaiser, Mark. 'P.N. Medvedev's "The Collapse of Formalism"', in B.A. Stolz *et al.* (eds), *Language and Literary Theory* (Ann Arbor, MI: Michigan Slavic Publications, 1984), pp. 405–41.

Keynes, Geoffrey (ed.). *Poetry and Prose of William Blake* (London: Nonesuch Library, 1961).

Kristeva, Julia. *Desire in Language: A Semiotic Approach to Literature and Art*, ed. Leon S. Roudiez, trans. Thomas Gora, Alice Jardine and Leon S. Roudiez (Oxford: Blackwell, 1980).

Leavis, F.R. *The Great Tradition* (London: Chatto and Windus, 1948).

Lips, Marguerite. *Le Style indirect libre* (Paris: Payot, 1926).

Lock, Charles. 'Double Voicing, Sharing Words: Bakhtin's Dialogism and the History of the Theory of Free Indirect Discourse', in Jorgen Bruhn and Jan Lundquist (eds), *The Novelness of Bakhtin* (Copenhagen: Museum Tusculanum Press, 2001), pp. 71–87.

Lossky, Vladimir. *The Mystical Theology of the Eastern Church* (Cambridge and London: James Clarke & Co. Ltd, 1957).

Lubbock, Percy. *The Craft of Fiction* (London: Jonathan Cape, 1921).

Lukács, Georg. 'Essay on the Novel', *International Literature*, 5, 1936, pp. 73–74.

——. *History and Class Consciousness: Studies in Marxist Dialectics*, trans. Rodney Livingstone (London: Merlin Press, 1971).

——. *The Theory of the Novel* (London: Merlin Press, 1971 [1920]).

Lunacharsky, Anatoly. *On Literature and Art* (Moscow: Progress Publishers, 1973).

Lyotard, Jean-François. 'Notes on Legitimation', *Oxford Literary Review*, 9:1–2, 1987, pp. 116–17.

MacCabe, Colin. *James Joyce and the Revolution of the Word* (London: Macmillan, 1978).

McHale, Brian. 'Free Indirect Discourse: A Survey of recent Accounts', *PTL: A Journal of Descriptive Poetics and Theory of Literature*, 3, 1978, pp. 249–87.

Macherey, Pierre. *A Theory of Literary Production*, trans. Geoffrey Wall (London: Routledge and Kegan Paul, 1978 [1966]).

Makhlin, Vitalii. 'Face to Face: Bakhtin's Programme and the Architectonics of Being-as-Event in the Twentieth Century', in Carol Adlam, Rachel Falconer, Vitalii Makhlin and Alastair Renfrew (eds), *Face to Face: Bakhtin in Russia and the West* (Sheffield: Sheffield Academic Press, 1997).

Manganiello, Dominic. *Joyce's Politics* (London: Routledge and Kegan Paul, 1980).

Mannheim, Karl. *Ideology and Utopia: An Introduction to the Sociology of Knowledge* (London: Routledge and Kegan Paul, 1966).

Markus, György. 'The Paradigm of Language: Wittgenstein, Lévi-Strauss, Gadamer', in John Fekete (ed.), *The Structural Allegory* (Manchester: Manchester University Press, 1984), pp. 104–29.

Marx, Karl. *Grundrisse: Foundations of the Critique of Political Economy*, trans. Martin Nicolaus (Harmondsworth: Penguin Books, 1973).

Matejka, Ladislav and Katerina Pomorska (eds). *Readings in Russian Poetics: Formalist and Structuralist Views* (Cambridge, MA: MIT Press, 1971).

Matthews, Caitlin. *Sophia Goddess of Wisdom: The Divine Feminine from Black Goddess to World-Soul* (London: Mandala, 1991).

Merquior, J.G. *From Prague to Paris: A Critique of Structuralist and Post-structuralist Thought* (London: Verso, 1986).

Mihailovic, Alexandar. *Corporeal Words: Mikhail Bakhtin's Theology of Discourse* (Evanston, IL: Northwestern University Press, 1997).

Ndebele, Njabulo S. *South African Literature and Culture: Rediscovery of the Ordinary*, intro. by Graham Pechey (Manchester: Manchester University Press, 1994).

Neubauer, John. 'Bakhtin versus Lukács: Inscriptions of Homelessness in Theories of the Novel', *Poetics Today*, 17:4, 1996, pp. 531–46.

Nielsen, Greg. 'Bakhtin and Habermas: Toward a Transcultural Ethics', *Theory and Society*, 24, 1995.

Nietzsche, Friedrich. *The Birth of Tragedy*, trans. Francis Golffing (New York: Doubleday, 1956).

Page, Norman. *Speech in the English Novel* (London: Longman, 1973).

Pain, James and Nicolas Zernov (eds). *A Bulgakov Anthology* (London: SPCK, 1976).

Pascal, Roy. *The Dual Voice* (Manchester: Manchester University Press, 1977).

Pechey, Graham. 'The London Motif in Some Eighteenth-century Contexts: A Semiotic Study', *Literature and History*, 4, 1976.

——. 'Formalism and Marxism', *Oxford Literary Review*, 4:2, 1980, pp. 72–81.

——. 'Mutations of Romantic Discourse', in Francis Barker, Peter Hulme, Margaret Iversen and Diana Loxley (eds), *1789: Reading Writing Revolution* (Colchester: University of Essex, 1982).

——. 'Bakhtin, Marxism and Post-structuralism', in Francis Barker, Peter Hulme, Margaret Iversen and Diana Loxley (eds), *Literature, Politics and Theory* (London: Methuen, 1986).

——. 'On the Borders of Bakhtin: Dialogization, Decolonization', in Ken Hirschkop and David Shepherd (eds), *Bakhtin and Cultural Theory* (Manchester: Manchester University Press, 1989), pp. 39–67.

——. 'Voices of Struggle', *Southern African Review of Books*, 3:2, 1989–90, pp. 3–5.

——. 'Post-Apartheid Narratives', in Francis Barker, Peter Hulme, Margaret Iversen and Diana Loxley (eds) *Colonial Discourse/Postcolonial Theory* (Manchester: Manchester University Press, 1994).

——. 'The Post-Apartheid Sublime: Rediscovering the Extraordinary', in Derek Attridge and Rosemary Jolly (eds), *Writing South Africa: Literature, Apartheid and Democracy 1970–1995* (Cambridge: Cambridge University Press, 1997), pp. 57–74.

——. 'Towards a Culture of Democracy: Ken Hirschkop on Bakhtin', *Dialogism*, 5–6, 2002.

——. 'Penultimate Words: The Life of the "Loophole" in Mikhail Bakhtin', *Literature and Theology*, 20:3, 2006, pp. 269–85.

Poole, Austin (ed.). *Poems of Gray and Collins* (London: Oxford University Press, 1961).

Poole, Brian. 'Bakhtin and Cassirer: The Philosophical Origins of Bakhtin's Carnival Messianism', in Peter Hitchcock (ed.), *South Atlantic Quarterly*, 97:3–4 (special issue on Bakhtin), pp. 537–78.

Rice, Philip and Patricia Waugh (eds). *Modern Literary Theory: A Reader* (London: Edward Arnold, 1996), pp. 61–68.

Ryan, Michael. *Marxism and Deconstruction: A Critical Articulation* (Baltimore and London: The Johns Hopkins University Press, 1982).

Rzhevsky, Nikolai. 'Kozhinov on Bakhtin', *New Literary History*, 25, 1994, pp. 429–44.

Shorter Oxford English Dictionary, On Historical Principles, ed. C.T. Onions (Oxford: Oxford University Press, 1955).

Shragin, Boris and Albert Todd (eds). *Landmarks: A Collection of Essays on the Russian Intelligentsia*, trans. Marian Schwarz (New York: Karz Howard, 1977 [1909]).

Simons, Anton. *Het groteske van de taal: Over het werk van Mikhail Bakhtin* (Amsterdam: Uitgeverij Sua, 1990).

Spencer, Jane. *Rise of the Woman Novelist: Aphra Behn to Jane Austen* (Oxford: Basil Blackwell, 1986).

Steiner, George. *Heidegger* (London: Fontana Press, 1978).

Steiner, Peter. *Russian Formalism: A Metapoetics* (Ithaca and London: Cornell University Press, 1984).

Stolz, B.A., I.R. Titunik and Lubomir Dolezel (eds). *Language and Literary Theory* (Ann Arbor, MI: Michigan Slavic Publications, 1984).

Tihanov, Galin. *The Master and the Slave: Lukács, Bakhtin, and the Ideas of Their Time* (Oxford: Clarendon Press, 2000).

Todorov, Tzvetan. *Mikhail Bakhtin: The Dialogical Principle* (Manchester: Manchester University Press, 1984).

——. *Literature and Its Theorists* (London: Routledge and Kegan Paul, 1988).

Ullmann, Stephen. *Style in the French Novel* (Cambridge: Cambridge University Press, 1957).

Uspensky, Boris. *A Poetics of Composition: The Structure of the Artistic Text and Typology of a Compositional Form* (Berkeley: University of California Press, 1973).

Williams, Rowan. *The Wound of Knowledge: Christian Spirituality from the New Testament to St John of the Cross* (London: Darton, Longman & Todd, 1979).

Wollstonecraft, Mary. *Maria: Or, The Wrongs of Woman*, ed. Janet Todd (Harmondsworth: Penguin Books, 1992).

Young, Robert (ed.). *Untying the Text* (Boston and London: Routledge and Kegan Paul, 1981).

——. 'Back to Bakhtin', *Cultural Critique*, 2, 1986.

Zylko, Boguslaw (ed.). *Bakhtin and His Intellectual Ambience* (Gdansk: Wydawnictwo Uniwersytetu Gdanskiego, 2002).

INDEX

Index

free indirect discourse 58, 60, 65, 66, 67–68, 70–71, 72–73, 208; in English writing 74–79
freedom 139
Freire, Paulo 31
French language 56, 67, 71, 73, 74
Freud, Sigmund 15, 81, 92, 94, 100–101
'From Notes Made in 1970–71' (Bakhtin) 135–44
Frow, John 211
Futurism 25, 49, 103

Gadamer, Hans–Georg 128, 133, 134, 136, 141
Geistewissenschaften 139–40
German language 67, 71, 74
German philologists 9
German philosophy 44–45, 162, 198
Glauser, Lisa 74
God 4, 8, 106, 110, 156, 161, 166, 175–76, 184, 197, 204; Blake and 120–21; as Creator 195; and gender 171–72; South Africa and 122, 125–26
Godwin, William 115
Godzich, Wlad 202, 203–4, 205
Goethe, Johann Wolfgang von 3, 15, 91, 103, 129
Gogol, Nikolai 64; *Dead Souls* 2
Golden Ass, The (Apuleius) 92, 93
Gorky, Maxim 9, 90–91, 93, 94, 96, 99, 100
Gospels 154, 155, 161–62
grammar 57–59, 61–62, 68
Gramsci, Antonio 22, 23, 24, 25, 27, 36
great time 10, 127–28, 129, 132, 148–51, 176
Greek drama 184
Greek language 83
Greek philosophy 83, 89
Greek romance 88–89, 92
Gregory, Michael 62, 69
grotesque 95, 99, 117, 130, 154

Habermas, Jürgen 52, 135, 138, 139, 146, 181, 202, 205, 219
hagiography *see* saints' lives
Harmer, L.C. 212
Hegel, Georg Wilhelm Friedrich 7, 10, 17, 87, 107, 139, 147, 150, 156–57, 158, 162, 202, 204; *Aesthetics* 95; anti–Hegelianism 14–15, 16, 17–18, 22, 24, 27, 29, 138
Heidegger, Martin 83, 137, 173, 184
Heine, Heinrich 108
hermeneutics 10, 132, 133, 136, 140, 141–42, 144, 147, 148–49, 150
hero/heroes: author and 153–54, 157–59, 164–66, 174, 176–77; in autobiography 177–79; Bakhtin's 2–3, 12; device as 38; in Dostoevsky 22, 47; epic 86, 87, 94, 97, 120; in folklore 96; meaning as 128; of polyphonic fiction 143–44; reported speech of 64–65; role of 28; slogan and 124; *see also* 'Author and Hero in Aesthetic Activity'
heteroglossia 59, 78–79, 111; Blake and 112–13, 116, 121; Christian 162; South African 122
Hildegard of Bingen 171
Hill, Geoffrey 2
Hirschkop, Ken 21, 22
historicity 27–28, 93, 128–29, 130, 186
history 92, 93, 95–98, 130, 134, 145–46, 166, 169–70
Homer 99, 102
homophony 23, 26
Horkheimer, Max 103, 140, 146, 201
Hughes, H. Stuart 218
human sciences 130–31, 132, 140–41, 147, 181, 207; *see also* Geisteswissenschaften
humanism, Western 28, 34, 171
Husserl, Edmund Gustav Albrecht 43
hybridity 205
hymns 125–26

I, the 157, 161, 163, 164, 167, 171, 172–73, 185, 190, 194, 195, 198, 200
idealism 16, 18, 21, 22, 27, 53, 139, 198
'ideological': replaced as term 51
ideology, autonomy of 49
image 145, 160; novelistic 114–15
imbongi 122
immortality 128–30
individualism 59–60; 'bourgeois' 21
individuality 26, 52